THE ENGLISH REFORMATION IN THE SPANISH IMAGINATION

Rewriting Nero, Jezebel, and the Dragon

DEBORAH R. FORTEZA

The English Reformation in the Spanish Imagination

Rewriting Nero, Jezebel, and the Dragon

UNIVERSITY OF TORONTO PRESS
Toronto Buffalo London

ISBN 978-1-4875-6350-9 (cloth)
ISBN 978-1-4875-6352-3 (EPUB)
ISBN 978-1-4875-6351-6 (PDF)

Library and Archives Canada Cataloguing in Publication

Title: The English Reformation in the Spanish imagination : rewriting Nero, Jezebel, and the Dragon / Deborah R. Forteza.
Names: Forteza, Deborah, author.
Series: Toronto Italian studies ; 69.
Description: Series statement: Toronto Iberic studies ; 69 | Includes bibliographical references and index.
Identifiers: Canadiana (print) 20210243821 | Canadiana (ebook) 20210243872 | ISBN 9781487563509 (cloth) | ISBN 9781487563523 (EPUB) | ISBN 9781487563516 (PDF)
Subjects: LCSH: Spanish literature – Classical period, 1500–1700 – History and criticism. | LCSH: Reformation in literature. | LCSH: Reformation – England.
Classification: LCC PQ6066 .F67 2022 | DDC 860.9/003–dc23

We wish to acknowledge the land on which the University of Toronto Press operates. This land is the traditional territory of the Wendat, the Anishnaabeg, the Haudenosaunee, the Métis, and the Mississaugas of the Credit First Nation.

University of Toronto Press acknowledges the financial support of the Government of Canada, the Canada Council for the Arts, and the Ontario Arts Council, an agency of the Government of Ontario, for its publishing activities.

Funded by the Government of Canada | Financé par le gouvernement du Canada

To my parents, Ernesto and Marlene Forteza, for their love and sacrifice all these years

Contents

Acknowledgments

Many people have made this book possible. I first discovered the complexity of Cervantes' *La española inglesa* through a paper I wrote for Joseph Buttigieg, one of the most brilliant and kind scholars whose genius conceived the PhD in Literature at Notre Dame, the program from which I graduated. Joe's relentless encouragement and expert counsel enabled not only the first proposal of this book but also the completion of my doctoral degree. Susannah Monta first drew my attention to the ecclesiastical histories of Ribadeneyra and Yepes, Michael Questier to Luisa de Carvajal, and Ernesto Oyarbide to Lope de Vega's epics. Those were the main components of a dissertation project, whose finished product I also owe to the generosity of my committee members Susannah Monta, David Dressing (unfortunately no longer with us), and especially my director, Encarnación Juárez Almendros, who spent innumerable hours reading and discussing my ideas for this book then and since that time.

Several other colleagues supported and enriched this work. Anne J. Cruz gave me valuable advice and insights, especially concerning Luisa de Carvajal, and Freddy Domínguez not only persuaded me of the need to publish this comparative study but also exchanged with me vital resources and thoughts that helped shape its arguments. I am indebted to GRISO, especially to Ignacio Arellano, Carlos Mata Induráin, and Mariela Insúa, for their support and warm reception during my research visit in Pamplona that enriched the chapter on Lope and Calderón. Antonio Sánchez Jiménez graciously corresponded with me about translations and resources, while conference attendance allowed me to connect personally with Javier Burguillo, Ernesto Oyarbide, and Alexander Samson, fellow early modernists with similar interests and expertise whose long conversations both energized and gave depth to my study.

My generous colleagues from Grove City College, Mark Graham, Rebecca Rine, and Gillis Harp, took time from their already very full schedules to assist me with the book proposal and funding applications. My extraordinary student assistants Emily Rosenberger and Rachel Wilhelm helped me with research, editing, and proofreading, while Stephanie Mills, Sabrina Stabler, and Moriah Bridges completed important tasks that freed up my time to write.

Of course, books cannot be written without funding. I am very grateful for the financial support of Grove City College to attend conferences, the diversity grant from the Renaissance Society of America to cover annual meeting expenses, and to Covenant College for their substantial undertaking of publication costs. I also wish to thank Suzanne Rancourt and the publication team at University of Toronto Press for their expertise and help throughout the publishing process.

Finally, I cannot imagine the completion of this book without the invaluable, extensive editing and logistical work of Brent and Lyn Marshall, personal friends who championed this project from the beginning and more than generously employed their time, skills, and resources to bring it to fruition. Moreover, the personal encouragement of my church, close friends, and family has been indispensable for finishing this arduous but enjoyable task.

THE ENGLISH REFORMATION IN THE SPANISH IMAGINATION

Introduction

In the flurry of celebrations as the Spanish Armada was preparing to leave for England in 1588, the Jesuit Pedro de Ribadeneyra published the first part of his widely read ecclesiastical history of the events that led up to the "English schism," the *Historia eclesiástica del scisma del reyno de Inglaterra*. Translating and adapting Nicholas Sander's *Schismatis Anglicano* (1585), a Latin text written by Elizabethan Catholic exiles, he contended that Queen Elizabeth was not only illegitimate but also born of an incestuous union – the monstrous culmination of Henry's lust and pride in taking Anne Boleyn and setting himself up as head of the church in place of the Vicar of Christ. Thus, according to Ribadeneyra, Elizabeth was a monster and a heretical tyrant who could not turn back to the Holy See without losing her right to the throne and therefore was irredeemable. Furthermore, she was ruthlessly cruel and without natural affection, as evidenced by her murder of innocent Catholics,[1] including her own cousin, Mary Stuart, Queen of Scots. For these reasons, Elizabeth had to be overthrown to win England back from apostasy and relieve the persecuted Catholics. Spain was the logical leader in this "English Enterprise" to protect the faith, and the Armada was sent with many prayers and blessings.[2]

After disastrous losses of Spanish ships by inclement weather that forced a retreat, Catholics were perplexed as to why God would allow his people to fail in a mission that so clearly seemed to be his plan. Ribadeneyra's *Tratado de la tribulación* (1589) describes the shock of Spaniards after the defeat:

> Mayor maravilla es que una armada grande y poderosa, y que parecía invencible, aprestada para volver por la causa de Dios y su santa fe católica, y acompañada de tantas oraciones y plegarias y penitencias de sus fieles y siervos, se haya deshecho y perdido por una manera tan extraña, que

> no se puede negar sino que es azote y severo castigo de la mano del muy Alto. (Rivadeneira 199)

> It is a greater wonder that a great and powerful Armada that seemed invincible, ready to return for the cause of God and his holy Catholic faith, accompanied by so many prayers and supplications and penitence from her faithful ones and her servants, would be destroyed and lost in such a strange manner that it is impossible to negate that it is scourging and severe chastisement from the hand of the Most High.[3]

For the Jesuit, the alarming failure came not only because the naval fleet was exceedingly powerful ("seemed invincible") but also because it went out for God's cause and that of the Catholic faith, with much prayer and sacrifice from God's people ("faithful ones," "servants"). Since Spain's status as God's chosen people and the rightness of their cause could not be doubted, the only explanation possible was the need to purge sin: the Most High, completely sovereign over events, allowed the failure as chastisement to expose his people's hidden sins, and now, like many of their biblical forefathers, Catholics had to endure patiently the evils and persecution of tyrants like Nebuchadnezzar, Nero, or Diocletian, as God was using this tragedy for the greatest good of his people. This humbler stance and focus on the providential strengthening the church through martyrdom with Ribadeneyra's *Tratado de la tribulación* as its theological basis was advanced in the second part of Ribadeneyra's *Historia*, published in 1593, and more thoroughly developed in the subsequent *Historia particular de la persecución de Inglaterra* (1599) by Fray Diego de Yepes, confessor of Teresa of Avila and of King Philip II. These works emphasized God's control over the continuing, albeit ultimately temporary, success of Elizabeth, her pirates Drake and Hawkins, and heresy, while carefully documenting the similarities between the persecutions and martyrdoms of church history from New Testament times and the present English Catholics, a link that evidenced the legitimate pedigree of the Roman Church.

The publication of Ribadeneyra's Spanish adaptation of Sander's *Schismatis Anglicano* in the first part of the *Historia* urged Spaniards to look at England in a specific light. They were encouraged to see the English Reformation as a horrific moral exemplum: a warning against apostasy and a mirror of Spain's potential future – and, like Peter Marshall argued, as an English "Black Legend." Ribadeneyra's *Historia* became so widespread and influential that Spanish authors who referenced events and characters linked to the English Reformation after the *Historia*'s two-part publication in 1588 and 1593 wrote in the shadow of that book, even as late as 1627. Two of Spain's greatest playwrights,

Lope de Vega and Calderón de la Barca, show clear personal and textual connections with Ribadeneyra's *Historia*, while Spain's greatest novelist, Miguel de Cervantes, has more oblique yet suggestive ties to the Jesuit's work.

Despite this deep imprint, Ribadeneyra's *Historia* has rarely been examined outside of theological and religious studies and has been almost completely excluded from the literary canon.[4] As Alison Shell has pointed out in her study of English imaginative works, the architects of the canon at times have neglected texts that were significant in their era – in her case, works by Catholics such as Crashaw that seemed to be excluded on the basis of "protestantised" criteria – thereby creating research gaps in the scholarship of literature and culture and obfuscating confessional fragmentation (*Catholicism* 3). In a similar approach, this book aims to recover Ribadeneyra's ecclesiastical history as a central text not only in shaping Spanish representations and perceptions of England, but also in crystallizing, if not enshrining, for Spaniards the discourse of anti-Protestant, Counter-Reformation debate and Spain's self-imaging in response to this conflict. The significance of the history by Ribadeneyra and the supporting role of Yepes' volume in uncovering Anglo-Spanish networks and their importance to early modern Spanish ideas and literature about England has been partially explored, mostly limited in scope to Elizabeth Tudor and to works that recognizably employed Ribadeneyra's *Historia*, such as Calderón's tragedy *La cisma de Ingalaterra*. To date, no single text explores all these connections systematically, as this book offers, to place them into a cohesive, historically situated framework in order to better understand the relationship between genre, form, and function among complex politico-religious literary texts.[5]

If one looks at Ribadeneyra's *Historia*, especially, as mere propaganda, as scholars in the past have done, it seems radical, ad hominem, and gratuitously pugnacious. However, the forceful, militant language in the history becomes more intelligible and purposeful when placed in the larger context of the Continental Protestant Reformation that influenced England to separate from Roman Catholicism, early modern ideas of religious toleration and persecution aptly outlined by Alexandra Walsham,[6] and when considering the high stakes of what England's actions meant for Spain and European Roman Catholicism. This is not to say that all Spaniards or Catholics were zealous and militant to combat heresy; in fact, the chapters in this book expose the ways in which authors, especially Ribadeneyra, aimed to persuade their audiences of their message, thus implying that a large group, perhaps the majority, were not convinced of the perspective espoused by Ribadeneyra, or at least of its urgency and call to action. Taking a closer look at the apocalyptic and biblical imagery employed in the history and its emphasis on persecutions and martyrs illumines the controlled efforts of Roman Catholic writers to connect current events to the early New Testament Church and thereby affirm Roman Catholicism's historical continuity. Moreover, an analysis of the production and literary features of the volume helps elucidate, first, how the book became so popular and influential among Spanish readers so that it shaped the Spanish imagination concerning England for centuries, and second, the intricacies of an Anglo-Spanish coalition that aimed to protect European Roman Catholicism from dissolution. These kinds of analyses are essential to understand European Roman Catholicism and for meaningful discussions about the Counter-Reformation and the Spanish "Black Legend" themes and tropes, which this study suggests also are applied to England.

Most of what is radical about Ribadeneyra's and Yepes' books has English, not Spanish, origins because it is drawn from English sources:[7] the scandalous details of the history of the English schism and of the horrendous persecutions and martyrdoms. Ribadeneyra's adaptation of Sander´s narrative in some ways is remarkably less radical – with a few exceptions, most obviously the conclusion to the first part where the Jesuit expresses the horror of the English schism embodied in Elizabeth Tudor's murder of Mary Stuart in Black Legend language applied to England and calls Catholics to support the Armada. Ribadeneyra omits some of the scandalous details in Sander's text, and he and Yepes employ common literary elements of their period to make the narrative more devotional and didactic: they heighten the Spanish contributions in England, frame the story as a mirror of princes from which to learn, strengthen the positive and negative portrayals of female characters by setting them against the familiar backdrop of Spanish female conduct manuals, and heighten the role of martyrdom and perseverance to offer hope and affirm the providential past and future continuity of the church.

Surprisingly, despite the gargantuan impact that the "English schism" had upon Spain, in the late sixteenth and early seventeenth centuries only a handful of Spanish literary works were written in relation to the subject. In theater, the first Spanish play borrowing from Ribadeneyra's history seems to have been Lope de Vega's obscure comedy, *El amor desatinado* (1597), followed by Calderón de la Barca's tragedy, *La cisma de Ingalaterra* (1627), both of which attenuate the *Historia*'s monstrous representation of Henry VIII and Anne Boleyn. Within poetry, Lope de Vega maintains Ribadeneyra's characterization of Henry, Anne, Elizabeth, and Mary Stuart – though he allows for complexity with "positive" non-moral traits in two epic poems written around this time, namely, *La Dragontea* (1598) and *La corona trágica* (1627), and in epitaphs from the second part of *Rimas Humanas* (c. 1603). In contrast, Miguel de Cervantes' exemplary novel, *La española inglesa* (1613), offers an unusually positive representation of Elizabethan England and its queen. All these works attest to the widespread influence of Ribadeneyra, at least, and deploy the ecclesiastical history's characters and message in works that are less about England and more about Spanish interests and concerns. As Spaniards look into England, they see themselves and write to take control of events and ideas that threaten to change their status quo, to celebrate and defend Catholicism against Protestant charges and Spain against Black Legend criticism, or simply to teach and delight.

The goal of this book is to examine the corpus of these histories, letters, plays, and poems, as well as the Cervantean novel about this watershed event in England that deeply transformed Spain and Europe in the broader context of the European Reformation, and to set these texts side by side to assess how rhetorical and genre distinctions open and constrain the representation of English Catholics and characters linked to the English Reformation. Additionally, this book will examine through these sources the complex fraternal and antagonistic links between England and Spain at this time – including Black Legend and Counter-Reformation exchanges – that show why a transnational study of this period is essential for a more nuanced understanding of the literature and the mindset of these regions. This study is limited to Spanish literature published between 1580 and 1630 because it is a period that marks the rise of England's power with significant concomitant conflicts and alliances between England and Spain.[8]

The comparative literary analysis of this book is more intelligible when framed both chronologically and thematically. While the first three chapters discuss the production, content, reception, and implications of the texts that shaped Spain's view of the "English schism" – the history by Ribadeneyra, sustained and expanded by Yepes' history – the last part of this volume centers on how the content of these histories is transformed by Lope de Vega, Calderón de la Barca, and Miguel de Cervantes through their works. The first chapter explains the historical and literary context of the European Reformations that was the catalyst for the publishing of ecclesiastical histories. The focus of this analysis is the continuities that exist between Protestant and Catholic sacred texts – since many of them were responding to one another – and the common generic and rhetorical features across confessional lines that made these texts persuasive and popular. Chapter 2 analyzes the specifically Spanish historical and literary context in which Ribadeneyra's *Historia* and later Yepes' *Historia particular* were produced and deployed. It centers on a rhetorical and literary analysis of the texts and the old and new elements they fused together to achieve their goal of defending the Roman Church and Spain against criticism. The third chapter departs from the chronological timeline to compare the letters of Luisa de Carvajal y Mendoza to the histories by Ribadeneyra and Yepes, thus concluding the study of the sources that established the "official view" in Spain. This chapter exposes generic constraints in the histories, hints at ways they may have been produced, and reveals some of the impact Ribadeneyra's *Historia* had upon Catholics like Carvajal. Chapters 4 and 5 are mostly framed thematically by author and genre to show that all Spanish literary works about England share Ribadeneyra's imprint on them. Chapter 4 begins with an analysis of Lope's works in chronological order and ends with a comparison of his early comedy and Calderón's tragedy. Though written in 1604 and published in 1613, the book ends with Cervantes' *novela, La española inglesa*, because it is the only novel and the most positive representation of England among all the works – a point that is better appreciated at the end of the comparative task. By analyzing these literary texts within their historical contexts from the perspective of their generic styles, this book uncovers their social and literary complexities. Contrary to what may be expected, Spaniards did not always reproduce Ribadeneyra's monstrous portrayal of Henry VIII, Anne Boleyn, and Elizabeth Tudor, even when they agreed with the Jesuit. I argue that these adaptations are polyvalent, in part, due to constraints of their respective genres and that they disclose a fluctuating Spanish interest in England that is primarily concerned with Spanish introspection and interests.

This study aims to provide a more nuanced understanding of early modern Anglo-Spanish relations and to avoid the oversimplification of neat us/them categories. While the texts sometimes reflect Spanish/English or Catholic/Protestant binaries, their production evidences mutual collaboration and contamination between categories.[9] In fact, Ribadeneyra and Yepes reproduced what some English Catholics were writing about the English Reformation and Elizabeth Tudor, and Catholic ecclesiastical histories responded to Protestant ones like Foxe's *Acts and Monuments* and the *Magdeburg Centuries*, employing similar strategies that made those books extraordinarily popular. The comparison of the Spanish texts addressed in this book also discloses fragmentation within Catholicism: neither English nor Spanish Catholics were monolithic in their stance towards Elizabeth Tudor or in their opinions of how they should respond to English Catholics who suffered persecution.

Moreover, the works examined in this study suggest that Spaniards turned Black Legend charges back on England, which can be seen in the way that the ecclesiastical histories and Lope's poems invoke the shock of the remotest and cruellest peoples if they were to hear about the horrors and cruelty that Henry's apostasy had produced.

When placed within the larger context of European ecclesiastical histories and biblical literature, Ribadeneyra's and Yepes' histories reveal a strong continuity with the past rather than innovative material, a concern to document sources and claims, and a deep anxiety for the future of the faith, since they advance that what had happened in England could have repeated itself anywhere – even in Spain. Since these Spanish theological concerns were intricately interwoven with political action, this book also addresses the historical and political landscape that is crucial to understanding the texts and culture of the period.

The final aim of my research is to contribute to a better understanding of early modern literature, particularly in Spain. This book recovers the knowledge of two Spanish ecclesiastical histories, highly influential texts that have not been studied within the literary canon and therefore have left literary and cultural gaps. For example, without this analysis it would be impossible to achieve a full understanding how radical Cervantes' *La española inglesa* really is, or whether the seemingly positive characterization details of Drake in *La Dragontea* are actually positive or merely adding complexity to a negative character. In fact, the idea for this book came out of a curiosity to find out whether Cervantes was the only Spaniard in his lifetime to portray Elizabeth Tudor in a jarringly positive way – a study that, astonishingly, no one had undertaken. Culturally, this study illumines one way in which many Spaniards acquired the language and arguments of Counter-Reformation and anti-Protestant debates and the challenges that had to be overcome to persuade Spaniards, who were not united in support for the Enterprise to England, whether to send the Armada or to accept English Catholics. More broadly, these studies illumine the defense of European Catholicism and how nations consumed and adapted ecclesiastical histories and Counter-Reformation ideas and texts.

This book has important limitations. First, while I have strived to gather published literature about England within the 1580–1630 time period in Spain, I have likely inadvertently overlooked lesser-known texts, and therefore, it is not an exhaustive study. Nevertheless, it is a comprehensive study in that the variety of sources and authors represent significant, popular trends in Spain. Also, as might be apparent in glancing at the table of contents, this kind of interdisciplinary and transnational study requires expertise in multiple areas, some of which

I do not claim to have. However, I have attempted to provide a competent amount of information in each of these areas with sources for further research to encourage exploration of areas of study that are sorely needed. In sum, this book aims to fill important research gaps in early modern scholarship by providing a more comprehensive study of the Spanish literary works related to the English Reformation than has been undertaken thus far, with special focus on literary analysis, in the hope of stimulating further interest in these kinds of transnational studies.

Chapter One

The War Brewing in Europe and Its Weapons: Ecclesiastical Histories and Martyrologies

With the erosion of the unity of knowledge and the unity of the church, by the late sixteenth century, Europe was flooded with ecclesiastical or sacred histories[1] disputing the authority of the Pope and the genealogy of the "true" church: the "war of words" had settled in.[2] John Foxe's *Acts and Monuments* (1563), Nicholas Sander's *Schismatis Anglicano* (1585), and Pedro de Ribadeneyra's *Historia eclesiástica* (1588), to name just a few first editions of these texts, sold widely immediately after publication and remained in print at least through the eighteenth century.[3] The subject of church history was relevant to all, and many of these volumes were published in the vernaculars and accessible to a broad audience. In the midst of Catholic and Protestant disputes concerning the authority of the Pope and the history of the church and church practices, the focus turned to producing and transmitting narratives of historical continuity that were supported by abundant documents and texts.[4] Catholics and Protestants alike established archives as repositories for the large number of supporting documents now being gathered and organized in one place.[5] These narratives were successful not just because they offered impressive knowledge and abundant ammunition for winning theological and religious debates but also because they were filled with sensational stories: stories of the lives and deaths of people of all classes that everyone was interested to read and that captured the collective imagination of nations. Thus, the focus of the war of words became the imagination, where the classical rhetorical elements of ethos and pathos (appeals to credibility and emotion) became at least as important as the logos (logical argumentation).

European Ecclesiastical Histories

Typically, early modern European ecclesiastical histories followed the basic model of Eusebius of Caesarea's fourth-century *History of the Church*, which was characterized by the systematic use of primary sources interrupting the narrative, as well as by technical innovations, such as including parallel columns, maps, and book and chapter divisions (Grafton, "Church History" 17–21). Writers of these histories sometimes followed Eusebius' example knowingly – as is the case of John Foxe, whose first copy of the *Acts and Monuments* explicitly mentions in the dedication to the queen that he is writing an "ecclesiastical history" and refers to Elizabeth as Constantine and to himself as Eusebius. However, authors transcended the model in scale by collecting massive archives and incorporating a larger volume of documentation in their texts and by taking advantage of the printing press, typography, and the reproduction of images to improve book design (Grafton, "Church History" 18–21).

Foxe's *Acts and Monuments* (1563), better known as Foxe's "Book of Martyrs," is a good example of this expansion of the ecclesiastical history model. The volume traced the history of the Church of England through independent groups of Christians who endured persecution through the ages, which aligned these groups with the "true church" united solely by the Holy Spirit rather than by the common institution of the Catholic Church. Counting around 1,800 pages in the first edition and 2,300 in the second (published in 1570), Foxe's *Acts and Monuments* was unprecedented in English history because of the wide range of its documentary base and reprinting of archival material: it was an incredible feat of publication for England's rudimentary presses at the time.[6] Though subsequent editions did not keep the label, the second edition of Foxe's tome featured the addition of "ecclesiastical history" to the title (*The Ecclesiastical History, containing the Acts and Monuments*), highlighting the importance of Eusebius' model for Foxe[7] (Ditchfield, "Sacred History" 75; Woolf, "Rhetoric" 245). Foxe's more expansive and hybrid kind of work is central in the discussion of early modern European ecclesiastical histories because his text was highly influential and shares similar literary features with contemporary and later European histories of the church.

In fact, Foxe's work shaped and was shaped by a Catholic response, both in content and possibly in form. In terms of content, Catholic authors sustained direct attacks against Foxe's book and its supporting evidence and offered alternative ecclesiastical histories that located the origins of the Catholic Church and its traditions in New Testament times. While the term is limited, this book will use "Counter-Reformation" to describe these Catholic responses to Reformation ideas in England and the Continent. The second expanded edition of Foxe's *Acts and Monuments* (1570) addressed an extensive list of charges from the Catholic Nicholas Harpsfield against the validity of Foxe's arguments and supporting data, published in the massive *Dialogi sex contra summi pontificatus, monasticae vitae, sanctorum, sacrarum imaginum oppugnatores, et pseudomartyres* (*Six dialogues*, 1566). In fact, both Foxe and Harpsfield wrote for sympathetic and antagonistic readers alike.[8] Harpsfield inadvertently strengthened Foxe's cause by his criticism because *Dialogi sex* forced Foxe to purge his book of unverifiable data and to bolster arguments and add documentation for historical claims that Harpsfield had questioned[9] (Freeman, "Harpsfield" [*ODNB*]). However, only the sixth dialogue (around 250 pages) of *Dialogi sex* addressed Foxe's volume. The remaining five dialogues largely refuted content from the other major Protestant ecclesiastical history of that time that had an important influence on Foxe: the *Magdeburg Centuries*.

Dissatisfied with histories patterned after Eusebius because they were "chiefly devoted to describing or praising individuals," Matthias Flacius Ilyricus produced a different kind of ecclesiastical history that would "show not only what doctrines existed in the church in each century, but also what sorts of ceremonies and songs … for all these things are organically connected to one another" (Grafton, *Worlds* 103). Flacius' goal was that as Christians were questioning traditions in the church, reconstructing the ethos of the primitive church would help sort out which doctrines and practices were aligned with that ethos and which were not. In order to write this ambitious history – the *Historia ecclesiae Christi*, known as the *Magdeburg Centuries* because it registered events century by century (1559–74) – Flacius gathered a team of Protestant Lutheran scholars based in Magdeburg, who came to be known as the *Magdeburg Centuriators*, among which Flacius was chief, guiding the research project (Grafton, "Church History" 16). The Centuriators relentlessly collected documents and information tracing the history of the Christian church following Luther's theology up to the thirteenth century (Cameron, "Protestant Visions" 48). The result was the first modern ecclesiastical history – produced in a research lab through collaborative effort and extensive archival material – that changed the classical model of ecclesiastical history produced by one person and whose methodology Foxe would also adopt. This method of collaborative research and archival collection triggered a similar production in Italy from a Catholic perspective – the *Annales Ecclesiastici* (1588–1607) by Cesare Baronio. The Italian volume was an impressive collective production grounded in extensive archives, particularly in the Vatican, and produced in response to the *Magdeburg Centuries* (Cameron, "Protestant Visions" 49; Guazzelli 53)). Foxe's volume and the *Magdeburg Centuries* showed English Catholics the need to produce a comprehensive historical account of the national, English church up to the present from a Catholic perspective[10] and to gather documents supporting this history. In this dynamic context of polemic debate that included similar research methods and opposing arguments at times supported by the same ancient sources and framed within various gripping literary genres familiar to an early modern audience, it would be difficult to maintain that Catholics and Protestants did not influence and shape each other's arguments and texts.

Translations of primary sources used as evidence also became essential, since translators showed mastery and intellectual authority, controlled interpretation, and were suspicious of interpretations that were not from their co-religionists (Oates 183).[11] This was one impetus for biblical translation and interpretive commentary, as found in the Geneva and Douay-Rheims Bibles. As part of this historical project of demonstrating the continuity of the Catholic Church in England, Thomas Stapleton translated and published in 1565 the venerable Bede's eighth-century *Ecclesiastical History of the English People* (Patterson 256), partially in response to a Protestant translation of the text (Oates 183). Other Catholics extended Bede's timeline to the reign of Elizabeth. The first to acquire some success in this was Harpsfield who, in addition to refuting the Protestants in *Dialogi sex*, was the first to compile an account of the church in England in his *Historia Anglicana ecclesiastica*, a manuscript that was not published until 1622 but had circulated widely since the 1570s (Highley 152, 158–9). Furthermore, Harpsfield's arguments became part of standard Catholic polemic writings of the time – originally reproduced by Thomas Stapleton and Robert Persons[12] – and later incorporated into other ecclesiastical histories (Freeman, "Hands" 97–8; Freeman, "Harpsfield" [*ODNB*]). The most widespread of these histories was Nicholas Sander's *De origine ac progressu schismatis Anglicani* (*Of the Origin and Progression of the English Schism*, known as *Schismatis Anglicano*) – written in 1573 and completed and published posthumously in 1585 by Edward Rishton – a work which would shape Spain's view on England's separation from Rome through the translation and adaptation by the Spaniard Pedro de Ribadeneyra, as will be discussed in the next chapter.

Sander's *Schismatis Anglicano*

By the time Sander's first edition appeared in print, its author was a well-respected historian among Catholic authors, especially because of his numerous publications in defense of the Roman Church (Domínguez, *Radicals* 20; Highley 153–4).[13] Nicholas Sander, an influential Oxford Catholic who had left England upon refusing to swear Elizabeth's Oath of Supremacy, died participating in a papal invasion of Ireland in 1581.[14] His book filled a need for Catholics to respond to the positive portrayal of Elizabeth and the English Reformation in Foxe's *Acts and Monuments,* which was already in its fourth edition when Sander's book came out (Highley 157). The historian J.H. Pollen says that Sander's *Schismatis Anglicano* "had in its day a larger circulation on the continent than any other book about England whatever" and counts fifteen editions of this volume within the first ten years of its publication in various countries (in Latin and in the vernaculars): nine editions in Germany; seven in France; six in Spain; four in Italy; and one each in Poland, Holland, and Portugal (41). Eusebio Rey points out that these are conservative figures because by 1595 Spain had fourteen editions in Castilian alone (860).[15]

Like the *Acts and Monuments, Schismatis Anglicano* drew its evidence from various sources: oral accounts, official documents – most notably Pius V's bull excommunicating Elizabeth – ecclesiastical histories, lives of saints, and biblical and patristic texts. It also gathered diverse Catholic polemic material that was already circulating clandestinely in print or in manuscript, such as *The Life and Death of Sir Thomas More*; Reginald Pole's response to the schism in *Pro Ecclesiasticae Unitatis Defensione* (*Defense of the Unity of the Church*); and Nicholas Harpsfield's arguments in *Dialogi sex, Historia Anglicana ecclesiastica,* and *Treatise of Marriage Occasioned by the Pretended Divorce of King Henry VIII from Queen Catherine of Aragon* – a well-known manuscript not published until the nineteenth century on the invalidity of Henry's divorce from his first wife (Highley 158–60). These diverse sources made *Schismatis Anglicano,* like the Protestant *Magdeburg Centuries* and *Acts and Monuments,* whose original model had been Eusebius, a collaborative work that gathered the research of many people. Moreover, *Schismatis Anglicano* had several English editors and one Spanish contributor. Sander died in 1581 before he could complete the narrative, and Edward Rishton, another English Catholic in exile, took over the project of correcting, editing, and adding materials until Rishton's death in 1585. In fact, Sander's work would continue to be revised and expanded until its final version in 1628, which in 1610 had incorporated a Latin translation of the second part of Pedro de Ribadeneyra's *Historia eclesiástica del scisma de Inglaterra,* showing a mutual Anglo-Spanish influence and cooperation (Rey 860). Moreover, these changes were only those made to the Latin version of *Schismatis Anglicano.* The volume was quickly translated into many languages, and these vernacular texts were sometimes closer to adaptations of the story tailored to different audiences rather than strict translations, as is evident with the Spanish ecclesiastical history by Ribadeneyra. The popularity of Sander's book augured that the later Spanish narration of the same events by Ribadeneyra would likewise attract a large readership. Nevertheless, although the content of the work – the arguments in favor of the Roman Church and against Protestants – was timely and relevant to everyone, the literary features and hybrid form of these ecclesiastical histories – the sensational stories and vivid pictures of characters and events – would cause them to grip the imagination of individuals from various strata of society.

Popular Genres in the *Acts and Monuments*

Scholars like John King and D.R. Woolf have advocated for more study of the literary hybridity of Foxe's *Acts and Monuments* and its strategic appropriation of literary elements not only from ecclesiastical histories, hagiographies, and secular histories, but also from "less serious" popular genres such as romances, comedies, and beast fables (King, "Fiction and Fact" 12–13; Woolf, "Rhetoric" 247). Woolf notes that the narrative freedom of movement in the episodic events in the *Acts and Monuments* that are unified by the quest of the true Christians seeking the true church resembles the pattern of romances rather than the pattern of histories[16] ("Rhetoric" 248). King analyzes specific episodes that employ witty wordplay, dramatic irony, biblical allusions and typology, beast fables, and romantic emplotment ("Fiction and Fact"). Building on King's and Woolf's works, Freeman shows the original sources, stylistic choices, and careful research behind Foxe's book to better understand episodes such as Elizabeth's imprisonment, which is clearly framed as a romance and therefore could be mistaken as completely fictional (*Great Searching*; "John Foxe's Notes"). Further, Woolf suggests that Foxe's use of repetition with variation in the martyr accounts, highly conducive for memorization and oral retelling, also mirrors romances and, coupled with the woodcuts to aid retention of the stories, may explain his appeal to those on the margins of literacy ("Rhetoric" 250–1). Authors point to Foxe's experience in writing two comedies as influential in his production of the *Acts and Monuments*, so that the text reveals grotesque details, "providential jokes" where God's enemies are punished in a Dantesque way according to their sin, and jesting comments from martyrs as they mock and intellectually humiliate their executors (Woolf, "Rhetoric" 247, 256–7). Woolf and King conclude that since Foxe realized the need to entertain his audience just as much as the need to teach them, the "less serious" and popular literary features in his text should be analyzed carefully, and because of its immense popularity, the literary influence of *Acts and Monuments* on later literature must also be studied (Woolf, "Rhetoric" 273; King, "Fiction and Fact" 34–5).

Given the mutually formative polemic exchanges and similar literary hybridity, sources, and patterns between Foxe's work and that of Catholic authors that later became integrated into ecclesiastical histories such as Sander's, a literary analysis of *Schismatis Anglicano* can be fruitful to examine the book's immediate appeal to broad audiences once it appeared in its numerous vernacular translations, including Ribadeneyra's adaptation in his *Historia.* Since Eusebius' *History of the Church* was the original model for both Protestant and Catholic early modern ecclesiastical histories, it could be argued that similarities between *Schismatis Anglicano* and the *Acts and Monuments* derive from this common source, especially since both texts also employed Eusebius' methodology. While this may be true in many instances, the differing goals of the ecclesiastical histories resulted in varying adaptations of the Eusebian model so that, in terms of content, the *Magdeburg Centuries* focused more on church practices than on individuals, as seen above, and the *Acts and Monuments* added to the original model an apocalyptic emphasis and a heavy reliance on oral accounts (Freeman, *Great Searching* 43–4, 66). Nevertheless, both *Schismatis Anglicano* – and later Ribadeneyra's adaptation – and the *Acts and Monuments* share literary features that are absent from their common source, which, of course, could derive from other common literary or cultural sources but remain intriguing.

At minimum, the rapid spread of Foxe's book questioning the Roman Church and offering an alternative, "pure" lineage of Christians tracing back to apostolic times and including recent Marian martyrs demanded a competing Catholic narrative that, in order to be sufficient, had to be persuasive and highly engaging. The earliest Catholic book to achieve this goal was Sander's *Schismatis Anglicano,*[17] though it was limited in language, being written in Latin, and in accessibility, since it was banned in England. This is not to say that Sander's book was intended as a direct response to Foxe in the way that Robert Person's *Three Conversions* was or in the way that Baronio's *Annales* responded to the *Magdeburg Centuries.* Rather, insofar as *Schismatis Anglicano* and the *Acts and Monuments* compiled arguments mutually shaped by Catholic/Protestant debates and to the degree that Sander employed engaging literary elements at times similar to those used by Foxe to capture the imagination of readers, it may be argued that *Schismatis Anglicano* was responding to a theological, literary, and cultural need generated by Foxe that would preserve Roman Catholicism. In the end, both Foxe and Sander understood that to win the theological argument, their sources could not just be persuasive to theologians through the logos: they had to be understood by and, most importantly, capture the imagination of lay readers[18] in a broad economic and social spectrum through the ethos and pathos, and to achieve that goal they had to produce narratives that were entertaining, moving, and memorable.

Among some of the numerous engaging literary devices in Sander's text – many of which appear in Ribadeneyra's – are dramatic direct dialogues,[19] emotive descriptions to soften characters, gruesome details, dark rhetorical flourishes that evoke fear, and numerous ironic providential turns to delight. One clear example of a dialogue that seems extracted from a comedy is the scene where Thomas Boleyn warns Henry Tudor that Anne Boleyn is the latter's daughter, and the king responds: "'Hold your tongue, you fool, hundreds are compromised; and be her father who he may, she shall be my wife. Go back to your embassy, and do not say a word of this.' The king went away laughing, Sir Thomas being still on his knees" (27–8). Henry's ridiculing words calling Thomas a "fool," the description of him laughing as he leaves, and the posture of Thomas on his knees is theatrical and foreshadowing, not unlike the representation of the stereotypical womanizer Don Juan, whose arrogance will set him up for a great fall and later satisfy the sense of justice in the audience, for example, as would later be depicted in Tirso de Molina's highly successful *El burlador de Sevilla*.

Another characterization strategy to protect the saintly representation of Catherine of Aragon and to move audiences through pathos is to add detailed descriptions to display her suffering and evoke compassion and indignation. After a pugnacious dialogue between her and Wolsey where she firmly sets the record straight that she is a victim of his ambition and unwarranted hatred for her uprightness, her emotional distress is displayed to soften her character and justify her actions before the readers with the following line: "Then, when [Wolsey and the other Bishop with him] saw her great distress, and the tears which she could not control, they thought it better to refrain from further discussion" (46). The narrator's comment of Catherine's "great distress" and tears she cannot control is unusual for this queen who is elsewhere in the text characterized as measured and reasonable. Moreover, the comment that the men who are her enemies see and, presumably out of compassion, respect her suffering shows the reader that Catherine, the strong, is also tender, full of feeling, and greatly suffering, thus inviting the reader to feel compassion for her and indignation at the unjust actions she must suffer.[20] Similarly, when she appears before the king, her husband, at court, and pleads with him, the narrator notes that those present "seeing the faces and the demeanor of both husband and wife, could not refrain from weeping" (53). The weeping of Catherine, Henry, and the audience signals to the reader the deep injustice done to Catherine in the breaking of a lawful marriage (for she is a dutiful wife) that causes sorrow to everyone, even to Henry, who is causing this pain, and thus is aimed at showing her as a victim and stirring up pity and a visceral aversion to the divorce in the reader.

Like Foxe's text, Sander includes gruesome descriptions of the executions of martyrs, though these kinds of details appear in Eusebius' history, for example, in the martyrdom of Polycarp in Book IV, chapter 15. The details of the quartering of the "first fruits of martyrs of Henry's schism" (Humfrey Middlemore, William Exmew, and Sebastian Newdigate) are vivid:

> And when they had been hung for awhile, were cut down, being yet alive. Then the executioner mutilated their persons, and threw into the fire that which he had cut off. That done, he laid their bodies open with a sword, wrenched out the entrails, and threw them into the fire before their eyes. Finally, he cut off their heads, and divided their bodies into four quarters, which were first boiled, and then hung up in divers places to be seen of the people. (119)

The details of the men being alive when they are mutilated, their body parts cut and thrown into the fire, being boiled, and finally displayed publicly would be horrifying and yet ghastly appealing to certain readers, searing into their minds the ruthlessness of persecutors who mechanically butcher men like animals and the heroism of those who faced that fate without wavering. This is only one example of many in Sander's volume. Though the events may be factual, the inclusion of such details is a creative choice that makes the text sensational and moving.

Additionally, Sander's volume presents dark, often apocalyptic rhetorical flourishes echoing biblical passages to signal to the reader the extent of fearsome, deeply tragic, or shocking events that supernaturally warn readers. The text uses apostrophe and personification to underscore the unbelievable blindness and hypocrisy of Henry Tudor in his judgment of Wolsey in this line: "Who would not imagine that the king would have wished now to abandon his evil purpose? But be astonished, O heavens, upon this. The very sin for which he punishes Wolsey so severely is the very sin in which the king obstinately persists" (77). The heavens who see everything, supernaturally, should be astonished at this extraordinarily ironic and hypocritical action. In the next lines the reader should recognize St. Paul's words in Romans 2:1–2, now used to dramatically condemn Henry: "Therefore, O king, art thou inexcusable; for wherein thou judgest another thou condemnest thyself, for we know that the judgment of God is according to truth against those who do such things." Implicit in this reference is the foreshadowing of God's judgment falling on Henry, according to the original context of the biblical passage, now meant to be imported with the quotation. At the closing of Book III, another dramatic, apocalyptic biblical echo appears after the death of Mary Tudor and Cardinal Pole: "Then came the hour of Satan, and the power of darkness took possession of the whole of England." The familiar reference to the "hour of Satan" and darkness engulfing the land echoes Jesus' words to the chief priests come to take him away in his darkest hour of Judas' betrayal (Luke 22:47–35) and echoes the apocalyptic darkness signaling God's judgment in the book of Revelation (16:10). The allusion, full of dramatic irony, foreshadows that Elizabeth's reign, controlled by Satan and his minions ("power of darkness"), will fill England with sinfulness, persecution, and death ("darkness"). These references link well-known biblical moments of violence, woe, and divine judgment with England's recent events, thrusting the present into the Apocalypse, as Foxe also had done. This connection moves Christian readers to fear from the imminent evil – with an effect perhaps akin to contemporary horror movies – and to hope for a future redemption, just as God had accomplished in some of the church's darkest moments.

Much like Foxe's *Acts and Monuments*, Sander's volume features entertaining ironic providential twists that justly recompense sinful actions. Thus, Henry Tudor replaces Anne Boleyn with Jane Seymour the day after Anne's execution, the author noting that "as Anne supplanted Catherine, so Jane supplanted Anne," and that "the judgments of God are not less marvellous than they are just, rewarding every one according to his works" (134). Thus, Henry's actions are placed in a providential framework of judgment against Anne, satisfying the audience's sense of justice and pity towards Catherine. Likewise, a dramatic end to Book II discloses that Henry's only legitimate son, Edward, dies as a judgment of Henry on the anniversary of Sir Thomas More's beheading (217), and the last paragraph of Book I notes that because none of his children built a monument for him, Henry himself lay "unhonored" in his grave, possibly as fitting recompense for being "a man who scattered to the winds the ashes of so many saints, and who plundered the shrines of so many martyrs" (165). In fact, Henry also receives in his body the just recompense for gluttony in a comically grotesque description where he is almost unable to pass through doors and cannot walk up stairs, so he is lifted by machinery in a chair to the upper level of the palace (164).[21] In this way, seemingly unconnected events are interwoven in a grand narrative of providential judgment, warning Catholics about their own actions but also giving them satisfaction in seeing the ironic ways in which their enemies are punished and justice is achieved.

Since the rhetorical appeal to pathos is not dependent on the logos, these highly memorable literary devices would imprint these interpreted historical moments and the characterization of historical figures on the imagination of readers, regardless of their accuracy or veracity. Thus, even audiences who did not know or understand the logical and theological arguments for the authenticity of the Roman Church could be persuaded of this point through these literary strategies that presented the historical events of the "English schism" and its consequences in imaginative ways. If nothing else, a vivid and entertaining historical narration was sure to please a large audience.

Conclusion

As discussed in this chapter, the late sixteenth century saw an explosion in the production of ecclesiastical histories – both Protestant and Catholic – tying the lineage of the "True Church" to New Testament times and the establishment of arsenals of documentation and translations to substantiate these narratives. Moreover, these ecclesiastical histories began with the pattern set by Eusebius, but soon the model was adapted to innovative printing press technologies and was outgrown by the need for massive supporting evidence, which in turn required teams of researchers and more expansive, hybrid volumes. As argued, what made these sources most successful, however, was not only that they were timely, relevant, and persuasive, but also that they were able to capture the imagination of readers through vivid, memorable stories and entertaining literary features most often found in "less serious" popular genres such as plays and romances. Scholars' exploration of these features in Foxe's *Acts and Monuments* invites a similar analysis, merely illustrated here, of Sander's *Schismatis Anglicano*, a book that in many ways was influenced by and responded to Foxe's text and which shows similar literary strategies that made the book a bestseller for many years. The common features in these ecclesiastical histories and plays and romances include dramatic dialogues, characterization details that soften strong women like Catherine, gruesome details of martyrdoms, apocalyptic or biblical language to evoke fear, and ironic providential turns to show God's punishment of one's enemies. Many of these elements carried over to adaptations of Sander's text into various vernaculars and, particularly in Spain, were preserved in Pedro de Ribadeneyra's wildly popular adaptation, the *Historia eclesiástica del scisma de Inglaterra*. As the next chapter will discuss, Ribadeneyra, in an effort to make his *Historia* specifically relevant and applicable to Spaniards, added Spanish literary strategies to the arsenal he found in Sander's *Schismatis Anglicano* and thereby was able to mould not only the Spanish imagination concerning England and the English Reformation, an influence evident in Spanish literature published after 1588, but also Spain's perception of its own identity in a time of crisis and external criticism.

Chapter Two

How English Monsters Overtook Spain: Ribadeneyra's Adaptation of *The English Schism* and Yepes' Sequel

Spurred on by Sir Francis Drake's first sack of Cádiz in 1586, Pedro de Ribadeneyra hurried to finish the first part of his soon to be extremely popular ecclesiastical history of the events that led up to what came to be known as the "English schism" under Henry VIII, the *Historia eclesiástica del scisma del reyno de Inglaterra* (1588, 1593) (Rey 864–5). Published in Spain in 1588 as the Armada sailed towards England, this volume provided a Catholic explanation for the existing reign of terror of Elizabeth, Henry's daughter, and justified the attack. In addition to the political and economic tensions between England and Spain, the religious changes in England were of great concern to Catholics all over Europe, but especially for Spaniards, who feared that the fate of England turning against the Pope would incite heresy in Spain. Although by 1588 the news of Henry's apostasy was half a century old, for Catholics the ramifications of that event embodied in Elizabeth Tudor were painfully current, and all previous efforts to bring England back to Roman Catholicism now seemed to have failed. Moreover, Elizabeth Tudor's horrific public executions of the Jesuit Edmund Campion and Mary Stuart, along with the daily martyrdom of Catholics in England, sealed for Catholics the ruthlessness of the English queen and demanded action.

Thus, in addition to setting the historical record straight from a Catholic perspective against Foxe and other Protestants about the English church, Henry VIII, and Elizabeth Tudor, Ribadeneyra's *Historia* had two aims. In the first part (1588), Ribadeneyra aimed to warn Spaniards of flirting with heresy and to enlist their support in the invasion of England and the establishment of a Catholic monarch on the English throne, appealing to Spain's responsibility to lead in this new crusade and thus defend Roman Catholicism and renew Spain's commitment to its defense. In the second part (1593), the Jesuit endeavored to encourage Catholics by linking their persecutions and suffering in England to those of the New Testament Church that providentially was ensured triumph and to promote English seminaries in Spain and missionary endeavors to England.[1] The ideas of this second part were supported and further expanded by another widely read text that adapted English polemic materials for a Spanish audience and bolstered Ribadeneyra's vision of the English Reformation, namely, Fray Diego de Yepes' *Historia particular de la persecución de Inglaterra* (1599).

That Spaniards like Ribadeneyra and Yepes would portray Elizabeth as an irredeemable monster – the product of lust, incest, and apostasy – and advocate for a crusade against England is not surprising. However, these ecclesiastical histories reveal that the monstrous characterization of Elizabeth had an English – not Spanish – origin and that Spaniards, for various reasons, hesitated to reproduce the most scandalous charges from English exiles and thus modified the representation.[2] Furthermore, as will be shown, the indictments and incendiary language against Elizabeth Tudor, particularly forceful in Ribadeneyra's first part, from the theological perspective of the Reformation debates and early modern ideas of heresy and religious toleration[3] are neither gratuitous nor unmeasured but rather reveal the real threat that the English Reformation became for Spain and Roman Catholicism at large and the fear of theologians like Ribadeneyra that Spain was far from being immune from the lures of Protestantism.[4] From this context arose not only the need to warn Roman Catholics against any small indulgence with heresy but also to assure them that any victory of Protestants was only temporary and under God's providential control. The antagonistic language concerning Elizabeth also includes a direct recasting of specific Black Legend and anti-Catholic criticism leveled at Spain and the Pope – most popularly disseminated through Foxe's *Acts and Monuments* – to fit English apostates. Nevertheless, though the language in Ribadeneyra's *Historia* against "English heretics" is strong, the text also displays fraternal relationships and attitudes towards England, also evident in Yepes' text. In fact, these works implicitly model a kind of Anglo-Spanish collaboration and reveal a network of people and resources that contributed greatly to the success of these narratives. More importantly, they offered a cogent theological explanation going back to New Testament times for Roman Catholics throughout Spain and the Continent to understand the terrible turn of events in England for the Roman Catholic Church[5] and to reclaim an honorable name and identity for Catholics who had been and were being called pharisees, idolaters, and traitors.

This chapter focuses on the various literary tropes and genres – sometimes inverting those of Protestant polemic sources like Foxe's *Acts and*

Monuments – that Ribadeneyra employed to seal into the imagination of his audience that Elizabeth I was an irredeemable heretic, condemned by God from her birth; that English Catholics were suffering brethren desperately in need of Spanish aid; and that the persecutions were a sign of the authenticity of the Roman Church. Its representations of Henry VIII, Anne Boleyn, and Elizabeth Tudor, in particular, left a deep imprint on the Spanish imagination that would have long-lasting effects that can be seen, most immediately, in works by Lope de Vega, Calderón de la Barca, and Miguel de Cervantes, as will be discussed in later chapters. In fact, so strong was the footprint of Ribadeneyra's narrative that it is possible to speak of "Ribadeneyra's vision" of England's separation from Rome as later becoming Spain's more or less "official" stance concerning the events, even if Spaniards questioned or modified this narrative for their own purposes. In effect, Ribadeneyra did for Spain what Foxe had done for England, according to Freeman: "Before Foxe wrote there was no popular history of the Reformation; after him, there was no other" (*Great Searching* 7).

In addition to drawing from the strategies and success of the European histories already discussed, the immense popularity of Ribadeneyra's *Historia* in Spain can be partially attributed to historical and literary factors particular to Spain that Ribadeneyra and later Yepes used to shape their volumes. Historically, their works resonated with the Spanish sense of messianic mission to lead in crusades defending the faith, the nationalistic pride in their heritage of guarding the faith from the Catholic Monarchs through Philip II, and many Spaniards' zeal for orthodoxy and fear of heresy.[6] From a literary perspective, this chapter will show that Ribadeneyra's history likely gained traction in Spain because, like the books by Foxe and Sander, it was hybrid, incorporating elements from popular genres of the time with the further addition of Spanish literary sources: it had the authority of histories and political treatises; the didacticism of ecclesiastical histories, conduct manuals, and martyrologies; and the entertainment value of novels and comedies. In many ways, like Foxe's *Acts and Monuments,* Ribadeneyra's *Historia,* true also of Yepes' sequel, was the best model of the Horatian principle of "teaching and delighting" that was ubiquitous in literature of the period[7] and that addressed some of the main Spanish objections against fiction: that of being salacious, full of lies, and a waste of time.[8] In fact, the histories by Ribadeneyra and Yepes were real-life "*historias peregrinas*" (strange stories)[9] with sexual scandal, incest, and even monsters and miracles that warned sinners against God's judgment and set the present into apocalyptic times. As such, they were widely endorsed and read by Spanish Catholics, especially after 1588.

The Historical and Theological Catalyst

Anglo-Spanish relations around 1588, of course, were complex. Although the kingdoms historically had generally been amicable, Henry VIII's declaration of autonomy from Rome and the Pope and the insult of repudiating his wife, Catherine of Aragon, and declaring his daughter, Mary Tudor, illegitimate offended Spain but did not elicit a military attack. After Henry VIII England would be torn between successors who supported the authority of the Pope or resisted it, influenced by ideas from reformers like Calvin and Luther. Henry's son, Edward VI, took a hard line in opposing Roman Catholicism in his short, six-year reign (1547–53), after which his half-sister Mary Tudor, granddaughter of the Catholic Monarchs, became queen (1553–8). Mary carefully employed parliamentary precedents to bring England back under the Pope with the help of Cardinal Reginald Pole (Wizeman 12). Though chastisement changes under Mary's rule were focused on restoring what had been lost under Henry and Edward,[10] the unprecedented burning of heretics in England became controversial and from that point alienated the moderate English from Roman Catholicism (Duffy 1; MacCulloch 273–7). Mary married Prince Philip (later Philip II) but died childless in 1558, and Spain's marriage ties with England were dissolved. To re-establish this alliance, Philip II offered his hand to Elizabeth Tudor, half-sister of Mary, but she did not accept. Nonetheless, as King of England with Mary, Philip had been involved first-hand with efforts to draw England back to Roman Catholicism and throughout his life for various reasons would continue to support efforts in achieving that goal, even while the English people would become increasingly polarized in their stance towards Roman Catholicism.

Elizabeth Tudor remembered Philip's kindness in interceding on her behalf before her sister in earlier years, but in time, the political relations between England and Spain became strained – especially when Elizabeth began to persecute Roman Catholics after Pope Pius V excommunicated her in 1570 and when she allowed, and sometimes endorsed, English piracy of Spanish ships (de Pazzis Pi Corrales 17–19). This led to the Anglo-Spanish War (1585–1604), a conflict which was not only economic but also involved interventions in the Low Countries, succession power struggles, and Catholic-Protestant rivalries. In this conflict, the language of religion was employed by both sides to give impetus to a war that was much more than just a religious war, and the status of Spain as the leader in the protection of the faith was brought to the forefront of the discourse.

In this milieu under Elizabeth I, the Spanish "Black Legend" defamation propaganda, often extended to Roman Catholics called "Papists," was popularized and gradually solidified in England. Though this term would become cohesive in retrospect and would not be coined until the nineteenth century, one useful definition that will be used in this book is that it refers to "a cohesive, but flexible system of anti-Spanish stereotypes that circulated in the XV–XVII centuries, representing Spaniards as beings who were especially tyrannical, cruel, intolerant, lustful, and avaricious" (Sánchez Jiménez, *Leyenda Negra* 22). Under this view, Spaniards and their monarchs, particularly Philip II, were covetous, lustful, and greedy, but also ruthless, deceitful, and proud – all of which was obvious in the Spanish Inquisition and the exploitation of the Americas, in which only barbaric peoples could have participated (Sánchez Jiménez, "Quevedo y Lope" 43–4). Samson convincingly argues that during the reign of Mary Tudor, though she and Philip II were sometimes criticized, a pervasive idea of the Spanish Black Legend did not yet exist in England. Rather, it was a retrospective construction that began with the Reformation, particularly with Bale and Foxe's *Acts and Monuments* and other polemic works by Marian exiles ("A vueltas" 93–4). As will be seen in chapter 3, in 1612 Luisa de Carvajal witnessed the English mocking Spain with this language, calling it "a land of most cruel savage beasts" and saying that Spaniards "[drank] human blood" and worshipped "the abomination of the antichrist and the Whore of Babylon," identified as the Pope[11] (*Epistolario* 374). Because of Spain's central role in defending Roman Catholicism, the image of a fanatical, greedy, and barbaric Spain transferred to Roman Catholicism at large, especially in England.[12] As the second part of Carvajal's quotation shows, Protestants associated the Pope with the Whore of Babylon and the antichrist,[13] while Catholics, as will be shown, linked these ideas to Elizabeth Tudor.

The Anglo-Spanish polemic intensified after two public executions of Catholics in England. First was that of Edmund Campion (1581), one of the first English Jesuit missionaries, and several other English Catholic priests who had been charged with treason. The second execution under the charge of treason for involvement in a plot against Elizabeth was that of Elizabeth's own cousin, Mary Stuart, Queen of Scots (1587). As granddaughter of Margaret Tudor, sister of Henry VIII, Mary had a legitimate claim to the English throne and embodied the hopes of many to restore Catholicism in England. Ribadeneyra and many Catholics throughout the Continent presented Mary's death as that of a martyr for the faith under the hand of a tyrant heretic, a shocking and horrifying event, although historical records show that matters surrounding the execution of Mary were much more complex, and many Catholics had not always supported her.

Mary Stuart had been complicit in a plot that, unbeknownst to her, was being monitored by Elizabeth's officials, so there was ample evidence against the Scotswoman.[14] Moreover, Mary's asylum had been a delicate political matter involving relations with Spain, Scotland, England, and France that Elizabeth was attempting to resolve, and even in the face of indisputable evidence against Mary, Elizabeth was reluctant to approve the execution until Parliament forced her to do so.[15] Nonetheless, because of Elizabeth's excommunication by Pope Pius V and her execution of Catholics, the English queen was perceived by militant Catholics as a heretical tyrant who had to be overthrown, and Mary's death projected her as yet another victim of the unjust oppressor. According to this opinion, to secure her position Elizabeth had framed and killed the legitimate heir to the English throne and her rival. In fact, Ribadeneyra closes the first part of his ecclesiastical history in 1588 with Mary's imprisonment and execution in England as the culminating demonstration of Elizabeth's ruthlessness and cruelty, and Antonio de Herrera presents a similar conclusion in his "secular" *Historia de lo sucedido en Escocia e Inglaterra* published in 1590 (173v). As will be discussed in more detail below, Ribadeneyra's *Historia* described Elizabeth's barbaric killing of her relative in language gesturing at an English Black Legend that even remote heathen peoples would condemn as the logical outcome of Henry's apostatizing out of lust to marry his own biological daughter, Anne Boleyn.

Ribadeneyra's work echoed writings by Richard Verstegan, Adam Blackwood, Thomas Stapleton, Cardinal Allen, and Nicholas Sander – English Catholic leaders who advocated for a Catholic crusade against England in the name of the Pope, who had a right to depose a heretical ruler (Highley 172). These ideas undergirded the expedition of the Spanish Armada,[16] which many considered inevitable once it was clear that Elizabeth was intractable in her religious – and therefore political – position. However, Ribadeneyra's appeal in the *Historia* implies that many Spaniards had yet to be convinced that Spain should intervene. Therefore, his ecclesiastical history was meant to buttress the efforts to reconvert England to Catholicism – which in 1588 Ribadeneyra believed would only happen with military intervention.[17] The history explained why the reconversion of England was essential for Spain and for Roman Catholicism and called for measures necessary to accomplish this worthy goal – from intercessory prayers, to supporting Catholic seminaries and missionaries, to the forceful removal of heretics from the English throne. Furthermore, Ribadeneyra's work vindicated the death of Catholics, stating that they were martyrs rather than traitors, contradicting Elizabeth and later James I on this point, and emphasized the spiritual obligation to intervene in seemingly foreign political events. Nevertheless, Ribadeneyra had a personal interest in England – he had been in London at the time of Mary Tudor's death, knew English,[18] and was well acquainted with English Elizabethan exiles – and as such remained an advocate for preserving brotherly bonds between England and Spain – at least among Catholics. Because of this, his *Historia* can be read not only as a polemic text, but also as a case for Anglo-Spanish cooperation and an appeal to the ancient fraternity between the two nations when such relationship was quickly eroding. His volume can also be studied as an effort to reclaim for Spain a wholesome and strong Christian identity at a time of internal perceived weakening and external Black Legend charges.

Enter Ribadeneyra and Yepes

The first part of Ribadeneyra's *Historia eclesiástica del scisma del reyno de Inglaterra* was essentially a dynamic translation of Sander's *Schismatis Anglicano* (1585) and a remaking of an Eusebian history with interpretive commentary by Ribadeneyra that fits with the militant spirit of 1588. In this volume, he claims to have a didactic goal along with a broader, national purpose for writing, and in his preface to "the Christian and pious reader" he spells out his theological commitments and reasons for publishing this text, which correspond to his being a Spaniard and a member of the Society of Jesus (Ribadeneyra 899–901). As a Catholic, Ribadeneyra will endeavor to "favor and advance all things pertaining to [his] sacred religion" (900) – which includes tracing and recording the sufferings of the church at large, of which the English Catholics are a part. As a Jesuit he avows he is obligated to defend Christianity against heretics and heathens, in this case, especially, Henry VIII, Anne Boleyn, and Elizabeth Tudor (900). Finally, as a Spaniard he writes to disclose the virtue and sufferings of the pious Spaniard Catherine of Aragon, the magnanimity of Philip II, and whatever is of "honor and profit [*provecho*] to [his] nation"[19] (Ribadeneyra 899–900). Ribadeneyra also explicitly writes to make known the sufferings of the English Catholics (Christian brothers and sisters) for encouragement to the faithful; to expose the heresy of Henry VIII, Anne Boleyn, and Elizabeth; and to rally support (political, missionary, and economic) from Spaniards for English Catholics (Ribadeneyra 1318–25). While these goals are noticeable throughout Ribadeneyra's history, the first part reflects a spirit of military crusade, focusing on Elizabeth as a tyrant to be overthrown, while the second part more humbly turns military disappointments to providential victories for the church through persecution and the martyrs, whose testimonies inspire many to return to Catholicism and encourage missionary support.[20] This second part of the book was largely a Spanish adaptation of Robert Persons' *Elizabethae Angliae Reginae* (1592),[21] which exposed and refuted Elizabeth Tudor's 1591 proclamation against seminary priests and Jesuits, and had a providentialist focus on martyrs drawing from Ribadeneyra's *Tratado de la tribulación*.[22] In 1610 this second part was translated into Latin and appended to Sander's history (Rey 860, 886).

The same spirit and goals of this second part were supported and developed in Yepes' *Historia particular de la persecución de Inglaterra* (1599). In this volume, Yepes consciously compiled information from published and unpublished early modern Roman Catholic writings – including the histories of Sander and Ribadeneyra – noting that the things described in his text were well known because they had been presented publicly in judgment of Catholics ("Prefacion al Letor"). Yepes' volume fleshed out in more detail the arguments in Ribadeneyra's *Tratado de la tribulación* as they related to the English persecution, arguing that since Elizabeth had been unable to stamp out Catholics from England despite intense endeavors, their providential survival thus far ensured that they would persevere until the end because God's people had always outlived persecutions.

Like Ribadeneyra, Yepes connected the English tribulations to the universal church, weaving in example after example of times when the New Testament Church's experience was very similar to that of the current Roman Catholics in England, and explicitly argued for the relevance of these links to Spaniards. His first connection to the early church is in the act of writing, observing that all the sufferings of the Catholic Church have always been recorded for its members in martyrologies and histories – citing the examples of Popes Clement and Fabian and the churches of Smyrna, Vienna, León, and others – as a testimony of the holy faith ("Prefacion al Letor"). He adds that he "knits" this "ecclesiastical history" of England – even though it is still unfinished and some parts are dangerous to disclose[23] – because particular details are more delightful to read and are better understood when connected to universal principles[24] and because the story of England's apostasy and faithful martyrs can be beneficial ("ser de provecho") for all, as an illustration of Saint Paul's warning for Christians not to shipwreck from the faith ("Prefacion al Letor" 3). In this way, the news from England about Catholic persecution was recast into a spiritual narrative of providence that argued for continuity between the English Roman Catholics and the primitive church of the New Testament and was thus transferable to Catholics everywhere, including Spain.

Unlike Ribadeneyra's *Historia,* whose reach seems fairly clear, it is very difficult to ascertain the Spanish reception of Yepes' *Historia* and the extent of its influence because very little has been written on this book.[25] However, the volume was certainly widely read, since copies appear in most library catalogues of the period, and other works by Yepes, such as the *Life...of St. Teresa,*[26] were also extremely popular. More importantly, although it has significant stylistic differences from Ribadeneyra's text, given its supporting role both in endorsement and in expansion of the second part of Ribadeneyra's *Historia,* a study of Ribadeneyra's imprint on Spain with respect to England would be incomplete without a discussion of Yepes' history as a complementary work. Thus, while the central text in this period is undoubtedly Ribadeneyra's, both histories will be discussed together to arrive at a fuller picture of the ways in which Ribadeneyra's vision of England may have become entrenched in Spain.

Both Ribadeneyra's and Yepes' adaptations of English material were to teach a Spanish audience not only how to think about England and Elizabeth but also how to think about Spain (renewing the tradition of a glorious past) and Catholicism (tying Roman Catholicism to the New Testament Church through suffering). Ribadeneyra heightened the role of the Spanish characters and their virtues – he added to Sander's narrative letters from Philip II and emphasized his influence in restoring Catholicism in England alongside Mary Tudor, among other details about Catherine of Aragon, Mary Tudor, and Mary Stuart – and he omitted prosaic portions unimportant to Spaniards, such as details about the legality of Henry's divorce.[27] Also, because Sander and his editor Rishton were dead by 1585, Ribadeneyra and Yepes updated the history after this time until 1599, especially with accounts of martyrs. Some of the particular martyrdoms have only survived in Yepes' history, thus preserving valuable information for Catholics.[28] Both Spaniards translated and compiled English Catholic texts and accounts and helped them circulate in Europe, since these texts, logically, were banned in England. As will be shown, they also encouraged Spaniards to see the English church as foreign, new, and foundationally flawed, tying these ideas to the imagination through bodily monsters and admirable saints. Thus, Ribadeneyra and Yepes were not merely reporting historical facts or creating an arbitrary defamation campaign of England, but rather, they were part of a transnational concerted effort in theological and political support of Catholicism against Protestant attempts to discredit the Roman Church by undermining the authority of the Pope as well as by associating Roman Catholicism with bloodshed, the antichrist, idolatry, Pharisees, and treason. While it could be argued that Catholic works produced in Spanish were of little help to the English (as Luisa de Carvajal often pointed out), the Germans, and others, they generally would have been intelligible to speakers of Portuguese, French, and Italian. Additionally, the breadth of Philip II's kingdom had extended the knowledge of Castilian not only to the Low Countries but also outside the Spanish empire, thus making Spanish works useful transnationally.[29]

The writings of Ribadeneyra and Yepes would be persuasive to Spanish Catholics not only because they were opportune to the historical moment but also because they used a hybrid genre of ecclesiastical history – an ideal package to convey the message, as Foxe had discovered – with other popular literary strategies that captured the imagination of readers and were aptly tailored to Spanish interests and preoccupations. In effect, Ribadeneyra set the tone and arguments for Spanish perceptions of England as the Armada headed to England (focusing on Elizabeth and Henry as monsters) and after the Armada's defeat (focusing on martyrs, perseverance, and providence), and these arguments were supported by Yepes. In the end, these histories contributed to the solidification of a particular image of Elizabeth and the English Reformation that originated in England, initially encountered some publication resistance in Spain, but would quickly become the standard and enduring Spanish vision.

The Challenges to Overcome

The task of persuading Spaniards to enlist in helping English Catholics was not easy. One of the main sources of anxiety and complaints during the reigns of Emperor Charles V and Philip II was precisely the depletion of Spanish resources in foreign religious wars outside of Spain. Furthermore, by 1588, Spain had already suffered three bankruptcies under Philip II (1557, 1560, 1576) and would undergo another one in 1596 (Kamen 177, Elliott 196–7, 207–8). In fact, even Philip II had been hesitant to invade England and was largely criticized for it (Hillgarth 9; Domínguez, "History in Action" 19). Thus, their resources were limited, and Spaniards had to be convinced that "the Enterprise of England"[30] was a worthy cause that had direct repercussions on Spain.[31]

In addition to being weary of spending money on great international enterprises, many Spaniards were suspicious of or strongly disliked the English and therefore were unwilling to shelter Catholic exiles in Spain. By the 1540s, Henry VIII's actions had brought about associations of England with a heretical/Lutheran "other," and the words "Lutheran" and "English" seem to have become interchangeable for some Spaniards

(Marshall 47–8). This is most noticeable in Lope de Vega's texts discussed in chapter 4, where for example in *La Dragontea* Lope refers to Drake's men as "the vile seed of infamous Luther" (188). During the Anglo-Spanish War English spies entered Spain disguised as pilgrims to Compostela, itinerant friars, or Scottish or French traders, enhancing Spanish suspicion of all foreigners (Loomie, *Spanish Elizabethans* 60–1). This Spanish anti-English sentiment extended to the English Catholics fleeing persecution in England to receive training at Saint Alban's Royal English College in Valladolid so that they could return to their land as missionaries to the Protestants.[32] A letter from Nicholas Sander's sister, Elizabeth, to an English gentleman living in Madrid in 1589 discloses that the English priests who came to Spain were confident to find at their destination "hospitality and charity, even though the masses ha[d] great aversion towards them because of the hatred that the English name has gathered in these years"[33] (Parsons 71). The correspondent goes on to make a sharp distinction between these priests and "English heretics" who are willing to do more damage (*agravios*) to their own countrymen than to Catholics of other nations, and the letter also gives reasons to dispel the anxieties of Spaniards who feared that the English who were coming to Spain could be spies (Parsons 71–2). The letter concludes with an exhortation to trust in God and to empathize with fellow Catholics from a nation of friends who have no other recourse than the help of Spain:

> We trust God that there will be much less danger in the negotiation of the Faith with receiving and sheltering these who are persecuted by the same Faith. Rather, it will be of great merit, glory, and honor for Spain, both before God and before men, to have succoured a nation of such friendship and so afflicted by God and by Spain itself, as is the English Catholic part. And this during a period of so much conflict and need, when they almost have no other refuge nor can resort to another part of the world because of the wars and heresies that exist everywhere, and when they await their total relief to come, after God, from Spain and Spaniards.[34] (Parsons 73–4)

The note encourages Spaniards to help by diminishing fears ("much less danger") and magnifying the rewards ("will be of great merit, glory, and honor"), by making the rewards both eternal ("before God") and earthly – and perhaps even political ("before men").

This excerpt not only evidences the atmosphere of dislike of some Spaniards towards the English but also rallies Spanish Catholics by appealing to the fraternal relationship that Spain and England have had in the past ("a nation of such friendship"), to the messianic sense of Spain in leading in Christian endeavors, and to the universal Catholic Church, outlining the responsibilities of its members towards one another. The text argues that Spaniards should hold fraternal compassion towards the English Catholics greatly suffering at the hand of English heretics because of "the same Faith," uniting Spaniards with co-religionist English people who were suffering unjustly, setting aside national identities and differences. Furthermore, the repetition of the adverb "so/such" (*tan/tanto*) highlights the dire situation of the English and Spain's obligation towards them. England is called "a nation of such friendship" (*tan amiga*) and "so afflicted" (*tan afligida*). Providentially, the perpetrators of the affliction are God (*afligida por Dios*) and Spain herself, and if this is so, these agents have an inescapable obligation to help the English Catholics in a time of "so much conflict and need" (*tanto aprieto y necesidad*). In effect, the English have nearly nowhere else to flee, and they hope in God and in Spain for relief. From the author's perspective, this plea could only be rejected by cold-hearted Spaniards who were not good Christians. The same argumentation employed in this letter of the requirements of a universal Catholicism transcending national boundaries was used in Ribadeneyra's preface already referenced, as well as in Luisa de Carvajal's letters when requesting support from her wealthy connections in Spain, as will be shown in the next chapter.

An important obstacle that Ribadeneyra had to overcome was obtaining permission to publish his narratives about England. Even the strongest supporters of the English Catholics, the Jesuits, had serious misgivings about propagating some of the scandalous charges against Elizabeth and her lineage. The vice provincial initially denied the request to print the first part of Ribadeneyra's *Historia*, and General Claudio Acquaviva wondered why Ribadeneyra would not just publish a strict Spanish translation of Sander's text (Rey 865; Domínguez, "History in Action" 5–6). Domínguez suggests that one of the main concerns of Society leaders may have been to avoid the perception that Jesuits were meddling in secular affairs and, more importantly, in inflammatory political matters, and that is one reason the *Historia* has a strong emphasis on spiritual lessons to be learned and Ribadeneyra was careful in choosing his words ("History in Action" 7–8; *Radicals* 69–70). Furthermore, Jesuit leaders were hesitant to approve the publication of the work because opening the English events to the unlearned "vulgo" could be dangerous, and the translation was only approved after much deliberation and assurances by the influential Cardinal Allen that it would not cause havoc (Domínguez, "History in Action" 6–7). Even the second part of Ribadeneyra's *Historia* was temporarily prohibited shortly after being published because Philip II was uncomfortable with the fact that

Elizabeth's proclamation of 1591 that included harsh criticism of the Spanish king had been put in the vernacular, and the section was edited out (Rey 885–6; Weinreich, "Introduction" 48–51). However, given that the *Acts and Monuments* and the *Geneva Bible* and other Protestant works were written in the vernacular and circulated widely, many Roman Catholics, including Ribadeneyra and Yepes, saw the need to correct these errors by counter-publishing works in the language people at large could understand.[35]

Adapting the Work of English Authors

The Anglo-Spanish cooperation in the production of Ribadeneyra's and Yepes' histories could only help to convince their audience by establishing rhetorical ethos, or credibility. As detailed in chapter 1, the English provided first-hand knowledge of events in England by "grave men" and a basic narrative framework of the schism and its aftermath that was already a publication success throughout Europe in Sander's *Schismatis Anglicano*. The Spaniards endorsed the information and effectively adapted the English narrative to address the interests and concerns of fellow Spaniards in Castilian, making it accessible to a broad audience of Catholics who could support their English brethren. Moreover, choosing the ecclesiastical history genre to show the need for a new crusade and a connection between the Roman Catholic and New Testament Church was masterful because the medium was flexible and authoritative. As histories debated by Reformation ideas and forced by skepticism in society towards an increasingly critical use of sources and copious documentation that made them more open to corroboration and disproof,[36] they were considered trustworthy.[37] Moreover, ecclesiastical histories interpreted historical events in light of the theological narrative of the church and connected history with biblical content, endowing their narratives with the indisputable authority of divine sanction. Thus, the best medium at the time to guide Catholic Spaniards' interpretation of the persecutions under Elizabeth and to persuade them to intervene was not the chronicle or even the hagiography, but the ecclesiastical history – and Ribadeneyra chose to model his after the most popular Catholic one: Sander's *Schismatis Anglicano*.

Like Foxe's and Sander's works, Ribadeneyra's text, and to a certain extent Yepes', was hybrid, patterned after Eusebius' story but also borrowing literary elements from hagiographies, martyrologies, and popular genres such as sermons, comedies, and chivalric novels. Both Spanish histories were in the vernacular, and their diction was direct and simple, with memorable rhetorical details suitable to be read aloud.[38]

Their narrative style, too – including revised chapter divisions and catchy titles that pointed to the plot of each section, such as "The trickery of the heretics to obscure the Catholic Faith is discovered: and how Faith began to shine again. Ch.X" and "Chapter XXV. The persecution that arose against the Catholics because they did not recognize the Queen as head of the Church"[39] (Yepes 15; Ribadeneyra 1102) – recalled the style in Spanish chronicles also used in chivalric novels and satirized in *Don Quixote*. Inverting the common beast fable pattern displayed in Foxe's text,[40] Ribadeneyra and Yepes present English Catholics as lambs who are being slaughtered by the monstrous tyrant Elizabeth and are in dire need of help from Spanish brothers and sisters. Both volumes – but especially Yepes' because it has a stronger focus on martyrs – collect comic, grotesque, or horrifying providential, miraculous signs or judgments that would grip readers, such as seeing live faces on quartered bodies of martyrs,[41] the instant striking of persecutors with illnesses where they expel urine orally,[42] and exorcisms involving vomiting of hair and iron pieces impossible to be found inside people.[43]

Additionally, the inclusion of direct dialogue and moving private letters, such as those penned by Catherine of Aragon and Mary Stuart that were not recorded in Sander's text, gave the protagonists a voice to disclose publicly intimate feelings of pain, fear, and faith akin to soliloquies on the stage for rhetorical pathos evoking sympathy or indignation, and it also gave the histories an aura of authenticity. Ribadeneyra's addition of Queen Mary Tudor's habit of disguising herself to visit her poor subjects in the village in order to comfort them and hear and remediate their complaints, even if it were factual, recalls kind princesses in folk tales (1090). Mary Stuart's moving speech to her audience as she steps on the scaffold for her execution, asking them to pray for her and for Elizabeth and resolutely affirming her faith and willingness to be an example of the evils of heresy, would have deeply moved listeners as if watching the end of a tragedy and sealed in their minds her innocence, as her forgiveness of her enemies and the committing of her soul to God emulated Christ's, Stephen's, and other saints' deaths (Ribadeneyra 1181–2). In fact, in an excursus on how Mary Stuart valued eternal over material things, Ribadeneyra adds, "she knew that this life is a play [*comedia*], and that all who live in it, though they be kings, are actors [*representantes*]," alluding to the common trope that the world is a stage and equating it to the scaffold (Ribadeneyra 1183).

The combination of these literary techniques, as well as a few other significant ones that will be discussed below, explain the Spanish ecclesiastical histories' readability and popular enjoyment, while their homiletic and devotional content ensured they were profitable (*de provecho*) and edifying to Catholic readers. In fact, Yepes made this point explicitly in his dedication to the king, saying that he wrote so that Philip II would have "holy entertainments according to his taste for the relief of his long infirmities" and that the confessor would tell the king details about the English persecution "because of the benefit and comfort" from their lessons that served to distract the king on his deathbed (4, 893).

Persuasive Elements of Ecclesiastical Histories

Like Sander, Ribadeneyra and Yepes used the logos and ethos of testimonies from authoritative authors, witnesses, and documents and appealed to the imagination through the pathos of various literary devices, including the use of exemplum and biblical typology – connecting early Christians, events, and martyrs to the present – and flat characters and monster rhetoric to vilify opponents. Ribadeneyra and Yepes added features especially appealing to a Spanish audience, including a more marked evocation of Spain's glorious past and heritage, an exhortation to the monarchy to fulfill the role of the great Spanish Christian princes of the past – such as was common in Christian prince treatises – and a strong alignment of female characters with the decorum of women dictated in early modern Spanish conduct manuals.

Like *Schismatis Anglicano*, all the added sources in the histories of Ribadeneyra and Yepes adjusted to the demand that historical accounts be supported by authoritative documents and witnesses. Ribadeneyra claims to write simply and truthfully ("con toda llaneza y verdad"), using as his sources early modern histories ("las historias de nuestros tiempos"), especially Sander's, who gathered his information from public documents and writings, oral and written testimonies from trustworthy men ("hombres gravísimos"), and from things he himself observed[44] (Ribadeneyra 905). In fact, the title page of his 1588 volume advertises that the history has been "gathered from diverse and grave Authors, by the Father Pedro de Ribadeneyra, of the Society of Jesus," ensuring the reliability of the sources and of the editor. Likewise, Yepes' 1599 title page also declares that his history includes "many strange things [*cosas curiosas*] not published until now, taken from grave authors," and he emphasizes the credibility of his sources by pointing out that they had circulated in Latin – implying scholarly scrutiny – and that they had been brought up in "public judgment [*juizio*]" against the Catholics and had therefore been widely examined ("Prefacion al Letor"). The title page advertises that the history was "gathered" by Yepes, adding his titles of "confessor of King don Felipe II" and "Bishop of Taraçona." If Ribadeneyra's name – denoting a well-known Jesuit leader and lauded writer who had been the companion and biographer of Ignatius of

Loyola – was not already sufficiently credible, Fray Diego de Yepes' endorsement of Ribadeneyra's *Historia* imbued it with such authority as to make it practically indisputable in Spain. In fact, although the Elizabethan exile Joseph Creswell heavily edited and supplemented Yepes' *Historia* to the point that he could be considered a co-author, Yepes' name alone appeared on the title page, apparently by consensus of Creswell and Robert Persons, another influential Catholic exile.

Rogers reasonably argues that Creswell was the master compiler and editor behind all the English Catholic polemic materials in Yepes' volume but that it was published under Yepes' name because of his prestige. For the letter where Yepes discusses this with Persons, see Forteza, "Particular Providence." Another persuasive strategy involving ethos and pathos used to convince Spaniards to help English Catholics was to appeal to Spain's glorious Christian past and advocate for its renewal. Implied in Ribadeneyra's argument, especially in the first part of the *Historia*, was the idea that participating in a new crusade would renew Spain's legendary legacy defending Christianity such as they had attained in the victories of Granada (1492) and Lepanto (1571). Moreover, such a victory would evidence a strong Christian nation under a strong Christian prince. Towards the end of the sixteenth century, some Spaniards were becoming concerned with a weakening of the monarchy and a rising dependence on favorites, or *validos*,[45] a fear that appears in literature and plays of the time.[46] In fact, the warning for kings not to over-rely on favorites was a feature of a prudent monarch and was already present in Ribadeneyra's portrayal of Cardinal Wolsey in the *Historia*, repeated in Yepes' volume, and was an explicit lesson to be learned not only from Henry VIII but also from his children Edward and Elizabeth, who had been led astray by heretical counselors. Thus, the appeal to the idealized glorious past of strong Christian monarchs in Spain and the suggestion that Philip III would be a strong Christian leader like his father[47] were certain to capture the imagination of Spaniards who may have been lamenting the present state or longing for the idealized Golden Age of the Catholic Monarchs.[48]

The Exemplum

The use of the medieval exemplum and biblical typology in the ecclesiastical histories by Ribadeneyra and Yepes heightened the persuasiveness, imaginative appeal, and justification for the disclosure of shocking events as spiritually edifying. While Sander had used the exemplum, Ribadeneyra and Yepes relied on it more heavily to intensify the focus on spiritual benefits and providence in the story. Historian Victoria Pineda traces the use of the exemplum from Aristotle's *Rhetoric* through the medieval and Renaissance periods, including in the works of Erasmus and Juan Luis Vives, who were especially influential in Spain. Pineda notes that, through analogies between the past and the present, the exemplum allows one to comprehend the extent of a particular situation and foresee its consequences, indirectly renovating the past and deriving general principles from particular cases[49] (32). In other words, the seemingly outdated stories of men and women in the Bible or in martyrologies are constantly renovated by analogy in figures of the present, who in turn endorse moral precepts and traditions of the past. Furthermore, the use of analogy and exempla in this way, particularly when relating contemporary figures to biblical or early church characters, contributes to the overarching argument for continuity of the Catholic Church so important in this period and, in turn, enhances the histories' authority and persuasiveness. Yepes acknowledges this renewal and continuity by means of exempla drawn from the English martyrs in his dedication to Philip III and affirms how edifying (*de provecho*) they are to those who read them attentively: "Because if the lives of the ancient saints and the brave combats of the sacred Martyrs who in other times have made the Church illustrious are of such benefit as experience teaches those who read attentively, much more will these examples be, that (shedding blood) not only in our days but also before our eyes renews the faithfulness and constancy of the first Christians"[50] ("A la real catolica magestad" 5).

In terms of particulars, Pineda notes that Vives preferred to use exempla – especially those closest to the audience – instead of precepts because the former were more powerful in persuasiveness (37), which is also an idea that Yepes' passage both supports tacitly and elsewhere, citing Cesare Baronio, makes explicit.[51] Thus, a compelling element of the histories of Ribadeneyra and Yepes was that instead of just lecturing with precepts about why it was expedient to obey the Pope and flee heresy, which in part they did, they vividly showed through the recent exempla of Henry VIII, Anne Boleyn, and Elizabeth I the tragic end of repudiating the authority of the Pope and orthodox teachings of the Catholic Church. This allowed the specific history of England to apply to the universal church, of which Spain was a part, and to help persuade Spaniards to support the English Enterprise. Furthermore, the shameful sins of Henry and Anne could be exposed as moral lessons, not mere gossip and salacious entertainment, thus justifying their inclusion for entertaining appeal.

To illustrate this, it is useful to examine the distinctive uses of exempla by Sander and Ribadeneyra. While Sander's work centers on a chronological history of the schism, Ribadeneyra's writing focused on individual exempla, especially in the first part. Their respective prefaces show these distinctions. Sander states: "The marvellous and amazing things that God wrought in that kingdom, after the beginning of the schism, for the purpose of bringing back the hearts of the children to the faith of their fathers, can never be thoroughly understood without a history of the schism; that history, strange and surprising, I shall now tell" (cxlvii). With a subtle allusion to Malachi 4:6 ("bringing back the hearts of the children"),[52] which speaks of Israel's Babylonian exile as a tool to reconcile them to God, Sander centers on the persecution under Elizabeth as a spiritual purging for apostate England to return to Catholicism. No mention is made here of the role of individual characters in this history, though it will be exposed in the body of the history. Ribadeneyra's "Prologue of the author," however, restates this part from his source and adds details about Henry VIII: "We see a powerful king who wants everything he craves and executes everything he desires; a blind and unbridled penchant, armed with fury and power, shedding the blood of exceedingly saintly men and robbing the temples of God, becoming impoverished with their riches; removing the true head of the Church and making himself her monstrous head and perverting all divine and human laws"[53] (895–6). Ribadeneyra here accumulates descriptive phrases and colorful adjectives to characterize the king, and this rhetorical exuberance characteristic of Ribadeneyra's writing contrasts with Sander's less ornate and more direct style. The Jesuit offers the reader a lively summary of what will come: Henry is a negative example of how blinding power and lust causes the monarch to murder saintly men, rob God's temples, and replace the true head of the church with himself as its monstrous head. Wordplay highlights the stark ironies: a powerful (*poderoso*) king has an unbridled (*desapoderada*) lust that is armed with power (*poder*); he is impoverished by the riches of the temples he robs; he substitutes the true and natural head of the church (i.e., the Pope) with himself as an unnatural head; and his perversion of the laws of God and man is seen in the monstrous spectacle of a strange head engrafted on a body. The monster is the product of an unbridled lust, and readers would do well to learn from Henry's case to control their passions.

If this were the only reference to an individual exemplum in the preface, the rhetorical departure from the source would be quite subtle. However, Ribadeneyra continues naming all the other positive and negative exempla in the story – Catherine, the Pope, Anne Boleyn, the ministers of the king, the martyrs, young Edward VI, Mary Tudor, Philip II, and Queen Elizabeth I – and declares what princes and monarchs, ministers, and Christians at large may learn from these characters and their stories (Ribadeneyra 895–905). In this way, Ribadeneyra's deliberate focus on particular characters specifies the lessons to be drawn from each protagonist, going beyond Sander's broader perspective of the history of the English church. In fact, Ribadeneyra's and Yepes' departure conforms to the renewed emphasis in Spain after

Trent on didactic literature and to the abundant *regimine principis* treatises of the fifteenth and sixteenth centuries on how rulers should govern, such as those responding to Machiavelli. A key concept in these treatises was "reason of state," a Machiavellian idea that the monarch was justified in using whatever means – good or evil – for the good of the state and that the appearance of religion, if it benefitted the state, was more important than true religion.[54] Christian anti-Machiavellians argued that true religion and faith in God were the only means to a successful kingdom. These treatises use the exemplum copiously as a means of persuasion, pausing to explain its importance and proposing that the sovereign to whom the work is dedicated be an "exemplary figure" for his subjects (Pineda 34). Ribadeneyra's *Historia* is dedicated to the prince, later Philip III, exhorting the youth to continue the great and pious heritage of his father and grandfather. He says: "The well-being of the kingdom is so great when God's hand gives it a pious king, guardian of his Glory, rewarder of the good, persecutor of the evil, just, peaceable, and moderate, that no other joy from those found here can be greater. Because as the king is the head of the kingdom and its life and soul, at the pace of the king, so goes the kingdom that depends on the King himself"[55] (Ribadeneyra 893). The Jesuit argues that, as head of the kingdom, the monarch determines the well-being or destruction of his realm, and this is the lesson of Henry VIII, whose counterexample is Philip II and, hopefully, Philip III. Yepes also dedicates his volume to Philip III, recently enthroned in place of his father, and concludes his book listing benefits (*provechos*) Catholics outside of England – including monarchs and clerics – can extract from England's history, one of which is how "the only and sure reason of state" is to align human action with God's will (Ribadeneyra 887).

Given that Ribadeneyra published his own response to Machiavelli in 1595 – *Tratado de la religión y virtudes que debe tener el Príncipe cristiano para governar y conservar sus Estados* – his use of the exemplum and directives for a Christian monarch are unsurprising. Nonetheless, the correspondence in the use of the exemplum in Ribadeneyra and Yepes with these *regimine principis* treatises sets the Spanish ecclesiastical histories apart from Sander's, especially when taking into account Maravall's observation that these treatises were not only for the monarch but also for those who criticized princes (221). Ribadeneyra's and Yepes' change can be understood as an adaptation that would resonate with a Spanish audience concerned with a weakening of Spain's strong Christian identity and leadership and eager that their Christian prince be like the "Golden Age monarchs" of the past, able to lead Spain and Christianity in the new crusade against the English heresy, whether in a military or an evangelistic expedition.

While the second part of Ribadeneyra's history necessarily turns away its focus from the lessons found in the detailed lives of a few important individuals to a broader martyrology and history of the church, the rhetorical liveliness remains and tends to focus on Elizabeth, the propagator of Catholic martyrdom. Similarly, though the history by Yepes mentions single individuals, especially Henry VIII, as examples, it is much more concerned with stressing the broader exemplum of God's providential acts. Yepes states:

> Finally I wish to warn you (Christian reader) that even though in some parts of this work *we have focused on more doctrinal rather than historical and narrative matters*, we have not departed from your benefit or our purpose, which has been *to show you with example of this persecution* how feared God's judgments should be, and how revered the secrets of his providence and loved his eternal goodness with which he always turns to shelter his own, keeping them and defending them with his grace and protection in such a way that no creature can harm them.[56] ("Conclusion desta Historia" 893; emphasis added)

Yepes concludes his work admitting that although he has reversed what readers would expect in some parts where his emphasis has been on doctrinal matters (explaining God's providence and connecting it to doctrine and examples) over history and narrative (discussing the English schism and persecutions), his main goal remains to use the persecution in England as an overarching exemplum of God's providence – containing smaller exempla like the miraculous deaths of persecutors or inexplicable escapes of English Catholics – to show how he protects his own and, therefore, how much God ought to be feared and loved.

This Spanish theological explanation of the English persecutions added to Sander's narrative is an expanded commentary of Ribadeneyra's *Tratado de la tribulación*, which, as mentioned, explained with copious biblical and patristic references that Spain's loss in the just and pious expedition of the Armada to stop Elizabeth Tudor's persecution of the church and spread of heresy was an act of God for ultimate good. Within a Counter-Reformation context, the effect of these explanations was to transfer the rising power of Elizabeth Tudor, England, and Protestants to God, who was ultimately in control of all things, and, therefore, to assuage Spanish fears as well as counteract the idea that God was no longer on the side of Spain and the Roman Catholic Church. In fact, in the *Tratado*, that God was willing to discipline Spain and Catholicism was a mark of approval and legitimacy, since this corresponded to the biblical chastisements and persecutions of God's people. Moreover, the perpetrators of the persecutions were aligned with the enemies of the church, confirming that the religion of Henry and Elizabeth Tudor and of Protestants in general was counterfeit. Thus, the examples in church history and the Bible were repeating themselves in the present condition of Spain and the Roman Church as well as in the condition of their persecutors.

Biblical Figures and Typology

As Ribadeneyra's *Tratado* illustrates, exempla were often aligned with biblical figures and typology that made the paradigm more forceful. Casting characters of the English Reformation in a biblical typology was a long-standing theological strategy that had already been liberally employed by Foxe[57] – but also by Sander and other Catholic authors. Many of the particular roles assigned in the Catholic writings to Henry, Anne, and Elizabeth were preserved in Ribadeneyra's and Yepes' texts, while others were omitted. Biblical typology was used to portray the English monarch as a tyrant, as Eusebius had done with persecutors of the church to connect the present to the past. Departing from Sander, in Ribadeneyra's history Henry[58] and Elizabeth[59] are equated to the Babylonian king Nebuchadnezzar, who erected a statue of himself that had to be worshipped and executed those who refused. The clear implication of this allusion is that the English Catholics were the new Shadrachs, Meshachs, and Abednegos – the children of Israel who were condemned to execution because they refused to bow down to the monarch's distorted image of headship – and were approved by God for their refusal to worship idols. Yepes, for his part, connects God's miraculous saving of English Catholics to God's extraordinary preservation of Daniel in the lions' den (35). This addition reclaims a pure name for Catholicism through its implied reversal of the Protestants' argument that Catholics were idolaters and construes the English monarchs as tyrants forcing others to sin, specifically by worshipping images in place of God. Ribadeneyra also explicitly equates Henry VIII's hardness to that of Pharaoh, the Egyptian who shows the futile efforts of tyrants – implicitly Henry and Elizabeth Tudor – to destroy God's children, while God makes them multiply[60] (994, 1201, 1306).

Biblical typology was also used to illustrate how current rulers were led astray by the deceitfulness and charm of women, as happened in biblical times. Sander, for instance, presented Henry VIII as a Solomon – that is, a wise king who would fall into false worship through the love of women, especially of one: the "Lutheran" Anne Boleyn (Highley 162). Ribadeneyra's text preserves Sander's account of a Carthusian monk about to be executed who asks the spectators to pray fervently for King Henry "so that, since in the beginning of his reign he had represented Solomon in piety and wisdom, he should not end up as him, ensnared and perverted by women"[61] (Ribadeneyra 975; Sander 118). Similarly, the recounting of Anne Boleyn dancing gracefully before Henry VIII – found in both the accounts of Ribadeneyra and Sander – would evoke in an early modern audience the image of the dancing of Salome, the daughter of Herodias, associating Boleyn with the sensual dance that causes the violent beheading of John the Baptist[62] (Highley 163; Ives 60). The sensuality of the dancing Herodias was a popular figure in Spain at this time; it appears, for example, in Cervantes' sexually charged entremés, *El retablo de las maravillas*, and assumes an audience familiar with this figure. The implication is that Anne Boleyn is the new Herodias/Salome, who bewitches the king and thus fulfills the type of the "bad woman" in literature and drama, particularly, the beautiful foreign women that led Solomon away from God and into idolatry.

Furthermore, the association of Anne Boleyn with seductive women in the Bible reflected and reinforced the early modern theological position that was held by both Protestants and Catholics alike since the time of the early church fathers, namely, that women were dangerous because they could easily embrace heretical views and lead men astray. This idea is derived from patristic and scholastic interpretations of the Apostle Paul's teachings, primarily in Ephesians 5:22–4,[63] which enjoins wives to submit to their husbands "because the man is the head of the woman; as Christ is the head of the church," and in the exhortation of 1 Timothy 2:8–15[64] that forbids women from teaching or "hav[ing] dominion over the man" because Eve was formed after Adam and "Adam was not seduced: but the woman being seduced, was in prevarication." The interpretation of these passages up to the early modern period maintained that Eve demonstrated that all women are more easily deceived than men, therefore women are inferior to men and should not teach. Juan Luis Vives summarizes this perspective in his internationally acclaimed female conduct manual, *De Institutione Feminae Christianae* (*Instruccion de la muger Christiana*, 1524):

> Therefore, since the woman is naturally a sick animal, and her judgment may not be in every way secure and can be very easily deceived, as our mother Eve has shown, that for very little she let herself be fooled and persuaded by the demon. Because of these things and others that are not disclosed, it is not good for her to teach. Moreover, because having harbored a false opinion in her head, she should not transfer it to those hearing with

the authority that she has as teacher and bring others into the same error, especially since disciples follow their masters.[65] (libro I, cap IV, 27–8)

Vives' statement that a woman is a "sick animal" comes from the scholastic tradition of Aquinas that follows Aristotle's definition of women as "deformed men" – an idea that emerges in the legal codes of Castile promulgated in 1505, which categorized women as "*imbecilitas sexus* [imbecile sex]," along with children, invalids, and delinquents (Cammarata 1–2). Thus, because of this "natural" weakness, these thinkers conclude that a woman's judgment is unreliable and that women are led astray like children. In fact, this was one reason that in Yepes' *Historia* Elizabeth is pitied, namely, that her womanly weakness along with her illegitimate birth and evil counselors forced her to act as she did – ideas also echoed in Ribadeneyra's text (Yepes, "Clausula de una Carta"). Despite this, Vives was somewhat unconventional in his conduct manual because he preferred educated and virtuous women over men to teach young women and even their own children,[66] although his objective was to instruct Christian women to overcome their natural weakness: "Therefore, how much more care should we place in the rearing and in the life of the Christian woman, being so crucial to human living that all the good and bad that is done in the world can be said without mistake that it be because of women, as will be understood in the process of this work?"[67] (libro I, cap I, 1). This traditional idea expressed by Vives that women hold great power to do good or evil is buttressed by the portrayal of female characters in the ecclesiastical histories of Sander, Ribadeneyra, and Yepes, which attribute the destruction and salvation of England to Anne Boleyn and Elizabeth Tudor, on one hand, and to Mary Tudor on the other.

Flat Characters

The medieval exemplum and biblical typology in the texts of Sander, Ribadeneyra, and Yepes generally rely on flat characters within a binary of good and evil according to their loyalty to or rejection of Roman Catholicism[68] – Catherine vs. Anne Boleyn, Mary Tudor vs. Elizabeth Tudor, Philip II vs. Henry VIII. This use of flat characters does not preclude a respectful or even possibly sympathetic description of enemies at times,[69] but rather, it means that their actions will be generally confined to good and evil protagonists who act according to their virtue or vice so that there is no room for wrongdoing in Catholic exempla and no room for good actions in fallen exempla, such as Henry[70] or Elizabeth. This is especially true of the women. For instance, nothing is said of Mary Tudor's persecution of those who resisted the restoration of Catholicism during her reign and alienated many English from Roman Catholicism, or of Elizabeth's reluctance to execute Mary Stuart.[71] Nor is Henry's theological concern because of lack of a male heir from his marriage to Catherine taken seriously, and even though Ribadeneyra critiques Philip II in other works,[72] neither he nor Yepes mentions any fault in the Spanish king in their histories. In Sander's book, Catherine's piety is generally contrasted to the licentiousness of Henry, but Ribadeneyra pits the good and pious Catherine of Aragon and Mary Stuart against the evil temptresses Anne Boleyn and Elizabeth. In an addition to Sander's text, following the death of Catherine Ribadeneyra explicitly compares her life and death to that of Anne Boleyn:

> This was the end of the holy queen doña Catalina, illustrious, certainly, for having been queen and daughter of monarchs, and of such great monarchs as were the Catholic Monarchs, of glorious memory; but much more illustrious and blessed for the excellent virtues with which she shone in the world and now reigns with Christ. Let us proceed and see the end of Anne Boleyn, who succeeded her in the kingdom and let us compare lineage with lineage, life with life, and death with death.[73] (Ribadeneyra 1001)

Ribadeneyra here shows that he is employing the classical rhetorical device of comparison consisting in an *encomium* of Catherine and a *vituperation* of Anne aimed at reinforcing the encomium. The characteristics of encomium and vituperation or invective – according to Aphthonius' rhetorical rules used in Jesuit training at this time – include descriptions of lineage (nation, birth, parents), body (beauty, strength), virtues, customs, and accomplishments. This is precisely Ribadeneyra's goal in juxtaposing "lineage with lineage, life with life, and death with death" with respect to Catherine and her foil Anne, and he does this throughout the history, necessarily resulting in polarized, flat characters. Moreover, this contrast allows Ribadeneyra to recall Catherine's parents with all the implications of their idealized Catholic identity and again remind readers of Spain's idealized glorious past with the goal of acting in the present and continuing that identity into the future, as well as pitting Anne and her daughter Elizabeth against everything Catholic and Spanish.

When compared to Sander's text, it is evident that Ribadeneyra underscores the sufferings, fortitude, and wifely devotion of Catherine amid Henry's open affront. He traces the life of Catherine and the other Spanish women in the pattern of the ideals of the good wife in Vives' manual and Fray Luis de León's late sixteenth-century treatise,

La perfecta casada,[74] which develops Vives' ideas by describing how early modern Christian women can imitate the virtuous wife of Proverbs 31. For Vives and León, the Christian woman above all must be chaste, obedient, and of great virtue witnessed by those around her – not vain, wasteful, or given to activities that will stimulate the passions, such as eating certain foods or engaging in activities like dancing.[75] In their dress and lifestyle, Catherine, Mary Tudor, and Mary Stuart display modesty, obedience, and humility, while Anne and Elizabeth are vain, arrogant, and seductive. Because the Spanish women's accounts are expanded and all women are deliberately set against this conduct manual construct, they are necessarily good or evil and cannot have much depth of character, appealing to Spanish religious conservatives and reinforcing concrete models of behavior for Spanish women while exalting the lineage of Isabella the Catholic.

Tropes of Monstrosity

Further limiting complexity, Sander and his Spanish translators use other literary conventions aligned with flat characters, such as early modern tropes of monstrosity, to vilify especially Elizabeth and her mother, Anne Boleyn, but also Henry VIII. In effect, as the narrative progresses and Henry, Anne, and Elizabeth distance themselves from the Roman Church, Catholic authors begin to reveal physical deformities that reflect their souls' corruption from having yielded to the sins of lust, vanity, and pride. These descriptions correspond with the Neoplatonic view common in literature and rhetoric of this period that the outward body portrays inner characteristics, whether beautiful or ugly, of virtue or vice, respectively. More importantly, these monstrous manifestations are used as "proof" of God's judgment on Henry's sins and as an explanation for Elizabeth's actions – a piece of evidence that would forcefully attach itself to the imagination of the audience. Thus, for Sander, Ribadeneyra, and Yepes, Henry finally becomes physically monstrous as fitting exemplary punishment for his lust – so obese that he cannot fit through doors – and destroys himself and his kingdom (Sander 164; Ribadeneyra 1038). Yepes replicates this Neoplatonist idea more explicitly: "as in the soul he was falling apart and with the multitude of his unbridled appetites he was losing his beauty, so in the body he was becoming disfigured until he reached such a monstrous state (caused by the intemperance of his life)" (8).[76] These events stand as a vivid warning of the dangers of flirting with heresy and of following one's passions in rebellion against the guidance of the Roman Catholic Church, aiming to regulate conduct. The fact that the punishment happens in this life and is visible to everyone makes the consequences more immediate and functions like a display of public punishment meant to deter sinners, so common in this period.

In fact, early modern readers would have understood the Latin word *monstrum* as a "portent or warning," but the term in other European languages also carried the ideas of extraordinariness, deformity, and "deviating from the natural order" (Bates 12–13). Sixteenth-century published accounts of monsters were numerous, which may be explained not only by curiosity but also by the increasing need for signs to validate competing religious and political systems and a need to preserve order in the midst of religious reform and heresy (Bates 16). This corresponds with Ribadeneyra's claim that Henry transgressed both human and divine laws and therefore became a monster. The depiction of monsters or monstrous births as a result of the judgment of God upon transgressions of human, social, or divine laws – for example, deviant sexual intercourse – warned sinners, showing them that these laws were connected, and promoted social and religious conformity and order (Bates 16–17).[77] In Ribadeneyra's case, the monsters in his narrative also serve as physical, visible "evidence" that Henry's actions had painful consequences in this life, that Elizabeth could not be redeemed, and that the English church was fundamentally corrupted. Still, Ribadeneyra does not replicate all the monstrous accounts in his source, but only those essential to prove his theological argument and capture his audience's imagination through the horror of pathos.

Ribadeneyra preserves Sander's portrayal of Anne Boleyn with monstrous characteristics that reveal her inner duplicity. On one hand, she is described as having a tooth protruding, a sixth finger, and a sagging under her chin, common identifiers of monsters and witches (Quintero, *Gendering* 135–6; Highley 163): "Anne Boleyn was rather tall of stature, with black hair, and an oval face of a sallow complexion, as if troubled with jaundice. She had a projecting tooth under the upper lip, and on her right hand six fingers. There was a large wen under her chin, and therefore to hide its ugliness she wore a high dress covering her throat" (Sander 25). The accuracy of these physical characteristics of Anne is debated.[78] An early modern author sympathetic to Anne admits that she had a small sixth nail on the side of her little finger and some moles on her neck, but even these admissions seem to indicate that Sander's description is at best exaggerated (Ives 50–1; Sander 25n2). On the other hand, she is presented as attractive and seductive: "The rest of her body was very proportionate and beautiful: she had much grace upon her lips, and great finesse, and agility in dancing and playing instruments"[79]

(Ribadeneyra 928). Although this part of Sander's account as translated by Ribadeneyra matches sympathetic descriptions of Anne, when read against Vives' and León's female conduct manuals, the implications are quite negative. Within that framework, Anne's dexterity in dancing and her fashionable dress are vain, immodest, and wasteful, especially in contrast with the attire of Catherine and Mary Tudor. Sander and Ribadeneyra then connect her appearance with her conduct, first stating, "as to the disposition of her mind, she was full of pride, ambition, envy, and impurity," and then describing her as sexually promiscuous and naming men with whom she was rumored to have slept (Sander 25; Ribadeneyra 928).

The vituperation ends with a theological explanation for Anne's behavior: "She embraced the heresy of Luther to make her life and opinions consistent, but nevertheless did not cease to hear mass with the Catholics, for that was wrung from her by the custom of the king and the necessities of her own ambition" (Sander 26).[80] What is important in Sander's account is that Anne's physical flaws could be concealed under clothing, just like her ambition, Lutheran inclination, and pride were disguised, and she could present herself as beautiful and innocent when she was really duplicitous and immoral. Coupled with her association with negative biblical types, these literary tropes conveyed that Anne bewitched Henry into heresy, a charge raised at her trial[81] (Highley 163).

Not only was Anne Boleyn presented as a witch and a seductress, Sander scandalously asserted that she was Henry VIII's own daughter, born of his sexual relations with Anne's mother. Scholars argue that rumors about Anne's mother being Henry's mistress may have circulated, but never before had anyone put this in print or in a manuscript widely distributed (Highley 164; Ives 60). In fact, Ribadeneyra seems shocked to reproduce these details which sound like gossip, but assures the reader that they are not only necessary (*provechosas*) to understand the history and Henry's blind passion (and by extension, the exemplum), but also that they are true because the "very grave and modest" Dr. Sander wrote them:

> I am aware that I tell some things that I could leave out, either because they are of little importance or because of their quality. However, looking into it, it seemed to me that I should write them, not only because they were written by a man so modest and grave as was Dr. Sander and because they are beneficial to the argument and truth of the history, but mostly because they declare better the blind passion of the King.[82] (929)

In order to expose this incest and the divine disapproval of their marriage, Sander employs another literary convention to describe Anne Boleyn: he says that she gave birth to a mass of flesh in place of a male child. As noted, delivering a fetus, or "mola," was considered a monstrous birth and a common symbol of God's punishment for deviant sexual acts and intermarriage with heretics (Highley 164–5; Burnett 65). Interestingly, even though the miscarriage was historical, Ribadeneyra does not reproduce this detail,[83] possibly to avoid what he considered unnecessary incendiary details not essential to the theological narrative. Along these lines, Ribadeneyra also omits Sander's comment that Elizabeth was not only among the vilest women of the Bible and history – Athaliah, Maacha, Jezebel, Herodias, Selene, Constantia, and Eudoxia – but also that "[she] ha[d] surpassed them all"[84] (240).

Eusebio Rey proposes that Ribadeneyra's interpretation of the events is "more moderate" than its source, as attested by Ribadeneyra's censor, López de Montoya, and that Ribadeneyra tells the story with "considerations and attenuations" and envelops it in "a discreet veil of priestly grief and melancholy" (873).[85] Although the motivation for Ribadeneyra's hesitation to reproduce some scandalous details in his source is unclear,[86] these instances stand to show that the shocking and monstrous details that were ultimately included in his *Historia* were neither arbitrary nor gratuitous, but were carefully selected "evidence" to support the broader goals of defending the Roman Catholic Church and its martyrs and clearing Spain's reputation against the vilifying charges of Protestants. As many scholars have pointed out,[87] the *Historia*'s "argumentation" is not primarily doctrinal – that is, arguing for or against theological points – but rather, exemplary and imaginative – namely, showing by "one's fruits" good or bad behavior tied to biblical and patristic history that evinces whether one belongs to the True or the False Church.

Nonetheless, Ribadeneyra, following Sander, implicates Elizabeth in all her mother's sins when he says about Anne that she is above all "most wretched [*infelicísima*] and abominable" for being the source and "fountainhead" (*fuente manantial*) of the schism and destruction of her nation and "for having left us a daughter that so imitates her and swells and fills up the measure of her mother"[88] (Ribadeneyra 1004). In fact, for Ribadeneyra, Elizabeth's lineage is tainted, and she herself is a monstrous child, albeit a tragic victim, having been the product of incest and heresy and a sign of God's punishment for Henry's transgression of natural and divine laws.[89] Yet the monstrous child here remains culpable for "imitating" her mother to the point of "filling up her measure" – that is, committing the same or even worse sins. Like father, like daughter, as

Ribadeneyra says in his history: "We see a woman, daughter and granddaughter of Henry VIII, and daughter and sister of Anne Boleyn … as an abominable monster and idol, seated in the temple of God, taking the office and name of governor and head of the Church"[90] (Ribadeneyra 1196). With echoes of the biblical image of the apocalyptic Beast (Rev. 13:1–14:13), Ribadeneyra points out that Elizabeth, like Henry, forces everyone into idolatrous worship of her own image, again throwing back on the English church and Protestants the charge of idolatry that was routinely leveled at Roman Catholics.

In fact, at the end of the first part of his history, Ribadeneyra greatly expands the story of Mary Stuart's time in England and her execution by Elizabeth to underscore the monstrous tyranny of Elizabeth and the need to overthrow her politically. After recounting Elizabeth's cruelty towards her cousin and Mary's moving self-defense and appalling execution, Ribadeneyra launches a series of poignant rhetorical questions and offers a horrific conclusion rejecting the heresy and exposing its inevitable fate:

> Who has ever seen or heard that an aunt and queen should have ordered to cut the head off of her niece, another queen, by hand of an ordinary executioner …? In which history of Indians and barbarians is it read that they had festival lamps and festivities and rejoicing upon the death of an innocent queen, and that the same queen that put her to death would wear elegant clothes and ride around the city on horse with joy, like someone who triumphs over her enemy? … Only in England has this been done in all the world, and by hand of heretics it was done and only by them it could have been done. Because as heresy is an infernal monster, all the fruits that are born from her are monstrous and infernal. And if to know this truth the innumerable examples that we previously had of cruelty, violence, and tyranny that the heretics have used in our times were not enough, this one only is enough for all, and will be enough in all the coming centuries. Because it is such that in Tartary and Scythia and in whatever nation, no matter how coarse, fierce, and inhuman it may be, the very barbarians, when they hear this, will not believe it.[91] (Ribadeneyra 1186)

In a kind of reversal of the Spanish Black Legend loaded with pathos, Ribadeneyra claims that only in England has been committed an act unheard of even in the shocking *relaciones* of atrocities practiced among barbarians in the Americas or in exotic stories told about Tartars and Scythians. Implied here is that if Spaniards had sent ships to the Americas to Christianize barbarians, should they not also intervene in England? In other words, Elizabeth has reached a point where her heartless acts towards a queen, even a relative, are unbelievable even to infidels and yet are publicly celebrated in parades and feasts. For Ribadeneyra, if all the atrocities committed by Elizabeth before this time were insufficient to expose her monstrosity, this one is enough for now and for all ages to come. Only one explanation for this barbarity is possible: all this came to be because of the monstrous heresy (*monstruo infernal*) of her father and mother that could only breed monstrous and infernal fruit, including Elizabeth. In fact, it is implied that tolerating heresy would allow the spread of these horrifying events to any Catholic country, including Spain, and therefore, attacking England was also an act of self-defense.[92]

Through this rhetorical diatribe and the use of tropes of monstrosity applied to the flat characters of Henry, Anne, and especially Elizabeth, Ribadeneyra aims to capture with pathos the imagination of his fellow Spaniards to support the "great cause" of stopping the atrocities against God committed by tyrants who, because of heresy, cannot do anything but evil in England and the Continent. Furthermore, this shows that Elizabeth cannot be redeemed or trusted in political negotiations: Ribadeneyra argues that she cannot back out of persecuting Catholics because she is illegitimate and would lose her right to the throne if she acknowledged the authority of the Holy See. Therefore, she has usurped the position of the Vicar of Christ, perverting all natural and divine laws. Because of this representation and Black Legend language, especially the first part of Ribadeneyra takes a more directive, forceful tone than its source, namely, Sander's history, even while the Spaniards omit certain indecent details. Nonetheless, the reason for the strong language is theological rather than personal, which is why she can at times be pitied and treated as a mostly passive recipient of her parents' judgment and the manipulations of her evil counselors.

Conclusion

In sum, in order for Ribadeneyra and Yepes to galvanize Catholics for a new crusade against England, they presented Elizabeth as a dangerous obdurate tyrant who could destroy Catholicism in all of Europe if unchecked and the English Catholics as brothers who needed to be rescued from their oppression by military force or missionary reconversion. The literary devices employed by Sander, Ribadeneyra, and Yepes show that these authors – in a sort of Anglo-Spanish cooperation of sources, narrative structures, and literary devices – produced narratives that were specifically adapted both to inform Catholic Spaniards about the persecutions in England under Elizabeth and to rally them in support for their English brethren despite publication obstacles and challenges that could make Spaniards indifferent to the cause, such as disenchantment with foreign expeditions and suspicion of English seminarians coming to Spain. These challenges were confronted with the use of the ecclesiastical history genre that tied the Roman Catholic Church and current events in England to biblical characters and teachings, authoritative sources – particularly coming from England – and influential endorsement of the histories by renowned Spanish leaders. These ecclesiastical histories traced the line of the Roman Church back to the New Testament through the sufferings of the martyrs and providential acts of God in the present that were identical to those of the church's past and by means of apocalyptic language that cast current events in an eschatological setting. Furthermore, the Spanish histories' employment of good stories of scandal, incest, and monsters, like their source, and also their fusion of rhetoric and literary genres particularly attractive in Spain made these stories teach and delight through the imagination. As a result of both historical and literary characteristics, the ecclesiastical histories of Ribadeneyra and Yepes remained in print for centuries and became two of the most important forces shaping the Spanish imagination concerning English criticism of Spain as well as the English and the English Reformation, as can be seen in early modern Spanish literature published in the seventeenth century and beyond.

Chapter Three

Who Gets to Be a Saint? Writing the English Reformation in Luisa de Carvajal's Letters

The previous chapter suggested reasons to explain how Ribadeneyra's *Historia eclesiástica del scisma del reyno de Inglaterra,* supported by Yepes' *Historia particular de la persecución de Inglaterra,* solidified a specific Spanish vision concerning the English Reformation and the persecution of Catholics in England by appealing to the imagination through literary strategies masterfully appealing to current Spanish interests and concerns. This chapter analyzes the production and reception of the ecclesiastical histories by reading them against the letters of Luisa de Carvajal y Mendoza, a Spanish aristocrat who was an eyewitness to the condition of Catholics in England during the first half of James I's reign and who was strongly influenced by Ribadeneyra's vision. This side-by-side analysis of writings of different literary genres – namely, ecclesiastical histories and letters – also offers a deeper analysis of the relationship between how the message of English events was shaped by the medium in which it was conveyed, specifically showing some of the constraints of Ribadeneyra's *Historia,* and enabling a more complex understanding of the multiplicity of reasons behind the narratological and rhetorical choices in the histories and what aspects of them appealed to Spanish readers.

Carvajal's extant writings include devotional poems, an autobiography, and abundant correspondence between 1598 and 1613. In 1965 almost two hundred of her letters were published in the series *Biblioteca de Autores Españoles* following Ribadeneyra's volume because its editor considered Carvajal's correspondence and poetry to be a fitting sequel to the Jesuit's work (Carvajal, *Epistolario* 4). However, this cursory reference seems to be the only effort to connect these texts, despite their significant historical, literary, and ideological continuity. Additionally, because Carvajal's circle of contacts included highly influential Spanish and English figures who shared Ribadeneyra's vision, supported

English Catholics, and participated in writing Catholic polemic literature, her life and letters reveal intricacies of the Anglo-Spanish network that cooperated in the English mission or, in other words, how Ribadeneyra's call to action was fleshed out and how the Spanish ecclesiastical histories may have been produced. Thus, for instance, Carvajal corresponds with Robert Persons and Joseph Creswell, Elizabethan exiles who were crucial in the production of the Spanish ecclesiastical histories, and, as will be seen, sends them eyewitness accounts of recent martyrdoms of English Catholics as well as English heretical books with notes refuting point by point their arguments against Roman Catholicism. These kinds of exchanges expose ways in which these men collected information for polemic texts. Moreover, since Carvajal and her close acquaintances echo Ribadeneyra's vision of England as well as language and arguments in the *Historia*, her letters implicitly offer valuable information about the reception of the *Historia*, including glimpses into its intended audience, which she represents, and the scope of its influence.

Finally, Carvajal's own act of writing, especially as far as it concerns the English mission, reveals the guiding force of inherited literary tropes and genres appealing to the imagination of early modern Spanish readers and opens questions about the challenge of representing the English Reformation and English Catholics in literature, including questions of accuracy and credibility, generic opportunities and constraints – a challenge that is fundamental to the writing of the Spanish ecclesiastical histories.

Most of Carvajal's correspondence was written several years after the publication of Ribadeneyra's and Yepes' volumes when the landscape was rapidly changing towards Anglo-Spanish rapprochement after the crowning of James I and the Treaty of London in 1604. Despite this movement towards peace, at least for Carvajal, who sided with the Jesuit mission to return England to Catholicism, not much seemed to have changed from Elizabeth Tudor's reign or from Ribadeneyra's concerns. Surprisingly, as will be discussed, Carvajal's letters argue that the Jacobean persecution of Catholics in England was at least equal to, if not worse than that under Elizabeth, and she disapproves of Catholics who praised Elizabeth as benevolent compared to James. Her writing coincides in outlook and tone with the second part of Ribadeneyra's *Historia* and with Yepes' narrative in that it shows a time of looking at martyrs and persecution through a lens of providence and connecting these events to the primitive church. Because Carvajal's writings cannot be fully understood apart from key points in her background and experiences that are essential to establish her familiarity with the literature of her time, the English mission, and the ecclesiastical histories by Ribadeneyra and Yepes, Carvajal's life must be briefly outlined first.[1]

Carvajal's Life

Born into the Mendoza and Pacheco families in the north of Extremadura in 1566, Carvajal was an aristocrat who would be connected throughout her life to prominent figures involved in Anglo-Spanish political relations. Orphaned at six years of age, for four years she was raised at the palace alongside the *infantas* Isabel Clara Eugenia and Catalina Micaela by her maternal great-aunt, Doña María Chacón (Carvajal, *Epistolario* 17). This personal connection around 1600 would allow Carvajal to relay messages to Isabel Clara Eugenia, Archduchess of Austria, through Magdalena de San Jerónimo, Carvajal's religious friend at the archduchess' court, in an effort to persuade Isabel to take the English throne as a legitimate successor. Her familiarity with the Spanish court would also embolden Carvajal in 1613, towards the end of her life, to write Philip III's right hand, the Duke of Lerma, to help her remain in England when high officials labored to expel her. Upon Doña María's death, the Carvajal girl went to live first in Pamplona and then Madrid with her maternal uncle, Francisco Hurtado de Mendoza, the Marquis of Almazán, ambassador to Vienna (1570–7) and later viceroy of Navarre (1579–88) (Carvajal, *Epistolario* 19–21; Bouza 248, 258–9).

After the death of her uncle and aunt in 1592, Carvajal moved to a small house in Madrid and traveled to Valladolid when the court settled there in 1601, living next to St. Alban's English College, where Jesuit leaders Robert Persons and Joseph Creswell became her acquaintances (Cruz, *Life* 35, 49, 59–60). Although she had refused to marry or join a convent, between 1593 and 1598 she wrote vows of poverty, obedience, "more perfection," and martyrdom[2] (Cruz, *Life* 48; Carvajal, *Escritos* 238–45). Carvajal remained in Valladolid until 1604, when she won a lawsuit for her inheritance, gave it to Robert Persons for a seminary, and began to plan a trip to England as a self-appointed missionary (Cruz, *Life* 61–2). With the help of the Jesuits and her aristocratic connections, Carvajal arrived in London in 1605, not knowing the language and six months before the Gunpowder Plot, which intensified English authorities' suspicion of Catholics, particularly Jesuits and Spaniards (Cruz, *Life* 62–9). In England from 1605 to 1613, Carvajal corresponded with aristocratic relations and acquaintances as well as religious men and women in Spain and the Continent and was incarcerated twice for public disturbance. She also helped recover the mutilated bodies of

Catholic martyrs and prepared them as relics to send to those who supported her financially outside of England. Her ambiguous mission as a Spanish independent religious woman who was a Mendoza and had ties to Jesuits caused many to question the wisdom of her remaining in England. After her second imprisonment on charges of having set up a small convent in London and publicly debating and causing disturbances, Spanish and English officials requested and obtained permission from Philip III to send her back to Spain (Redworth, *She-Apostle* 220–3). Shortly before the order was carried out, Carvajal died from a disease contracted while in prison. Although her confessor and others compiled several documents to request her beatification, it was never granted.

Extraordinary Circumstances

Carvajal's extraordinary life was the product of intersecting circumstances: her gender, her aristocratic credentials and connections, her close bond with Jesuits, her unique childhood and upbringing, and her love for martyrs and martyrdom. Being a woman sometimes limited and other times expanded the scope of her writings and service, since Catholic men were more carefully surveilled by English authorities and, as a woman, she was more likely to be overlooked. Likewise, her deep sense of God's calling and the privileges of her social status occasionally offset certain restrictions for women,[3] such as allowing her to travel to England,[4] but at other times drew too much political attention and stood in the way of her goals, for example, of suffering for Christ or remaining in England.

Carvajal's membership in the powerful Mendoza and Pacheco families put her in a unique position with respect to the English mission and Anglo-Spanish politics and perceptions. Indeed, her trip to England was possible precisely because of her privileged financial and social position (Cruz, "jesuita"). Her contacts were notable. In England, Carvajal was personally attended by three Spanish ambassadors to London, Don Pedro de Zuñiga, Don Alonso de Velasco, and Don Diego Sarmiento de Acuña, and she received a stipend from Philip III (Carvajal, *Epistolario* 417). In fact, several of her letters were sent to her powerful cousin, Don Rodrigo Calderón, the notorious *valido* of Philip III,[5] and to her brother, Don Alonso de Carvajal, who had been a candidate for ambassador to London, but Carvajal encouraged him to reject it (Carvajal, *Epistolario* 383–5). These and other prominent correspondents in Spain and Flanders allowed Carvajal not only to be informed first-hand of political matters and tensions, but also to convey current information to individuals who were in a position of political influence. As will be further discussed below, from this perspective Carvajal's letters disclose the complexity of Anglo-Spanish relations and perceptions, including fraternal and antagonistic links.

Another determining circumstance that enabled Carvajal's extraordinary life and works was her family's close association with Jesuits.[6] Fulfilling the desire of his dying father, her uncle Don Francisco had placed himself under Jesuit teaching, visited Francisco de Borja at St. Magdalen's hermitage near Oñate, and later lauded General Diego Laínez, claiming a warm, fraternal relationship with the Society because of their superior[7] (Carvajal, *Epistolario* 20; Bouza 257). Hurtado de Mendoza's library, available to Carvajal, evidenced his predilection for the Society and included volumes by Ignatius, Manuel da Costa, and Ribadeneyra, among others, as well as a Jesuit comedy (Bouza 281, 283). Carvajal's own paternal grandfather had attended the Council of Trent and enthusiastically favored the Jesuit order (Cruz, *Life* 17–18). Carvajal, also retaining a similar affection for the Society, from London exhorted her brother to be devoted to the Jesuits, noting that their family was greatly indebted to them[8] (*Epistolario* 291). She loved the Society not only because it had enabled the salvation of her grandfather, father, and other close relatives, but also because she believed the Jesuits were bringing many souls to God through their missions and allowing the sacraments to be administered more frequently. She felt an obligation to support them and did so, both with her inheritance and with her work in London.

Critics agree, however, that one of the strongest shaping forces for Carvajal seems to have been the strict spiritual and corporeal discipline to which she was subjected as a young girl, especially while living with her uncle, the Marquis of Almazán, and his family. Carvajal reports that her nursemaid (*aya*) Isabel de Ayllón, who stayed with her until she was thirteen years old, was often harsh in disciplining her; still, Carvajal loved and defended Ayllón against criticism because the aristocrat felt that the chastisement was inflicted "to straighten her in virtue and destroy what could impede it"[9] (*Escritos* 139–40).[10] Carvajal also speaks highly of her uncle's devotion and discipline, noting that "he greatly enjoyed making great penance, ordinary and even quite extraordinary"[11] (*Escritos* 151). Under his guidance,[12] at fourteen years of age Carvajal was submitted to rigorous spiritual and physical disciplines, such as lengthy mental prayers on sin, hell, and Christ's passion, and secret, harsh humiliations and flagellations by female servants with the goal of breaking the girl's will (*Escritos* 157–63).[13] According to Carvajal, by the time she was seventeen years old, she was well acquainted with mortification – physical and spiritual – and began to have a strong desire to become a martyr. She writes:

> Being seventeen years old, and I do not know if even younger, in my private prayer I began to have a strong desire for martyrdom: that is, to die for the sweetest Lord who died for me. And for a very long time I sometimes found myself absorbed in a profound and vivid thought that they were tearing me apart for the holy Catholic faith, in which my spirit found the greatest satisfaction imaginable and great delight. And from there I would emerge with a great inclination towards a true imitation of the sufferings and cross of our Lord.[14] (*Escritos* 18–19)

Here it is evident that mental prayers and vivid meditations akin to Ignatian exercises of identifying with Christ in his death and with others martyred for the Catholic faith had a strong influence on her imagination and not only gave her great satisfaction and delight but also drew out her desire to suffer the same fate. As Carvajal explains in her autobiography, she came to associate corporal pain with imitation of Christ's suffering, and this precedent would be important in her decision to go to England and in the shaping of her writing and her thinking (*Escritos* 162; Cruz, *Life* 31–2).

Carvajal and Her Literary Heritage

According to her biographers, Carvajal's unusual religious zeal, essential to her work and her relationship to religious literature, seems to have been present before her teenage years, since as a child she was modest, honest, and grave and loved the poor and suffering[15] (*Escritos* 132–7). These early practices and inclinations were also nourished by the teachings of the Roman Catholic Church, largely mediated through Jesuit and devotional writings by Fray Luis de Granada, John of the Cross, and Teresa of Avila, among others. Critics argue the extent to which Carvajal's life and writings resembled, intentionally or not, those of Teresa, especially in her autobiography.[16] Since Carvajal only mentions Teresa's *Vida* once,[17] it is difficult to determine how influential this book was in Carvajal's conception of martyrdom and roles for religious women or whether she identified at all with the saint.[18] What is clear, however, is that rhetorical strategies in Carvajal's writing, like that of humility, resemble Teresa's and writings of other religious women of this period, as will be further discussed below.

Carvajal's literary formation, however, was not limited to books that women were expected to read because her uncle expanded her education. Carvajal recounts that she would sit by him as he read to her from the Bible and the church fathers, sometimes in Latin,[19] while he paused from conducting business with his secretaries:

> My most common company was the presence of my uncle; and seated next to him I spent a large part of the dạy: he in his chair, writing alone or with his secretaries or scribes; and I on the floor ... When my uncle would stop writing, or while his scribes would write a clean copy of what was written, he would then speak of our Lord with me ... very regularly he would read the Holy Scriptures and Holy Doctors of the Church; a reading which he very much loved.[20] (*Escritos* 156–7)

These early experiences made her proficient in Latin and exposed her to her uncle's governmental business. They also seem to have turned her into an avid student of theological discussions, somewhat uncommon for women, and given her a keen knowledge and interest in political affairs, especially insofar as they intersected with religious matters. In fact, her letters echo statements by Jesuits when she says that she is averse to meddling in "temporal things," but that her involvement in them was only necessary because they were tied to the success of the church[21] (*Epistolario* 164). Abad, one of her biographers, states that before leaving for England Carvajal "had procured a very complete knowledge" of the Catholic religion by speaking with priests and learned people and by reading and rereading Granada's *Summary of Christian Doctrine* and books by Augustine, Aquinas, and "some books of controversy against heretics in Latin and in English" (Carvajal, *Epistolario* 45). It is important here to note that most of the arguments of these "books of controversy," learned people, and priests were included in Ribadeneyra's and Yepes' ecclesiastical histories, so even if the latter are not listed, she would have been familiar with their contents directly or indirectly. Throughout her adult life, high-placed acquaintances kept her informed by means of letters and conversations of religious arguments and political negotiations and ensured her access to polemic texts from their private libraries. In fact, in London around 1610, Carvajal would continue to correspond with Jesuits and study all the Catholic polemic materials that she could find in order to improve her arguments to persuade "heretics."

Carvajal's knowledge of martyrs came both from written and oral stories. According to her beatification proceedings, a fifteen-year-old Carvajal had read a letter from the Spanish ambassador in England, Don Bernardino de Mendoza, recounting the execution of the Jesuit missionary Edmund Campion in England – a letter which some scholars believe triggered Carvajal's longing for martyrdom specifically in that land[22] (Mendoza; Muñoz 95; *Epistolario* 29; 165, n. 9). She also read lives of saints,[23] martyrologies, accounts of English martyrs in letters and books, and heard first- or second-hand the stories of Jesuits and English Catholics who were being killed in England for their faith. Isabel de la Cruz testifies that, while living in Madrid, Carvajal would host visiting English priests and eagerly hear for hours their stories of persecution under Elizabeth Tudor (Carvajal, *Letters* 1: xiii-xiv). Her letters from England are filled with accounts of various Stuart Catholic executions, showing that she felt that recording these stories was crucial for the encouragement of Spanish Catholics – as they had moved her – and for the support of their English brethren as Ribadeneyra and Yepes believed. Carvajal points to these accounts as inspiring her to practice increasing self-abnegation and seek martyrdom, eventually in England. Clearly, then, Carvajal patterned her life and writings after the religious texts she prized, including the Bible, lives of saints, ecclesiastical histories, and literature of suffering.

In addition to revealing shaping forces in her life and mind, Carvajal's description of her youth and her spiritual mindset inadvertently discloses aspects of her as reader that would also leave an imprint on her writing, and more broadly, how readers and writers of the period were affected by the literature available to them. For instance, the occasion for the excerpt cited above about desiring to become a martyr cannot be ignored, since it does not appear in a private letter to a religious friend, but rather in her autobiographical writings, which had a specific audience and a specific goal. While she labors to justify her remaining in the country, she writes these thoughts from England at the request of her confessor, the Jesuit Michael Walpole, who enabled her English trip and would initiate her beatification process with these materials.[24] Thus, Carvajal perceives and self-consciously writes about herself as a martyr: her self-inflicted spiritual and physical suffering that aims to unite her with Christ's passion out of love for him authorize her to participate in the real sufferings of Catholics in England, even to the point of death, like other martyrs and saints of the past and present. Given this scenario, Catholics who wanted her out of England would have to argue against this self-sacrificial and unusual love for Christ that merited her continuance in that land. Moreover, her meditations and prayers are detailed to show that she had the same kind of extraordinary devotion that only saintly women had, such as Teresa of Avila, and, therefore, Carvajal's experiences could only come from God and thus put her in a privileged position. Additionally, the details were meant to show that her beliefs were orthodox and compliant with the teachings of the Roman Catholic Church, especially if the Spanish Inquisition were to inspect them. Thus, according to this logic, those who attempted to stop Carvajal's work in England opposed God himself. The patterning of her spiritual experience after religious literature of the time to identify with saints and validate her mission as God's call was common, especially among religious women of this period who otherwise might come under the scrutiny of the Inquisition.[25] Writing about herself as a saint and a martyr, Carvajal seems to have full authority to give an account of the martyrs in England and to participate in the English mission, despite not being a man, a Jesuit, or a priest.

While she appears to be sincere in her piety, the autonomy that living in England gave an intelligent and decisive woman like Carvajal cannot go unnoticed. As a woman of her time Carvajal supported male hierarchy,[26] and her biographies presented her as a woman in subjection to her male superiors, including her uncle and her confessors (Carvajal, *Epistolario* 24, 28). However, through what she believed to be God's will for her life and his greater cause, Carvajal resisted her uncle's desire that she marry and decisively directed her confessor, albeit politely, concerning the management of her belongings after her death (Cruz, *Life* 34, 14). Furthermore, as will be shown, being in England fulfilling a divine calling about which she had read so much and doing certain work usually reserved for men gave her much more self-assertion than she ever would have attained in Spain.[27]

Carvajal and the Ecclesiastical Histories

Although a direct, explicit connection between Ribadeneyra's and Yepes' histories and Carvajal has not yet surfaced, multiple factors make it practically impossible for her not to have been very familiar with their contents, if she did not personally read them. First, a possible indirect reference to them came during her first imprisonment when Carvajal argued for Elizabeth Tudor's illegitimacy, telling the judge that she had learned those things from "printed chronicles and histories of that time"[28] (*Epistolario* 272). Since she mentions "chronicles and histories" as her source, rather than treatises or pamphlets, the histories available that discussed Elizabeth's illegitimacy were Sander's, Ribadeneyra's, and Yepes'. Additionally, she mentions "learning" from "printed" sources, implying that she did not hear these things from a priest or scholar or read a circulating manuscript or letter.

Second, Carvajal certainly had access to copies of the Spanish ecclesiastical histories through her uncle's library, in Valladolid at St. Alban's English College, and at the Spanish ambassadors' homes during her time in London, most notably at Diego Sarmiento de Acuña's, whose private library was extensive and who was known to lend books.[29] A 1591 catalogue of the library of the Marquis of Almazán produced upon his death includes a copy of Ribadeneyra's *Historia* and of Nicholas Sander's *Schismatis Anglicano*[30] (Bouza 272, 281, 283, 298), though not of Yepes' *Historia* because it was published later.

Third, Carvajal had read and prized accounts that were later incorporated into Yepes' *Historia* and was well acquainted with the English authors of these accounts, making it unusual for her not to know about one of the most important works they helped produce. Her close friend, Inés de la Asunción, testified that, while still in Spain, Carvajal had become very fond of Creswell's Spanish edition of the *Life and Martyrdom of Henry Walpole*[31] – a stand-alone text that by 1599 became part of Book V of Yepes' *Historia particular* (Muñoz 95; Carvajal, *Letters* 1: xiv; Rogers). In fact, she exchanged books and extensively corresponded with Joseph Creswell,[32] one of the main sources and behind-the-scenes editors of Yepes' volume (Rogers Allison and Rogers 40–3), sending him information that could be used for polemic publications. Unsurprisingly, the principal subjects in Carvajal's detailed letters from London to Creswell in Madrid are the persecution of Catholics in England and martyrdom accounts, thus making the Spaniard a valuable part of Creswell's extensive network of information.[33] Also, in 1606 Carvajal mentions sending Creswell a book of "the laws" of England – presumably the laws against Catholics – and in 1611 she sent him a copy of "the book of the English religion," that is, the Thirty-Nine Articles,[34] with marks on each page of "every lie and contradiction" (*Epistolario* 330; *Letters* 2: 169). This kind of work often preceded a lengthy, written refutation and was circulated; used in personal debates, as in the case of Carvajal; and sometimes published. Thus, these details offer a glimpse into the production of ecclesiastical histories and polemic texts and present an unusual case of a woman being involved in theological debate.

Although the books Carvajal read and exchanged are not always individually identified, they included ecclesiastical histories: in one letter she asks for Cesare Baronio's *Annales ecclesiastici* (*Epistolario* 135), as mentioned in chapter 1, an early response to the *Magdeburg Centuries*. Given this relationship between Carvajal and Creswell and their mutual interest in the subject of ecclesiastical histories and polemic literature, it is likely that the Spaniard had read Creswell's other publications and, after 1599, Yepes' history that collected many of those accounts into one volume.[35] Furthermore, in addition to knowing Creswell, Carvajal's acquaintance with Robert Persons extended to trusting him to manage the donation of her inheritance and to bury her body (Cruz, *Life* 60–1,

100–1). Persons had been central in the publication of Ribadeneyra's *Historia* and wrote several Catholic polemic treatises that also were incorporated into Yepes' volume (Rey 883–7; Weinreich, "Introduction" 57–8).[36]

Finally, the immense popularity of the ecclesiastical histories by Ribadeneyra and Yepes coupled with Carvajal's background, acquaintances, love for Jesuits and their writing, and interest in English martyrs and polemic texts make it highly unlikely that she was unfamiliar with those works. Also, as mentioned at the beginning of this chapter, Carvajal's letters disclose significant overlap with the content and vision especially of Ribadeneyra's *Historia*, which could indicate that she was one of the early modern Spaniards whose thinking concerning the English Reformation was moulded or at least informed by Ribadeneyra's narrative.

Carvajal as Reader of the Histories

Carvajal's background and interests would have made her an ideal reader of the Spanish ecclesiastical histories – a Catholic aligned with Ribadeneyra's vision and ready to follow his call to action, although in some ways her situation is exceptional because she had first-hand information about England and the world of the histories. For instance, she delivers their arguments as trustworthy: when citing in public debates or in private letters the sources affirming Elizabeth Tudor's illegitimacy or material from other Catholic polemic works, Carvajal almost always does so without qualification, indicating that she believes that they are reliable and authoritative. The exceptions to this pattern are significant and revealing, so they will be discussed in some detail below, but Carvajal's endorsement of Ribadeneyra's vision in the Spanish histories suggests that they shaped her thinking, or at least affirmed her beliefs and gave her shared language to discuss arguments advanced by her co-religionists. In fact, she echoes the language of the histories on several issues.

For instance, she adopts the monster rhetoric when speaking of Queen Elizabeth. In 1600 she writes from Madrid to Magdalena de San Jerónimo that she has heard rumors that Elizabeth "the monster" was negotiating peace treaties with the Spanish monarchs, and although this could be convenient, she fears her cunning and deceit because of "the ruses and wiles which that monster of a woman is used to employing to make war surreptitiously against God and his church and the souls of her subjects"[37] (*Epistolario* 100). Carvajal adds many warnings meant for Isabel Clara Eugenia about the hypocrisy of Elizabeth in negotiations aimed to destroy the church and her own subjects and concludes that section clearly associating Elizabeth with the apocalyptic Whore of Babylon:

> That most perverse woman should be contented with the blood of the martyrs she has drank, is drinking, and will drink (if she lives in her intransigence) every time she seizes in her kingdom a priest or religious person, or another of her Catholic enemies. She should be contented instead of going so far as to want capriciously and with golden hypocrisy to induce so great Christian and religious princes as ours to participate in such a foreign thing to them as is her malice and misery, which is so characteristic and natural to her.[38] (*Epistolario* 101–2)

Carvajal's "extremely perverse" woman who drinks the blood of the martyrs and her enemies vividly recalls Revelation 17:4–6[39] where John, the Apostle, sees a woman "drunken of the bloud of the Sainctes, and the bloud of the martyrs of Iesus" (*Douay-Rheims 1610*). As seen in chapter 2, the image of the Whore of Babylon, at once familiar and exotic, was used by both Protestants and Catholics to ostracize their opponents by categorizing them as a sexual and racial Other (Dolan 5–8). It also cast current events into a biblical framework. While the Protestant reformers believed the apocalyptic woman to represent Rome,[40] Carvajal and other Roman Catholics saw in her the evil persecutors who shed the blood of saints and persecuted the true church[41] – though, along with more militant Catholics, as chapters 2 and 4 show, Carvajal specifies that the whore is Queen Elizabeth.[42] Her representation of the queen recalls Ribadeneyra's: she is a deceitful, ruthless, bloodthirsty monster whose only goal is to destroy the Roman Catholic Church. Nonetheless, though Carvajal mentions her in a few instances, this is the only time that she refers to Elizabeth Tudor as a monster, perhaps because, employing a strategy similar to Ribadeneyra's, Carvajal's goal is not merely to slander gratuitously but to convince the archduchess through an analogy full of pathos that the English queen is essentially and irrevocably deceitful because of her unnatural, monstrous self and, therefore, not to trust her perverse negotiations that "make war surreptitiously." Also, for Carvajal as for Ribadeneyra, current events echo ancient biblical warnings that the current church must heed.

On a different occasion she seems to affirm Ribadeneyra's vision of Elizabeth as a victim of her parents' sins – though culpable for persisting in evil actions – who is tragically destroyed. While still in Spain and immediately after the death of the queen in 1603, Carvajal writes to

Magdalena de San Jerónimo to learn news about England and its priests and reflects upon the fate of the monarch:

> How short it must have seemed to that wretched [*misera*] woman, madam, the time of her reign and prosperity! And how long, like years, will seem to her that her torment endures! Hers was an infelicitous [*infelicísima*] soul, indeed, as will be forever and ever. And her judgment before the divine tribunal must have been astounding, and very peculiar, and I think that it must have been above any of those that have been for her sex in many years.[43] (*Epistolario* 131–2)

Although these words carry the stern weight of judgment – indeed, the greatest on any woman in years, echoing Sander's words omitted by Ribadeneyra – it may be possible to infer some compassion in "wretched woman" and "infelicitous soul," especially if the catalyst for Elizabeth's wrong choices were the sins of her parents, as was commonly held among Catholics and recorded in the Spanish ecclesiastical histories. Perhaps Carvajal had in mind a similar reflection of Anne Boleyn's life in Ribadeneyra's text that reads: "sad [*triste*] woman, who was born, raised, married, and died in such disgrace and infamy! ... But, above all things, infelicitous [*infelicísima*] and abominable, for having been the source and fountainhead of the Schism and destruction of her nation" (1004). Thus, for Carvajal and Ribadeneyra Elizabeth and Anne are not only "wretched" (*mísera, triste*) women but also the most "infelicitous" or "ill-fated" (*infelicísima*), and they have a tragic ending because of their persistent opposition to the church and their role in the spiritual destruction of England.

Carvajal's letters suggest that she is an ideal reader of Ribadeneyra's *Historia* in that they also display Ribadeneyra's spirit of Spanish nationalism and sense of the Spanish messianic mission that the histories targeted in their audience, especially at a time when Spain and Spaniards were being criticized. In 1612 she tells her brother that the English bring out infamous mockeries of Spain in plays and that from their pulpits they say "that it is a land of most cruel savage beasts and that they drink human blood; that they are idolaters who worship sticks and stones, and the worst, that is, the abomination of the antichrist and whore of Babylon, which is the Pope, and a small bread that we say is our God"[44] (*Epistolario* 374). This excerpt confirms the notion implicit in the Spanish ecclesiastical histories about the need to defend Spain against criticism, including Black Legend charges that were prevalent in England ("savage beasts," drinking blood), and also the need to defend Spain and Roman Catholicism against charges of idolatry and of worshipping the Pope, who was identified as the antichrist and the Whore of Babylon. As already noted, Ribadeneyra's *Historia* and other Roman Catholic polemic literature threw these charges back at the English and the Protestants, especially in the representations of Henry and Elizabeth Tudor.

Moreover, Carvajal shares Ribadeneyra's goal to vindicate and eulogize Spain and its monarchs. Her letters praise Spain for sending financial aid for the English Catholic cause[45] and for being a bastion of the true faith and express gratitude for its pious monarch, Philip III,[46] of whom she says: "What a pity that our king of Spain not be king of all the world! How respected would our Holy Catholic Church be and how many more souls would be saved! May God keep him long years, for it would be madness not to wish his life a thousand times over ours"[47] (*Epistolario* 397). These words echo the prevalent sense of messianic mission – Philip III would save the church if he just had more territories – and nostalgic appeal in Ribadeneyra's *Historia* for Spain to take the lead in defending universal Christianity. Carvajal also remarks favorably that the Spanish ambassador to London, Don Diego de Velázquez, advanced the honor of Spain and Christianity[48] and notes that such a goal was an important part of the Spanish embassy in London[49] (*Epistolario* 291, 383).

Throughout her letters, her Spanish identity is proudly emphasized, and comparisons between Spain and England in terms of food and customs reveal that England's only advantage for her is that of being the location where she can fulfill a spiritual cause.[50] In fact, in Carvajal's opinion, the superiority of Spain is precisely what allows England to serve as her "great purgatory" on earth and identify with the sufferings of English Catholics on some level. She writes:

> The plague increases more these days, though it has been here already twelve years, according to what some say, and a little or much is never absent. England has such graces that it lacked nothing, indeed, but this one to seal them all! It is an intolerable land; it does not disappoint me in anything concerning the assurance I had of being able to suffer a great purgatory in it, because for that, only the remembrance that one lives here is enough.[51] (*Epistolario* 191)

For the Spaniard, England seems to be unhealthy for the body ("plague," persecutions) and the soul (heresy), a place of purging like purgatory in a sort of Neoplatonic identification of the material and the spiritual. In this excerpt, she sarcastically boasts that she had expected to suffer greatly in England, though her bitter complaint seems to indicate that she had not expected these kinds of mundane trials. In fact, although

Carvajal had arrived in England prepared to suffer, her spiritual "purging" seems to have most often come from unexpected fronts, such as cultural difference, language barriers, and disappointment in the actions of English and Spanish Catholics. Carvajal's hyperbole that just remembering that she lives there is already a great torment ironically belies not only nationalistic superiority but also her resistance to suffering in these particular, pedestrian ways.

Also like Ribadeneyra and Yepes, she writes to make known the sufferings of the English Catholics (Christian brothers and sisters), to encourage the faithful, to expose the persecutions that continue under James I, and to gather support from Spaniards for English Catholics. In a letter to Creswell she refers to the exchange of news with him that is mutually comforting, including the example of two martyrdoms whose story of constancy she had recounted for him, and then goes on to describe the joys brought to her by her own imprisonment: "I receive much grace and comfort with your grace's letters and hope that your grace has received comfort with my latter ones, seeing the great constancy of the holy martyrs Jarves and Fludder"[52] (*Epistolario* 245). A different letter to Creswell congratulates him upon the death of two Englishmen, whose faithfulness to the end she narrates in some detail[53] (Carvajal, *Epistolario* 240–1). Writing to Magdalena de San Jerónimo, Carvajal also includes at least one account of an execution that she says English officials later regretted because it had been instrumental in encouraging the Catholic cause:

> Father Al was taken with his servant outside of London to a place where he used to live and both were killed. At the gallows he declared to have never known anything about the gunpowder and spoke with such spirit and tone, that more than five hundred people were seen weeping. Cecil later said that he would give three hundred ducats to prevent his death for it resulted in a great benefit of souls.[54] (*Epistolario* 174)

This martyr, named Al Oldcorne, had been charged with being involved in the Gunpowder Plot and, therefore, with treason. Carvajal, however, appropriates the narrative like Sander and Ribadeneyra had done and includes telling details: the priest's declaration of innocence regarding this charge; the weeping of the large, surrounding crowd, presumably of Protestants who knew him ("where he used to live"); and the powerful witness that he gave. The inclusion of these specific details, though they may be factual, especially Cecil's regret and the assertion that his opponents wept and believed in his innocence, adds pathos and ethos, drawing both sympathy from readers and instilling belief in the good character of the man to validate as genuine the priest's testimony and to prove that the execution was that of a martyr rather than a traitor. While Carvajal does not indicate that she is an eyewitness ("were seen," "Cecil said later"), that she is a credible source lends authority to the account, even if some of the details were not verifiable.

These stories implicitly offer data concerning the socio-political landscape at the time. They were not only to encourage Catholics on the Continent and promote the idea that Catholics were superior over Protestants in character and behavior – as Foxe and others would also do – but they could also supply valuable information necessary for Anglo-Spanish political advocacy on behalf of English Catholics. Additionally, they reveal fissures and conflicting information within Catholicism in Spain.

Carvajal's letters detail the persecutions of Catholics to contradict false information on the Continent about the oppression diminishing, being only political, and being less harsh than it had been. In April of 1608, she writes: "they tell us here that some there tell and persuade others that the persecution is not great, nor particularly because of religion" (Carvajal, *Epistolario* 238). Here it seems that some Spaniards were actively discouraging others from assisting the English mission through what Carvajal considers misinformation: minimizing the persecutions and attributing them to political, not religious, causes. Carvajal recounts different times when she had to defend martyrs from being called traitors,[55] a recurring theme in her letters, but usually this was among Protestants, not Catholics. Yet her letters to Creswell suggest that Catholics in Spain were divided concerning the English martyrs, possibly in part because the Jesuits who spearheaded the missionary work had a reputation for being "scheming Machiavellians" (Domínguez, "History in Action" 7). Also, some Spaniards were suspicious of Jesuits, in general, since the Society was relatively new, and thus, Weinreich has aptly argued that Ribadeneyra's *Historia* was meant to teach Catholics about the Spanish Jesuits and seminaries ("Introduction" 58–66). The testimonies Carvajal sends Creswell aim to correct the misconceptions in Spain that she had heard by detailing the harshness of the persecutions and affirming that English Catholics were being executed solely for their beliefs – not treason, as Elizabeth Tudor and James I claimed – and, therefore, that they deserved the status of martyrs and the support of Spaniards.[56] Religious leaders like Creswell could use this kind of information – as he did – to plead with the Spanish monarch to negotiate with James I concerning the hardships of innocent English Catholics or to appeal for financial support of the seminaries.[57] These stories were also passed on to seminarians and future missionaries outside the Continent as a glimpse into the value of their studies and the overall mission. Thus, the distribution of this information put Carvajal in a larger Anglo-Spanish coalition aimed at turning England back to Catholicism and disclosed antagonistic Anglo-Spanish perceptions, especially emerging after the Gunpowder Plot.

Furthermore, like the Spanish ecclesiastical histories, Carvajal also writes to rally support from Spain for English Catholics, though her efforts, unlike Ribadeneyra's, focused on gathering individual assistance – spiritual, economic, or political – rather than corporate. To her, prayer was one of the most urgent needs, and she requested it from almost everyone to whom she wrote. Shortly after arriving in London, she earnestly tells Magdalena de San Jerónimo that the English are so pressed that they urgently need prayers for God "to assuage the fury" in the hearts of his enemies (*Epistolario* 150). Yet prayers alone were insufficient. Thus, Carvajal also writes to her aristocratic and wealthy contacts for more tangible help, such as financial donations or assistance to be given to young Catholics who were leaving England for Continental seminaries. She asked Magdalena de San Jerónimo in Flanders to do all she could for English Catholics and sent a message to Archduchess Isabel Clara Eugenia charging her to protect and provide for them[58] (*Epistolario* 111). Carvajal also boldly solicited the services of those who had promised to help her, as in the case of one "licenciado Juan Manrique," of whom Carvajal requested personal and financial help[59] (*Epistolario* 200). In procuring sponsorship and shelter for Catholics leaving England, Carvajal was anything but half-hearted or timid. Instead, she personally recommended them and earnestly pleaded with her correspondents to do unto the English as they would do unto her. This earnestness is evident, for example, in a letter she writes to Joseph Creswell:

> Along with Father John, who is leaving for Spain, I think will go a young gentleman named Brigman, eldest son of a schismatic, who I think has a good fortune and the youth is reputed of being a good student here in London, and is good in his mettle. Our Lord has touched him, as can be discerned, to leave comfort and go to a seminary: he is sharp in intellect and shows great devotion. He goes with hope that my intercessions will help him to be accepted at Valladolid: I beg your grace for this on my knees, for I will appreciate it as if it were done to myself.[60] (*Epistolario* 250)

The young man, presented by Carvajal as having worthy credentials to be a seminarian – a sharp and diligent student of a good family who was full of devotion and ready to give up comforts – expected that Carvajal's "intercession" would open a door for him at St. Alban's College in Valladolid. Carvajal notes that the youth is the son of a "schismatic," evoking the hope of restoring to the faith the children of those who had turned back from God. Given the youth's credentials and Carvajal's recommendation and personal acquaintance with Creswell, her pleas were likely to be heeded. This was a tangible way in which Carvajal could use her acquaintances and position to link Spanish resources with the English cause and therefore contribute to an Anglo-Spanish coalition that relied on a fraternal view of England. Though her requests were individual, she had powerful contacts, and her letters attest to her success, especially in raising funds.

Carvajal's letters also confirm the implication in Ribadeneyra's and Yepes' works that many Spaniards were reluctant to help non-Spaniards, and she discloses prejudices against foreigners. Speaking to Mariana de San José about starting a convent in Flanders, Carvajal says: "If it were known in Spain how much Spain owes to God and how much less need it currently has of similar spiritual help, there would not be so much assiduousness in works there, and so much repugnance towards helping the souls of other lands"[61] (*Epistolario* 232). Again, like Ribadeneyra, here Carvajal appeals with pathos to their compassion, sense of duty towards brothers regardless of nationality, and even guilt: she charges Spaniards with taking for granted their privileged position of not needing this kind of spiritual help in the present and forgetting that they had help in the past and that they therefore owed assistance to the English, who were in a similar situation as Spain had been. She also implies that part of their problem is lack of awareness of the condition of the English Catholics, a deficiency which the information in her letters seeks to remediate. Nonetheless, that she was concerned for the English and was able to secure help for them from some of her Spanish correspondents shows that not all Spaniards were averse to the English: some even loved them and attempted to move other Spaniards to do the same. In fact, Carvajal's work to support the English mission was carried out in different ways – some highly unusual for anyone, and some extraordinary for an early modern woman – but it offers a glimpse into underground networks and texts.

Carvajal and the English Mission

Carvajal smuggled Catholic devotional and polemic texts in and out of England through the diplomatic privilege of the Spanish embassy and would read them not only for devotion or personal curiosity but with an apologetic goal. Her reading would become quite practical after 1605 once she was in England and had opportunities to converse with "heretics," although her inability to communicate in English was a barrier and constant frustration to her. She mentions pointing out to a Protestant the theological errors in Calvin's *Institutes*, especially in reference to Christ's descent to Hades (*Epistolario* 331). She also writes to Mariana de San José that she had been trying to persuade a Flemish painter named Alonso Sánchez to become a Catholic, of whom she says: "he understands Spanish very well and speaks it well; and thus, I was able to press him greatly, and Our Lord serves himself by helping my memory to remember important and very conclusive reasons that I have read and heard"[62] (*Epistolario* 290). His knowledge of Spanish enabled Carvajal to put him in a corner ("press him greatly") with good reasons for him to convert to Catholicism that she was able to recall from oral and written sources. In 1611, she asks Creswell to send her books and to pray for the salvation of souls of heretics that she encounters, especially for five or six (*Epistolario* 334), indicating that she had many potential converts and was using smuggled Catholic books to teach them. As mentioned, Carvajal also sent Creswell a copy of the Thirty-Nine Articles with Thomas Rogers' commentary with her marginal notes of the "lies and contradictions" she discovered (*Epistolario* 330; *Letters* 2: 169). In other words, she read Catholic and some Protestant theological and polemic materials specifically to have the arguments necessary to convince English men and women about the heresy imposed by Elizabeth Tudor and James Stuart and to defend the validity of Catholicism and the Pope. As an aristocrat who had received an unusual education at her uncle's house, she had the tools to obtain and critically weigh information, form opinions, and offer logical argumentation for her requests and advice. Her sending these arguments to Creswell reveal that women were also sometimes involved in these debates, even if not regularly, and perhaps had a part in shaping polemic literature published by men.

Because the information that Carvajal was disseminating had been censored in England and priests risked exposure if they became known, she felt all the more responsible to study and relay those arguments to English heretics. She vividly describes the situation, full of pathos, to the Marquis of Caracena:

> It breaks the heart to see so many thousands of souls drowning in an abyss of error without anyone to tell them; because the priests and religious men by no means are able to speak in public; and if they are known to some of the heretics they cannot go out on the streets by day without notable

> danger of being then caught; and therefore it seems that the conversion of these people is dependent upon persons of such little importance, like me and other similar ones.[63] (Carvajal, *Epistolario* 45, 270)

Carvajal here portrays Londoners as a great multitude of souls drowning, ignorant, innocent, and condemned to believing a fatal error because men cannot teach them the truth. Thus, the only possible solution seems an unconventional method: for "insignificant" people – presumably women – to take on the role of teaching them. With this rhetoric of humility similar to what women like Teresa of Avila employed,[64] Carvajal emphasizes how insignificant these messengers are while justifying them and ironically belying pride in her ability to participate in evangelizing and do the work normally reserved to men.

In 1609, Carvajal proudly tells her friend Mariana de San José that she had been able to "dispute for the faith," obliquely in imitation of Paul, although severely limited by knowing little English: "if your grace were able to see me before the judge and in jail, I think that you would be very much comforted, and what I disputed there and said for the holy faith in terse English, remembering that from the Holy Apostle: that the word of God *was not bound in his prison*"[65] (*Epistolario* 263). In this statement she boldly equates God's word with her arguments – metaphorically imprisoned by her location and inability to speak the language – and praises God's ability to overcome her weakness to communicate his message. That God could providentially, almost supernaturally, use weak vessels to powerfully speak his message was an important biblical mark of authenticity in Eusebius, later renewed by Foxe and Catholic ecclesiastical histories and martyrologies, and here in Carvajal's words. Her allusion connects current events in England with similar New Testament events, sometimes inexplicable – many recorded in Yepes' history as part of God's "providential acts" on behalf of his people – proving the divine origin of Carvajal's message. By extension, this reproduction of a New Testament providential act in Carvajal's time also vindicates the Roman Church.

In this vein, Abad celebrates that she converted to Catholicism a "very learned" (*muy docto*) Calvinist minister: when asked by Michael Walpole how he remained unpersuaded by priests and learned men but was convinced by a woman, the man replied that he found an irresistible force in her words (Carvajal, *Epistolario* 45). Carvajal and her biographers agreed that, as an exceptional case, God must have authorized her to speak because he extraordinarily used her words despite language and gender limitations – the conversion "proving" the validity of the means. Abad calls these activities Carvajal's "apostleship with the heretics" and uses them to support his beatification request (Carvajal, *Epistolario* 45).

These biblical allusions were important, too, because in the debate of vernacular translations of the Bible, Catholics often pointed to women reading and discussing the Bible as proof of the depravity of Protestantism, and Carvajal seemed to be doing the same. She was perceived by her opponents as a masculinized, disorderly woman (Cruz, *Life* 73–4), a charge often brought up against outspoken Protestant women like Anne Askew and others whom Foxe and Bale similarly defended with associations to New Testament martyrs.[66] Carvajal wrote in two separate letters recounting her second imprisonment that Londoners called her a "Roman priest in woman's clothing"[67] (Carvajal, *Epistolario* 254, 264). Redworth adds that Archbishop Abbott derisively called her a "Jesuitess" before the famous Englishwoman Mary Ward[68] received this mock title (*She-Apostle* 220). Whether these were rare or recurrent appellations, Carvajal seems gratified by these intended insults because she saw herself as filling the void men could not easily fill, and this task made her stay in England valuable and even necessary.[69] As a woman, she could not be a priest or a Jesuit, but precisely because of her gender she could draw less attention and perhaps be effective. She considered it an honor to be able to occupy the space of Jesuit missionaries whom she so highly regarded, and it has even been suggested that she saw herself as a female Jesuit (Redworth, *She-Apostle* 155).

Carvajal's involvement in apologetics in England that made even some of her supporters question whether she exceeded the Christian expectation of humility and silence for women reveals some of the leeway in the application of this Pauline restriction among Spanish theologians. Muñoz had to justify that Carvajal's actions were not against the teachings of the Holy Scriptures about the woman's place in teaching. To this end, the biography he wrote for her beatification includes a chapter titled "That the venerable Doña Luisa in the way in which she dealt with the cause of Religion with the heretics, and in her benefits to the English Catholics, did not exceed the limits that, in this, the Church has placed upon women"[70] (122). Here Muñoz argues that she was aligned with other female saints, citing from the Bible and ecclesial writings. He begins by asserting that since the beginning, the apostles and early church fathers had understood Paul's dictum that "women should not preach but keep silent" as restricted to public preaching and the *office* of teaching. He cites Paul, Clement of Alexandria, and Chrysostom to show that church leaders always traveled with learned, pious women to help evangelize noblewomen otherwise unable to hear the gospel and that the men considered these females "coadjutors of men"

(122v). Muñoz adds that the church has always accepted that women teach in private and "from person to person," like Priscilla with Apollos and wives with their unbelieving husbands or children, but that sometimes God made their testimonies public, as in the case of St. Catherine, Marcela, and Teresa of Avila, whose writings are "full of celestial doctrine" (124v). Muñoz concludes that in extraordinary circumstances when men were absent or unable to preach and defend the church, God used women as instruments to fill this need, and the church lauded these women. Thus, Carvajal's example was perfectly in accord with all these teachings of the early church (124v). More research is needed to gauge how widespread Muñoz's views were in Spain, but what is interesting is that at least some theologians welcomed the help of women in the English mission, since it was considered an exceptional time when regulations could be softened, and Carvajal herself held this opinion.

The letters of Carvajal expose an important underground activity during her time in England: the acquisition and contraband of relics. One way she would show her gratitude to donors was by sending them relics of English martyrs, an act that was important for the English mission in further linking England and Spain, in some ways permanently. Her recovery of these bodies was audacious and allowed her to fulfill yet another role she could not have had outside of England. As Carvajal writes, she would receive mutilated corpses of English Catholics that were stolen by night from common grave pits and brought to her house at great risk so that she could clean and preserve them. The love with which she describes her work with these bodies – cleaning them, kissing them, wrapping them, labeling them, and putting them in lead boxes – shows the great devotion she had for Catholic martyrs and the way bodily sacrifice further inspired her to imitate them and desire their fate. For her, martyrdom was not something just read in books, distant and merely used to win an argument. Her example also emboldened other Catholics, fueling this illegal activity. Cruz notes from Carvajal's canonization documents one witness who testified that on one occasion the Spanish ambassador's servants stole parts of two bodies by night from the graveyard, underwent great danger, and partook in gruesome work of digging and sorting through partially decomposed bodies because they were strengthened by their esteem for Carvajal, her saintly devotion, and her gratitude towards anyone who helped her (*Life* 86–7).

As stated in her letters, Carvajal's primary reason for sending these out of England seems to have been to repay Spaniards and other contacts for financial and spiritual support, but this exchange reveals other assumptions and effects achieved by relics in the English mission that relate to the broader context of the European Reformation. First, these relics provided another venue to vindicate the English martyrs by confirming that they truly were martyrs and not traitors, as the English monarchs so often insisted. Further, these relics would keep the English persecutions in the minds of Spaniards and inspire them to offer recurrent prayers, almsgiving, and physical help for seminarians, as well as provide hope for Catholics everywhere to find comfort and encouragement in the confirmation that the blood of the martyrs was the seed of the church. In fact, that pious people were willing to give their lives for the Roman Church supported the idea that this church was the true church, and, therefore, the relics served as "proof" that Roman Catholicism was the true religion, especially if the relics were validated by miracles, giving Catholics an advantage over the popular imagination that Protestants did not have.[71] In effect, every time Spaniards and other Continental Catholics looked at these relics, they would be reminded of these things, and if the relics were passed on to their descendants, as they were, they would keep alive the memory of the English martyrs perpetually, thus creating a strong and enduring Anglo-Spanish connection and adding to the proof in favor of the validity of the universal Roman Catholic Church.

Moreover, the preparation and traffic of these relics also gave Carvajal a strong sense of purpose in England, relief from her discouragement and sufferings, and much more autonomy than she would have had in Spain as a woman. When Carvajal arrived in England, her intent was to be martyred, but in time she realized that God was not granting her this desire and that she was unable to communicate in English, further limiting her role. Eventually she came to understand that there were other ways in which she could be useful to the English mission, one of which was in the recovery and preparation of relics. She told her cousin: "The work of burying these dead ones and wrapping them in linens cannot be done in Spain, nor other works of this great value. When did I deserve, Lord, to partake in them!"[72] (*Epistolario* 347). In addition, as Cruz notes, the risk of being caught stealing bodies, which was illegal, to make them relics increased Carvajal's chances of becoming martyred, as she hoped she would be (*Life* 85). Presumably, the sense of mission in England and comfort during times of discouragement attained from the traffic of relics would have been available to other English Catholics who participated in that activity and, therefore, can illumine the different ways by which Catholics remained encouraged and persevered during a time of great difficulty.

Generic Challenges and Opportunities

Because of her affinity with Jesuit ideas and exposure to Catholic polemic literature, Carvajal is closely aligned to Ribadeneyra and Yepes ideologically, but her letters provide a point of view that at times challenges the histories, largely due to her writing in a different genre for a private readership. Ecclesiastical histories were produced for a broad audience and, in Spain, ultimately had to be approved by the Inquisition before publication.[73] Thus, they had to be carefully crafted and aligned with the views of approving bodies, and they had to follow the teachings and literary patterns of sanctioned sacred literature. As discussed, ecclesiastical histories were read and challenged by opponents and were often didactic, including general exhortations to do good or reproof to deter from evil through exempla and precepts. Because publishing histories took time, they were necessarily somewhat distant from the events they narrated, but they were authoritative. Furthermore, their goal was to provide continuity with the early church and, in the case of the histories by Ribadeneyra and Yepes, to show the aberration of the English Reformation and rally Catholics to counteract its effects.

Letters, naturally, had fewer restrictions and were ubiquitous in the early modern period (Rico 68). They were the most important medium to deliver news of small or large importance, and, since antiquity, the epistolary genre was found alongside the autobiography (Rico 66–7, 71). Though sometimes written for circulation,[74] they were generally aimed at one reader and were therefore personal (Demers). They tended to be intimate and even confidential, especially when they disclosed incriminating or sensitive information. In that the letters recorded immediate responses to current events, they were ephemeral, and they were often written hurriedly and without a telos or an overarching narrative (Demers 119–20). Women's epistolary writing, when autobiographical, is included in the category of "ego-documents," or documents about the self (Howe; Mascuch et al.). As such, early modern women's letters share the traits of women's autobiographies, including the anxiety of having an authoritative voice or of instructing men – or in Spain, of coming under the scrutiny of the Inquisition – as well as the fear of writing too much idly, without being asked, and without a clear purpose. Therefore, the rhetoric of humility and justifications for writing are pervasive in women's letters, and as seen, Carvajal's letters are a prime example of these strategies.

Discontinuities between Histories and Letters

Despite the many continuities in subject, ideology, and rhetoric with Ribadeneyra's and Yepes' works, Carvajal's letters present important departures that are essential to understanding the complexity of the English mission and its representation. In many ways, Carvajal's letters from England reflect the climate of the second part of Ribadeneyra and of Yepes – a post-1588 period of disenchantment that had turned its focus to explain the military defeat and the persistent tribulations of English Catholics to the spiritual benefit of purging and expanding the church through suffering.[75] In fact, Carvajal's letters are generally encouraging to Catholics, but when read against the histories, they are less optimistic about the martyrdoms and the positive outcomes of the persecutions. In other words, Ribadeneyra and Yepes emphasize the conversions and fruit of the tribulations and present a more flatly positive version of the martyrdoms in England, while Carvajal depicts the full complexity of the situation, not omitting the discouragement that comes from those who were turning away from Catholicism, the contested opinions within the church, or the failure to reconvert. She writes to Inés de la Asunción in 1606:

> The news from here are all sorrows upon sorrows, and pain upon pain. The events that over there terrify and cause tears that are not wiped away in a year, here are daily bread, and its vivid objects are seen with serene and dry eyes, for the most part, because there is no strength to even begin to weep over such horde and continuation of harm of soul and body. And the worst part is that the harm of soul reaches some friends, who with exceeding affliction falter and give in to sin, even though, infinite thanks be to God, many and even most are strong in loyalty to religion, and some convert again even though only a few in this hardship.[76] (*Epistolario* 183)

The first part of this paragraph is not unlike portions in the Spanish ecclesiastical histories discussing the horrors that Catholics suffered daily in England, though from the perspective of an eyewitness who also suffers. Poetically repeating "sorrows" and "pains," the sentence describes horrific events that in Spain make a person weep for a year, but in England occur daily and are faced without tears because of the inability to weep so much. The second part, however, laments that many have become weary and have given into heresy ("harm of soul"), and few have reconverted to Catholicism. Because Carvajal's report is a private unburdening of her heart through writing to close acquaintances who needed a realistic view of the condition of the Catholic cause, she can discuss the weaknesses or potential failures of the missionary endeavor, whereas the histories of Ribadeneyra and Yepes are constrained to emphasize the global, positive outcomes of the persecutions and minimize the setbacks.

Although Carvajal echoes Ribadeneyra's view on several points, her letters expose some of the complexities underlying the neat polarization of "Catholic" and "heretic" into "wholly good" and "wholly evil," with the possible exception of Elizabeth Tudor, whom she believes to be essentially flawed, as discussed. However, even if Carvajal's view of Elizabeth seems flat and polarized like the representation in the histories by Ribadeneyra and Yepes, she disagrees with their positive representation of Philip II, illustrating some of the criticisms Spaniards leveled against Philip. In her opinion, Philip II was not the best example of a Christian prince, and not all his decisions were commendable. In fact, in a letter to her cousin, Don Rodrigo Calderón, she states that Philip III was a better monarch than his father, writing that "even though he was good in the beginning, and in his youth, and at a few other times, he really was not so good and so greatly virtuous as is and has been his son"[77] (*Epistolario* 396). Carvajal's political knowledge and views aligning with Spanish Christian prince treatises like Ribadeneyra's surface in this letter. She argues that Philip II's bad decision of compromising with Elizabeth Tudor for "reason of state" rather than trusting in God and opposing Elizabeth may have caused God's displeasure and therefore brought about the defeat of the Armada and the terrible current situation in England. She explains:

> He was faced with strong occasions in which God, perhaps, was very displeased, both in domestic affairs as in other very great ones concerning the state. And if this were so, that because of reason of state, as it was said and understood in the world, he favored Queen Elizabeth and did not oppose her when taking possession of her kingdom in England (so that France would not take over its right through the Queen of Scotland, Mary Stuart, married with the Dauphin, heiress of that kingdom), for occasion was given to such loss as is seen in this kingdom (although this was not, but should have been considered at the time) we must not be shocked that one and even many armadas should be lost.[78] (*Epistolario* 396)

Carvajal's words, "we must not be shocked that one and even many armadas should be lost," signal that her argument is a specific application of Ribadeneyra's general argument in *Tratado de la tribulación*. The Jesuit had stated that it was a great "marvel" that God sometimes allowed sins to be punished by greater sins and atrocities and specified that the defeat of the Armada was "scourge and severe chastisement from the hand of the Most High" (Rivadeneira 199). As Abad notes, this letter shows the extent of Carvajal's political knowledge. She was well informed about Philip II's proceedings during the first years of Elizabeth as well as the international ramifications of his decisions (*Epistolario* 397, n. 3). She was also aware of the profound complexity of the situation: "and I confess that the reason of state was great and strenuous to the extreme." But she echoes Ribadeneyra, who advocated in his

Christian prince treatise for trusting in God concerning political matters rather than taking the humanly logical path: "but despite all, the rectitude and justice and glory of God, and more in such cases, should trample and overcome whatever opposes it, and the hope in God, for he remedies inconveniences" (*Epistolario* 396). Looking back on the events, she points out calamities that resulted from that lack of faith, particularly in relation to the tragic death of Mary Stuart and the current reign of her son: "The Dauphin had no children and died young, and his wife, whom she was, returned to Scotland as a widow with little strength and persecuted by the heretics. And in the end, she was decapitated by their hands, after imprisoning her over twenty years. And this, her son, who now reigns in her absence, was brought up as a heretic" (*Epistolario* 397). As far as Carvajal was concerned, Philip II was responsible for England's long imprisonment and decapitation of Mary Stuart and for now having a heretic for a king.

The frank tone of Carvajal's letters is determined by the private and intimate nature of the epistolary genre, in contrast to Ribadeneyra's and Yepes' histories. Because Carvajal is writing privately to her cousin, Don Rodrigo Calderón, she is able to judge the king's political decisions, saying to her relative, "I would like to tell your Lordship my thoughts plainly" (*Epistolario* 396), perhaps in the hope to influence future political decisions at court. However, if Ribadeneyra and Yepes disagreed with Philip II's political decisions, the ecclesiastical history genre constrained them from voicing these opinions. In fact, Ribadeneyra in his *Principe Christiano* (1595) had openly expressed a similar opinion to Carvajal's concerning how important it was for kings to make political decisions by trusting in God rather than in "reason of state."[79] But public negative comments about Philip II in his ecclesiastical history would be inappropriate and undermine the primary goals of the work. Nevertheless, Domínguez argues that it is possible to read in the *Historia* a veiled critique of Philip II's dealings with Elizabeth by his relatively scarce protagonism and the heightening of the positive exempla of Catherine, Mary Tudor, and Mary Stuart over the men ("History in Action" 15–22). Furthermore, there was a generic reason: just like hagiographies tended to gloss over weaknesses of saints after conversion in order to emphasize the pattern to follow, so including Philip II's flaws in the histories would weaken the exempla in those texts, rendering only part of his behavior as worthy of emulation and making it hard for the reader to follow.

Moreover, departing markedly from Ribadeneyra's tendency to show heretics as irredeemable, Carvajal does not seem to view King James as wholly evil simply on account of being Protestant, probably because, unlike Elizabeth Tudor, his birth did not demand it. Her letters reveal that even though at times the persecutions of Catholics under James I seemed to be worse than those under Elizabeth,[80] the English king's evil actions did not prevent Carvajal from commending him when he brought to London the bones of his mother, "the holy queen Mary Stuart," and reinterred them in Westminster Abbey (*Epistolario* 374; *Letters* 2: 265). She introduces the surprising event to her cousin, Don Rodrigo Calderón, saying: "This King has done a very good thing, and none other in all his life, I believe, and all the bells of London could toll even if no one were ringing them for all its strangeness" (*Epistolario* 378). Carvajal goes on to describe in detail the only good thing that she believed James had ever done, which was honoring Mary Stuart's body, and concludes by discussing how encouraging this has been to Catholics.[81] Emphasizing her role as informant in the Anglo-Spanish network, Carvajal passes on the details of this event that she claims were being kept secret because it was a public honoring of the body of a Catholic in ways that seemed unfitting for a Protestant king.

In Ribadeneyra's view, heretics are praised for actions before but not after their apostasy because all subsequent actions follow a downward pattern which proves that heretics are unrepentant and ultimately destroyed. Yet Carvajal does not seem to apply this pattern to James. She explains his actions against Catholics as the logical result of having been raised "among Puritans without his holy mother and without his Catholic father," and in 1608 she even states that she likes him – at least in comparison with Elizabeth (*Epistolario* 258).[82] She seems to take into account one important difference between the monarchs that Garnet had argued before his execution – a testimony that she transcribed for Magdalena de San Jerónimo in a letter. Garnet maintained that Elizabeth Tudor had apostatized from Catholicism and therefore could not turn back, while James Stuart was raised Protestant and could eventually be converted (Carvajal, *Epistolario* 173).

Furthermore, Carvajal was hopeful, as many Catholics had been, about James I restoring the ancient faith in England and ultimately avenging his parents: "if the new King wanted to be a man of good, he has plentiful and strong motives to be so" (*Epistolario* 132). However, Carvajal understood that those in power would not have admitted him as their monarch had he not given proof of not being faithful to his parents' beliefs and added that those men were guilty in the death of Mary Stuart. Despite this bad start, Carvajal believed that in time God could "touch his heart" and turn him away from following the counsel of those who placed him on the throne[83] (*Epistolario* 132). Unlike Elizabeth, he was the legitimate heir, and his parents had been Catholic and pious, so there was hope of return to his parents' faith. In Carvajal's lifetime, however, she did not see James softening towards the Catholics, but the reverse, and thus she was surprised about the only good act that she had seen him do during his reign – that of honoring his mother's body. However, even though his persecutions of Catholics were relentless and increasingly harsh, Carvajal's writings present him as a complex character, rather than a flat enemy.

Carvajal's letters also expose fissures within English Catholicism. In the histories by Ribadeneyra and Yepes, English Catholics seem to be a monolithic group that stands against heretics and, despite persecutions, flourishes and enjoys spiritual success. Once more, behind the differences between the letters and the histories lie distinct rhetorical situations of audience and goals. Ribadeneyra's discussion of Catholics is clearly to set them up as examples and to encourage others to help them, and therefore they must represent the strengths of a unified church despite the hardships imposed by her enemies. As Monta notes, "even in the face of significant intra-Protestant or intra-Catholic fissures, most Protestant and Catholic martyrologists are reluctant to admit intra-faith divisions and instead labor to rally their co-religionists into an integrated opposition to a clearly demarcated religious Other" (2). By contrast, when writing privately to her close acquaintances, Carvajal is able to disclose factions and disagreements among co-religionists that Ribadeneyra and Yepes are not free to reveal directly but that are implied, at least in Ribadeneyra's text, in the very points he is forced to argue.

For instance, Carvajal tells Magdalena de San Jerónimo that among English Catholics there were differences of opinion concerning the Oath of Allegiance of 1606. This oath, endorsed by the archpriest George Blackwell, did not require subjects to affirm the monarch's supremacy over the English church, but forced them to disavow that the Pope had a right to dethrone princes (Carvajal, *Letters* 1: 195). After mentioning that the impoverishment of Catholics by the new laws was making many fall back and take the oath, even though in their hearts and words they seemed sincere Catholics,[84] she adds: "although there have been priests who remove scruples about this, approving it as permitted, but none from the Society, nor many of the important priests because, although they esteem the principal one, they do not wish to follow his opinion on such matter"[85] (*Epistolario* 190–1). For Carvajal, Catholics who believed the oath to be justifiable were lukewarm and had "fallen back," since no Jesuit or "many of the important priests" agreed with this opinion. The Jesuits' special vow of obedience to the Pope made their choice to reject the Oath of Allegiance clear, but other English Catholics were not as certain. Nonetheless, Carvajal's opinion was that, because the oath challenged the authority of the Holy Father, no devout Catholic could swear it. Although Carvajal's division here of devout and lukewarm was related to the oath and is technically only for English Catholics, the implication is that she and the Jesuits outside of England, including Ribadeneyra, agree with the devout Catholics and belong to the same group. As mentioned above, not all Spaniards agreed with Ribadeneyra's view and obligation concerning England, and those would not be considered as devout by Carvajal.

Moreover, Carvajal points to a more specific group of "weak" Catholics, called "schismatics" (*cismáticos*), whom she describes in a letter to Inés de la Asunción as "Catholics in their hearts" but who outwardly conform by taking the Oath of Allegiance and attending the English church (*Epistolario* 267, 350).[86] According to Carvajal, schismatics sometimes bribed or even physically attacked government officials to help their persecuted Catholic friends (*Epistolario* 280, 340). It was also not uncommon for close relatives of schismatics – children, spouses – to convert to Catholicism and suffer the consequences for publicly professing their faith (Carvajal, *Epistolario* 227, 250). However, Carvajal argues that, since schismatics did not fear God, they were ultimately not trustworthy (Carvajal, *Epistolario* 343). In fact, unlike Ribadeneyra and Yepes, Carvajal makes clear that not all Catholics were to be trusted: some of them praised Elizabeth in order to vilify James' persecution (*Epistolario* 303),[87] while others changed sides when they arrived in England from the Continent[88] (*Epistolario* 319, 405). Even those she considered to be genuine Catholics, including priests, had flaws. Some were not judicious in what information they shared, causing problems. She explains to Inés de la Asunción: "I do not wish for the English students to know these particular things because when they arrive here they tell everything in the houses of Catholics, which is a great inconvenience, and say that I write long about what happens in England. And not all Catholics are trustworthy, even if they be constant in the faith, since some have a hundred impertinences, and priests also"[89] (*Epistolario* 267). Here, Carvajal does not gloss over the weaknesses and disputes of Catholics with each other; instead she presents the Catholic situation in England as complex and messy. The description of these struggles and weaknesses, acceptable in private letters, would have been unfitting in widely printed ecclesiastical histories. In fact, Carvajal believed that her information had to be restricted, at times, even from Catholics because it had the potential to backfire.

In her letter above, the detail that people complained that she wrote too much suggests that not everyone had been comfortable with her sending detailed information about Catholics in England and that Carvajal was suspicious of her co-religionists. Moreover, the seminarians who had heard her reports on the Continent seem to have brought them back to England and caused inconveniences. For these reasons, she attempts to keep the information that she sends away from seminarians, at least, though others are also not to be trusted. Furthermore, she tells Creswell of a related problem: that English Catholics objected to their being represented as better than they were in publications printed in Spain on the ground that the narratives were not truthful:

> The book against the proclamation and recent laws[90] is very good; but it is in Spanish, which here is worth little or nothing. I think it will be of great benefit in English to encourage and fortify Catholics. They are not, your grace should know, so fervent as it is presented over there, and this is a great inconvenience, because they themselves undervalue the book seeing something in it that is not true, even though it may be in their favor; and I have seen it, indeed, and heard them say in a similar case, why do they write those lies in books?[91] (*Epistolario* 333)

The letter shows that, clearly, the book used stories of the perseverance of English Catholics to encourage co-religionists, but their idealistic portrayal undermined the credibility of the book because it lacked verisimilitude and was considered deceitful. Implied in this statement is that several books printed on the Continent had this kind of idealistic representation, since Carvajal emphasized that she saw and heard Catholics comment on other books ("in a similar case") that had a similar representation to the one she discusses with Creswell, perhaps even the Spanish ecclesiastical histories, since those were books that published "current events."

Furthermore, Carvajal denounced as being lukewarm and cold Spanish Catholics who minimized the English persecution and argued that they could do so because they themselves were in a privileged position of safety: "it is clear that they are not suffering from it. I don't know why they want to burden their consciences with such a grave matter, and it is the cause of lukewarmness and coldness in those who over there can help in various ways these people so extremely afflicted and hard-pressed"[92] (*Epistolario* 238). For Carvajal, transnational solidarity with suffering Catholics was a matter of conscience whose neglect was a grave sin of omission. More importantly, these reports are damaging to the English, who, "when learning about them, grew discouraged and faint" (*Epistolario* 238). Thus, the position of these Spaniards was not simply comfortable and callous but also involved a sin of commission:

it damaged the church by disheartening those who were going through tribulations. By telling her correspondents about the impact that these kinds of attitudes and reports from Spain have upon the English, Carvajal hoped to effect change for the encouragement of English Catholics. Additionally, Carvajal warns those in Spain that James' amiable and diplomatic front with Catholic rulers was deceitful because, while their friendships seemed stronger than ever, his Catholic subjects were oppressed as never before during his reign, and this was intensifying. Carvajal emphasizes the urgent need to relieve these hardships and calls James' actions tyrannical and exorbitant, even for heretics[93] – a judgment that surprisingly echoes what was being said of Elizabeth Tudor in the ecclesiastical histories (Carvajal, *Epistolario* 327).

Just like Carvajal's representation of Catholics is complex and realistic, so is her description of herself and her work. Her labor in England does not always seem to be rewarding, and she is sometimes very frustrated with Catholics, especially when they criticize her. In fact, her defense of why she writes letters seems to indicate that more than once her writing was thought to be excessive and perhaps idle – common criticisms of female writing. She says:

> I don't know how writing is considered there. I write God's servants because I have need of their prayers, and we cannot keep from writing those who give alms and write to us, if we are going to receive alms, since it strengthens us. And even if we were not to receive alms, I would show them gratitude and love. And I do not know what spirit it may be – being as I am always dealing with such perverse demons of people as there are here and with so much sterility of spiritual help – that may prevent me from writing to those I write in Spain who are very few and on account of very convenient reasons. And the things here are so burdensome that I count it a great prudence to unburden myself somehow.[94] (*Epistolario* 300)

Here Carvajal gives five reasons to exonerate herself of idleness: that she requests prayers from religious people, that she is obligated to correspond with donors to receive funds and to express affection and appreciation, that her correspondents are few, that she writes for good reasons, and that writing for her is therapeutic. The first two reasons are virtually indisputable, since they are directly tied to the English mission and devotion. Next, her language vividly turns to her personal suffering in a sterile land from which she personally needs relief. She finds this respite in writing to a select group of correspondents in Spain, not idly but with founded motives, and to escape metaphorically the spiritually suffocating atmosphere around her. A valid implication is that were she not undergoing these trials, perhaps her writing would be excessive for a woman. In addition to her letters being criticized, her prized imprisonment apparently also came under attack. She describes some of the ingratitude that English Catholics have demonstrated towards Spain and towards her – including their belief that her incarceration had been for political murmuring against Elizabeth rather than for religious beliefs (*Epistolario* 299). In other words, she withstood the same criticism that English martyrs had received when considered traitors.

Carvajal, in sum, confides in Inés de la Asunción that she is discouraged and that her relief only comes from the pleasure of serving: "I do not have among Catholics one single drop of comfort or relief, other than what I extract somehow in serving them" (*Epistolario* 299). Similarly, she tells Rodrigo Calderón, "I always find England very sweet" and says that she forgets that it is "a sea of bile" when she spends entire nights caring for the bodies of martyrs and when she argues with heretics about the truth and they listen[95] (*Epistolario* 389). Neither of these tasks was possible in Spain. Despite the ugly and disappointing things that Carvajal had heard, seen, and experienced in England among Catholics, her location enabled her not only to write about herself as a co-sufferer and perhaps, as she had hoped, a martyr, but also to participate actively in a mission that she could not be part of while in Spain. Moreover, her desire to imitate these martyrs in their lives and in their deaths, and to write about herself as if she were one of them, persists to the end of her life. When she is imprisoned, she tells the judge that she had come to England "to follow the example of many saints of the Church who voluntarily forsook [*desampararon*] their country, family and friends and went to strange lands to live there in poverty and forsaken [*desamparo*]" (*Epistolario* 259).

Four years later in 1612, she continues to imitate this life of martyrs and hopes for a death like theirs, even though it was extremely unlikely that a foreign woman from an aristocratic family would ever suffer that fate in England. She writes to Don Rodrigo Calderón: "if I were to become a martyr and it be possible to recover my body, your lordship should place it where you would please, giving some part to the English Novitiate of the Society of Jesus that is in Louvai," and she finishes her instructions saying, "not being a martyr, I do not deserve burial" (*Epistolario* 351). To Carvajal, her body was only valuable if she could physically suffer and die for the church and become one of the stories she had heard of, seen, or read about. Then her life would be of comfort to others, and the life she had seen herself living as a martyr would be achieved and her body, turned into relics, would continue to inspire and help others. Moreover, by writing about herself in this way, in a literary style familiar to readers of saints' lives, she is able to defend as exceptional piety what others may have considered to be questionable or illegal actions, and she can place herself as another Christian saint in the long line since the primitive church.

This intense desire to be martyred is used even in her final letter, written to the Duke of Lerma, to beg her recipient to intercede for her so that she is not forced to leave England, where her experiences have confirmed that her living and dying in England is God's will[96] (*Epistolario* 416). Her desire in the letter is clear: "The vivacity and valor of don Diego have thwarted me from a glorious crown that it seems I saw up close, and leaves me great confidence that they will find a way and time that don Diego ignores, unless Our Lord desires to defer it more than the ambassador will be here"[97] (*Epistolario* 416). Upon her second arrest in November of 1613, she had anticipated that she would be martyred ("glorious crown") but believed that the intervention of the ambassador Don Diego Sarmiento de Acuña had prevented it, though she believed that the English would eventually circumvent the Spanish diplomat and execute her, which was highly unlikely since it would have created a colossal diplomatic problem. Not long after this letter, she died in her bed, and although she was not directly killed by English heretics, in her beatification process it was argued that she died from an illness acquired while in prison from which she never recovered, and therefore died in active service for God (Cruz, *Life* 92–3).

Conclusion

What is clear from Carvajal's life is that her work was an important asset to the Catholic cause, even if it is difficult to gauge how much of a difference, in the end, it made. Although Carvajal's letters were private and somewhat narrow in scope, they provided valuable information to people like Persons and Creswell and were directed at individuals who were influential and in a position to help bring about the twin goals of bringing England back to the Catholic fold – whether politically or through missionary work – and of assisting English Catholics. Moreover, Carvajal's involvement in polemics – sending heretical books to Spain with notes, smuggling Catholic texts into England, and persuading English people about the validity of the Catholic Church and the Pope – was also valuable and offers a glimpse of the transnational network that was behind the production of ecclesiastical histories and polemic literature. Furthermore, Carvajal helped to forge stronger Anglo-Spanish fraternal links in her work of recovering mutilated bodies of English Catholics, preparing them as relics, and sending them to the Continent to those who supported the English mission.

In the end, Carvajal's letters echo the theology and ethos of the works by Ribadeneyra and Yepes, continue their narrative of recalling the New Testament Church, and ultimately seek to accomplish the same goals. In fact, her upbringing and beliefs resonate so strongly with Ribadeneyra's call to give everything for the "great cause" of winning back England that it is possible to suggest that her thinking about England was influenced by the histories, and her imagination was captured. Consequently, she refused to support the enterprise only in ways expected from aristocratic women like her, such as giving and praying, as her female noble correspondents did. Instead, her life's goal shaped by experiences and books is not just to support the mission but to *be* a missionary to England, to suffer persecution alongside English Catholics, and to finish her life as a martyr – actions largely restricted to men, but available to women in extenuating circumstances. Indeed, her devotion to God and her modeling of her life after saints and martyrs would authenticate her writings, make them more credible, and even inspire others to imitate her, especially readers of devotional literature and the lives of saints. A case in point is the testimony of the witness who, recounting the motivation for the men who risked their lives to steal the bodies of English martyrs, states that they were inspired by her devotion. Carvajal's requests for money and personal sacrifice were also backed by the rhetorical ethos of a wealthy soul that had herself given all, and reports about English Catholics were supported by a track record of truth-telling and candid admissions, making them more reliable, even when the details of the information she received may not have been accurate.

Even though she had seen first-hand the weaknesses of Catholics in England and the sometimes many setbacks in the mission of bringing back that country to her original faith, she remained convinced that the Roman Catholic Church would succeed on earth as well as in heaven and that the blood of the martyrs played an important role in bringing about that success, just as the New Testament claimed and just as she saw around her. Therefore, at times her letters departed from the flat representation of good and evil with respect to English Catholics and heretics in the Spanish ecclesiastical histories because, for her, writing about the church and the martyrs without glossing over the unseemly parts would still encourage the faithful and would help them know how best to take part in helping the worthy cause.

Even though an explicit, direct connection with the histories by Ribadeneyra and Yepes has not yet surfaced, the evidence from her life and letters shows that it is likely that she was familiar with them, if she had not read them, and that she had ready access to their contents through libraries in Spain and in England. Moreover, Carvajal's writings and life offer windows into the Anglo-Spanish networks of cooperation that enabled the production of the histories by Ribadeneyra and Yepes and the work of the English mission. Therefore, it is valuable to read Carvajal's writings side by side with these important texts in order to acquire a richer understanding of this complex period of fraternity and antagonism between England and Spain, the fractures within Catholicism, and the constraints and opportunities of Spanish literature in shaping the imagination of its readers and writers.

Chapter Four

Monsters and Saints in Poetry and the Stage: Lope and Calderón

As seen, Ribadeneyra's *Historia* supported by Yepes spread a particular interpretation of the English Reformation that Spaniards at large adopted: Elizabeth Tudor and her parents persecuted Catholics because personal sins had irreversibly turned the monarchs into tyrannical monsters. As such, they belonged to the evil forces of darkness that the light, the Catholics, had to resist. These portrayals and ideas and the specific language in the Spanish ecclesiastical histories were echoed, refashioned, and sometimes challenged by authors who were familiar with the original texts and appropriated them for their own ideological and aesthetic goals. One such author is Luisa de Carvajal, as the previous chapter proposed: a woman in ideological agreement with Ribadeneyra's vision and mission yet whose letters present a more complex view of the persecution of Catholics in England and of James Stuart and a less unified Catholic front.

This chapter argues that two other authors who engaged Ribadeneyra's vision in different genres to speak to Spanish and European Catholic interests were Lope de Vega and Calderón de la Barca. Calderón's tragedy *La cisma de Ingalaterra* is clearly a dramatic adaptation of Ribadeneyra's *Historia*, and Lope's comedy *El amor desatinado* has too many parallels with Ribadeneyra's account to be coincidental. Moreover, Lope's antagonistic characterization of Elizabeth in his two epic poems *La Dragontea* and *La corona trágica* seems heavily influenced by Ribadeneyra, and while the dramatist maintains the grotesque representation of Elizabeth Tudor in his poems, both his and Calderón's plays attenuate the monstrous portrayal of Henry VIII and Anne Boleyn that distinguishes Ribadeneyra's text. These echoes and adaptations reveal, first, the pervasive shaping force upon the Spanish imagination of Ribadeneyra's *Historia* and, second, some of Spain's responses to England and Europe in the face of Spanish Black Legend criticism, military and economic losses, and the challenging of Roman Catholicism by its opponents.

Representing England in early modern Spain had cultural and political implications: negative portrayals fed stereotypes, suspicion, and animosity, adding distance between Spaniards and the English, while positive or even neutral portrayals brought the two nearer and challenged essentialist depictions. Positive and negative images of England were also sure to influence Spanish popular opinion concerning war and peace negotiations between the kingdoms, such as the Anglo-Spanish War, the Treaty of London, and the Spanish Match. Most importantly, however, importing English events and players into Spain served to transport Spanish concerns to a different, defamiliarized setting to warn readers about pressing current issues in Spain, such as becoming religiously lax, settling for an imprudent king, or deviating from the traditional models prescribed for female conduct. For these English events and characters to connect with Spanish readers, the representations would have to be simultaneously foreign and other, estranging England, and yet familiar and same, seeing England as fraternal, as a mirror of Spain. As will be shown, transformations to Ribadeneyra's vision can be partly attributed to aesthetic choices and generic necessities, but they also reveal ideologies, prejudices, and, possibly, changing perspectives over time. Thus, Calderón's tragedy, for example, may show a waning animosity towards the English queen, now more distant, different from the lingering bitterness expressed in the older Lope, probably intensified from his involvement as a soldier in the Anglo-Spanish War. Nonetheless, what is clear in these depictions of England by both Lope and Calderón is that they are relevant to Spaniards primarily because of what they say about Spain and how they respond to Spanish criticism outside Spain. Many of Lope's representations also serve a larger purpose of defending Roman Catholicism as the true church in a European Reformation context, predominantly through biblical and mythological symbolism and intertextuality appealing to the imagination instead of employing prosaic argumentation.

Because Anglo-Spanish relations and perceptions changed quickly between 1580 and 1630, this chapter will examine these works following their chronological order of appearance and will conclude with a juxtaposition of Lope's early comedy *El amor desatinado* (1597) and Calderón's tragedy *La cisma de Ingalaterra* (1626) to examine their thematic parallels and contrasts. Since Lope's earliest text in this group is *La Dragontea*, and since it also reveals most explicitly his perspective on England and its queen during the Anglo-Spanish War, it is most suitable to begin by analyzing this text.

La Dragontea (1598)

La Dragontea is an epic poem of ten cantos in imitation of the *Aeneid* that diffuses the power of "the Dragon" Sir Francis Drake by recounting the failures of his final expeditions to the Canary Islands, Puerto Rico, Panama, Nombre de Dios, and Portobelo and ending the account with the Englishman's demise in hell. With a mixture of historical facts and poetic license, Lope guides the Spanish imagination to see England and Spain through a providential lens where English victories are limited and costly and Spain's losses are only a test to expose their perseverance, valor, and faith.

La Dragontea was conceived after the economic stability that the successful playwright Lope began to enjoy in the 1590s was disrupted in 1597 when the theaters of Madrid were closed to mourn the death of Philip II's daughter, Doña Catalina (Sánchez Jiménez, "Introducción" 13–14). The two-year extension of the closure forced the writer to find other sources of income and experiment with other genres, which resulted in the production of a verse trilogy patterned after Virgil's that brought him renown as an eminent Spanish poet: *La Arcadia* (1598), *La Dragontea* (1598), and *El Isidro* (1599). While *La Arcadia* and *El Isidro* achieved great literary success, *La Dragontea* was criticized by Góngora and others and for years was considered a lesser work that did not receive much scholarly attention (Sánchez Jiménez, "Introducción" 14, 16–17; García Rodrigo 329). Lope seems to have written *La Dragontea* by commission from someone in the Duke of Lerma's circle to prove himself with historical materials and secure a position in the new government of Philip III, perhaps as the royal chronicler (Sánchez Jiménez, "Introducción" 14, 46–9, 62–78, "Lope y la Armada" 276; Wright, *Pilgrimage* 27–32).

Lope dedicated this work to the prince right before his investiture as Philip III, telling the royal that he wrote, first, to remember an important victory and to show the king the great courage of Spaniards and the debt the monarch owes to those who offered him their lives and, second, to disenchant the "vulgo" concerning the success of Drake and to show the end that awaits the enemies of the church[1] (Lope de Vega, *Dragontea* 120). These goals of exalting Spaniards, especially in light of Black Legend criticism, and exposing the fate of those who oppose the true, Roman Catholic Church – particularly with reference to the English – coincide with Ribadeneyra's goals in writing the *Historia*. Lope's effort to deflate Drake's powerful image is a poetic application of Ribadeneyra's arguments in the *Tratado de la tribulación* that placed the success of England within the inscrutable will of God to purify his church. Lope's correspondences with Ribadeneyra are not surprising given that, in addition to having similar theological commitments, the poet had studied with and admired the Jesuits throughout his life and seems to have read all of Ribadeneyra's works (García Morales xxii, xl).[2] Like Ribadeneyra, Lope was a son of the Catholic Church and a son of Spain, and in *La Dragontea*, as in other texts, he would champion through the imagination both his religion and his nation against English heretics and criticism, even through not wholly negative depictions of his opponents.

In fact, Lope had been a soldier at the height of enmity with England and implies in various texts, including *La Dragontea* and *La corona trágica*, that he participated in an expedition to the Azores in 1582 and sailed with the Spanish Armada in 1588.[3] As Sánchez Jiménez points out, although these claims have been difficult to corroborate, Lope clearly projected himself in the literary persona of an experienced soldier at sea and an eyewitness in the expeditions to England ("Lope y la Armada" 274–8). Sánchez Jiménez concludes that the effect of this first-hand experience upon epic poems especially about England that claimed to be historically accurate, such as *La Dragontea*, was to imbue the texts with an aura of authority and present the author as a knowledgeable and competent historian and poet who had faithfully served the king in the past and was the perfect candidate for a royal chronicler position ("Lope y la Armada" 276). This goal to seek royal rewards, as will be seen, would drive certain stylistic choices in the poem.[4]

This rhetorical strategy of appealing to eyewitnesses for historical proof of a narrative is the same strategy employed by Ribadeneyra and Foxe in their ecclesiastical histories. Though it was common for ancient and medieval epic poems to blend facts and fiction and be presented as true, what seems unusual in Lope's poems is an effort to employ verifiable historical sources.[5] From this perspective, both Lope's epic poems about England and the Spanish ecclesiastical histories overlap in adjusting to the demands of early modern historiography of providing documents and witnesses to validate the historicity of their information, even if others disputed the accuracy or grand narrative of the accounts.[6] Both authors also weave historical facts with elevated diction and literary elements appealing to the imagination, such as monsters and biblical or mythological figures, and both emphasize continuity between the experiences of the people of God in the Bible and those of Catholics, especially Spaniards.

The difference between the poems and the ecclesiastical histories is a difference in the degree of poetic license each takes. The poems, true to their genre, take more license than the histories, for example when in *La Dragontea* the Captain ends in hell, a theological location but one that is not historically verifiable. Since epic poems do not simply record what happened but what could have happened with verisimilitude, they do not use direct and realistic language like history, but evocative, imaginative discourse that includes legends and myths (Lope de Vega, *corona* 52). Although Ribadeneyra's history includes monstrous descriptions, for example of Anne Boleyn and Henry Tudor, these are subtle and realistic and presented as plausible and, coming from a trustworthy witness, true. Nonetheless, the effect of mixing poetry with history in both literary genres is to create a powerful account aimed at persuading readers through logos, ethos, and pathos and is, therefore, not only convincing on the logical plane through verifiable historical sources, but also on the emotional and imaginative levels through authoritative biblical intertextuality and positive and negative popular mythical associations. Thus, in addition to writing *La Dragontea* to promote himself as a careful historian, Lope crafts a powerful text to vindicate Spain and Roman Catholicism through gripping characters and stories, which he did across various texts throughout his life, including *La corona trágica*, published late in his career.

La Dragontea begins lauding the unsung Spanish hero Diego Suárez de Amaya who had stopped the advance of Sir Francis Drake: "I sing the arms and the famous man / who barred the pass of the daring Englishman, / that new prodigious argonaut, / who frightened the stars of the West"[7] (Lope de Vega, *Dragontea* 143). With the title, a clear *imitatio* of the opening lines of the *Aeneid*, and the allusion of the term "argonaut," Lope primes the audience for a nationalist epic of Spanish heroes cast in mythological references to Aeneas and Jason, who would overcome in perilous voyages at sea metaphorical sirens, harpies, seductive witches, and even a dragon – recurrent imagery throughout the poem. In the next few stanzas, the poet appeals to the Spanish muses for aid and identifies don Diego as a "new George" who rescues the Indies from the fury of the "oriental Dragon, / Hydra of [Hercules] and Python of [Apollo]," also called "that filthy Dragon of Scripture" (Lope de Vega, *Dragontea* 144–5). By introducing references to St. George and the apocalyptic "Dragon of Scripture" Lope makes his epic not merely national, but also religious, especially when in the following stanzas Religion personified asks for God's intervention as a matter of justice and vindication of his people and his name. Towards the end of canto 1 the poem states that Religion "was heard" and Covetousness approaches Drake to entice him into a deadly, greedy expedition, ending in canto 10 with Religion praising God with biblical apocalyptic language for making war with "the Great Dragon and the seated woman who conceals the infamous abomination in the golden cup of venom"

(Lope de Vega, *Dragontea* 1: XXVIII; 10: XLIX). Thus, the narrative of the poem is framed by a theological explanation of why Drake rose and fell, namely, God's providence, and the fall metaphorically coincides with the victory of God over the Beast and the Whore of Babylon in the Apocalypse. The poem also reinterprets Drake's relative success as God's will to destroy him through greed, and Religion speaks for Spaniards and Catholics at large saying that because of God's actions, she no longer fears fierce barbarians, the dragon, England, or anyone else[8] (Lope de Vega, *Dragontea* 10: L).

Wright's analysis of the literature that contributed to the creation of the myth of Drake as hero surveys Spanish sources that heightened his cleverness, royal support, and courtly manners, glossing over violent or questionable actions. She includes *La Dragontea* among these texts, exposing narratological choices that indicate that Lope omitted negative details from the historical accounts and offering the weak contrast of Diego Suárez de Amaya and the title of the epic as indications of the heroization of Drake ("From Draque" 34–6). To be sure, this analysis shows that Lope refrained from presenting Drake as a wholly negatively character, but Lope's choices find a cohesive explanation within the strong religious framework of the poem that seizes the epic genre and transforms it for Christian purposes. Within this frame, the paradox of the weak being strong is in operation, so that Diego Suárez de Amaya is the human Aeneas who providentially defeats the dragon, but the real defeat comes from the Virgin and God himself, and, therefore, the human agent receives honor for his faith and courage but is equated to David, the inexperienced youth who defeated the giant Goliath. The dragon, like Goliath and the Devil himself, must be acknowledged to be clever, powerful, and dangerous, and his defeat brings greater glory to God. Thus, situating *La Dragontea* in a biblical and religious context is essential to understanding Lope's creative choices as an experiment in fusing the classical epic with Christian theology and ideals to create a Christian epic, as Edmund Spenser would do in the *Faerie Queene*.

The description and language of Religion in *La Dragontea* clearly point to Spanish Counter-Reformation arguments in defense of Catholicism, especially those of Ribadeneyra against England: It applies biblical, apocalyptic language to the church's enemies; it brings biblical eschatology into the present; and it offers continuity between the New Testament Church and early modern Catholics. *La Dragontea* goes further in linking its battles against Drake to holy wars such as those of Hezekiah against Sennacherib, David against Goliath, and the Maccabees against Rome, as well as victorious Spanish crusades against Islam on the peninsula, such as those of the Cid Ruy Díaz (8: II–X, XXII). Thus, warring against Drake and his vituperation is not simply to protect Spain's economy but also to stop God's enemies and defend God's name.[9]

Religion, described as a beautiful woman shining as the sun, approaches God's throne alongside three other beautiful allegorical women, who are all dressed in mourning and enter weeping: Spain, Italy, and the Americas – the last bastions of Catholicism for Lope (Lope de Vega, *Dragontea* VII–X, n. 138). Religion's request echoes Ribadeneyra's notion in the *Tratado* that God had allowed the success of the English heretics as chastisement on his church for her sins:

> Sometimes God raises the evil and gives them the sceptre and lordship for the punishment of the people ... At other times he allows barbarians and cruel and impious men to tyrannize and afflict people, and with their cruelties to purge the filth of their great wickedness. Because of this through Isaiah he calls the king of the Assyrians rod of his fury and through Ezekiel he calls Nebuchadnezzar his servant, because he employed them to chastise the ten tribes of Israel and the tribe of Judah.[10] (*Rivadeneira* 195)

Ribadeneyra explains here the providential use of tyrants or heathen kings, like the Assyrian king or Nebuchadnezzar and, by extension, Henry and Elizabeth Tudor, by calling them "rods" of chastisement. Using this language, Religion begs God to relent from punishing his people: "If you send chastisements to earth / with the immense power of your rod, / how long will I say with Jeremiah: / "Oh spear of the Lord rest and cease!", / and [how long until] these afflicted daughters of mine / see your divine face serene?"[11] (Lope de Vega, *Dragontea* 153–4). The second half of Religion's words are a citation of the prophet Jeremiah, not explicitly referenced in the *Tratado*: "O sword of our Lord, how long wilt thou not be quiet? Get into thy scabbard, be cooled, and be still"[12] (Jer. 47:6). Though in Jeremiah's text the sword or rod is applied to enemies, Religion's statement that the chastisements are brought with the power of God's "rod" (*vara*) most readily recalls the rod of correction in the book of Proverbs and in the psalms, where God's rod disciplines his children for their good,[13] several of which are cited and explained in the *Tratado*, as hinted in the citation above.[14] Thus, the poem implies that Religion pleads on behalf of Christians who are suffering in Spain, Italy, and the Americas ("these afflicted daughters of mine"), later noting that suffering is unavoidable to show the true church when it says: "this cost their lives, immense Father, / but it was necessary, because with this blood / is confirmed the divine Mother" (1: XIX).[15] In other words, because martyrs prove the true church ("the divine Mother"), the Catholic Church is legitimate. Moreover, Religion's asking "how long?," her desire that the afflicted women "see [God's] divine face serene," and her request that God revert the situation, appealing to a list of biblical martyrs,[16] echoes the pleas in the psalms, such as this excerpt from Psalm 79 (80:4–7 in the *King James*) that parallels how Spaniards felt towards England after 1588: "O Lord the God of hosts, how long wilt thou be angrie upon the prayer of thy servant? Thou wilt feed us with the bread of teares: and give us drinke with teares in measure. Thou hast made us to be a contradiction to our neighbors: and our enimies have scorned us. O God of hosts convert us: and shew thy face, and we shal be saved" (5–8). The appellation "God of hosts," used to denote God's military power, indicates that the Israelites did not believe that they were oppressed by their enemies because their God was weak, but rather because God had allowed it, and therefore they want God's favor restored ("shew thy face"). They continued to weep and plead with him to save them, even though they had sent up numerous prayers that remained unanswered, and their foes laughed at them because their God had not yet delivered them.

Such was some Spaniards' perception, which has been described as a period of "disenchantment" (*desengaño*) towards the end of the sixteenth century with some of the outcomes of Philip II's reign and doubts about Spain's strength to defeat English heretics (Domínguez, *Radicals* 66–70). Addressing some of these concerns in the *Tratado de la tribulación* and the second part of the *Historia*, Ribadeneyra identifies with similar feelings upon the defeat of Spain's Armada, "destroyed and lost in such a strange manner" (Rivadeneira 199). Not stated here were all of England's taunts for having defeated the "Invincible" Armada[17] that Spain had to endure, replicating the mockery of the psalmist's enemies. For the Jesuit, the only reasonable explanation was that "the Most High" – a title akin to "Lord of Hosts" in that no one could be more powerful or act above him – allowed the failure as discipline ("scourging" and "chastisement") (Rivadeneira 199).

This reasoning and feeling are echoed in *La Dragontea* when Religion explicitly acknowledges that persecution "confirms the divine Mother" or proves that the Catholic Church is the true church (1: XIX) but entreats God to look at England and its queen, Elizabeth:

> But turn to look at England,
> who so quickly loved you …
> you will see how she banishes me,
> because on account of your faith and divine name
> she has so many martyrs, Jesuits,
> Carthusians, priests, and Levites …

look at the queen of the Dragon, Medea,
who roams the coasts of America.[18]
(Lope de Vega, *Dragontea* 157–8)

England, once faithful, has exiled Religion and is now full of martyrs. The idea of "looking" (*mirar*) is a recurring trope in the poem: in the first canto, Religion uses the imperative six times directed at God to look at England. In similar biblical contexts in the psalms and the prophets the plea to "look" comes from the oppressed, who pray that God see the wrongdoings of their enemies in order to act, to impart justice, and to take vengeance.[19] These biblical intertextual connections imply that Elizabeth ("the queen of the Dragon, Medea") is a tyrant oppressing God's people, the Catholics, and that God should hear his people's prayers and rescue and avenge them from her. As noted, God answers Religion's request, and the repeated trope of "looking" in canto 10 ends by pointing the reader to look at Drake and his state of misery as a kind of negative exemplum: the poetic voice calls him "infelicitous" and notes "now that defeated by the eagle / you no longer arrogantly surround yourself with seashells, / the most saintly Christian Religion / places her sole on your Briton neck"[20] (Lope de Vega, *Dragontea* 10: XIII–XVII). Religion stepping on Drake's neck and, by extension, on England ("Briton neck") conflates two religious allusions introduced earlier in the poem: the most obvious is the promise to the woman in Genesis, equated with the Virgin, that her seed would wound the serpent's head,[21] but the words also evoke the image of St. George towering over the dragon. These references have the dual function of, first, renewing biblical and religious ideas by showing their application to contemporary circumstances and, second, showing Drake's demise as a grand example of the tragic end of all who oppose God's people, deflating his aura of power, and mitigating Spanish fears.

In addition to upholding Roman Catholicism, *La Dragontea* echoes Spanish nationalistic works concerned with vindicating Spain, especially against Black Legend indictments that, as seen in chapter 2, encouraged imagining Spaniards as greedy, fanatical, and barbaric. Lope, a pioneer in awareness of and response to these anti-Spanish stereotypes,[22] featured in *Jerusalén conquistada* and other texts and plays Spanish characters in Europe responding to the charge that Spaniards were arrogant and belligerent by explaining that they were merely exceedingly courageous (Sánchez Jiménez, "Quevedo y Lope" 44–9). In *La Dragontea*, Spaniards are noble and virtuous – likened to David, Judas Maccabeus, and the brave Argonauts (8: V–VIII) – with don Diego, who is the Spanish St. George, Jason, and Aeneas, as the example *par excellence*, although as noted, he was lauded for his piety and courage but was given the victory by God's and the Virgin's intervention. Contrasting these, Lope throws back on England Spanish Black Legend slurs by linking Drake, his men, and his queen with arrogance, greed, barbarism, and cruelty.

The Englishmen are arrogant, "armed with hubris more than steel" (5: I), and parade like proud peacocks and Titans (2: XXIII; 3: I). Drake, of course, is the foremost arrogant figure throughout the poem, and his humiliation is described in a lavish metaphor of the fall of the great Behemoth in Job, a proud, powerful creature who after God's judgment humbly eats grass like an ox (10: LI–LVI; Job 10:15–24). That Drake and the English are avaricious and covetous is central in the poem. This is evident from the linking of the English with images of greedy figures, such as the dragon itself, Midas, and harpies (10: XI; 5: LXXVII); to the allegorical woman Covetousness, a basilisk who entices Drake "to arms, to arms, to gold, to gold";[23] to explicit references in the narrative, such as the statement that Drake's men "satisfy their covetousness in the saints" they rob (5: XIX). Moreover, epithets like "the barbarian Protestant" for Hawkins (3: XVIII), "the indomitable British beast" for Drake (8: XXII), and "the monsters of Luther and Calvin" for the Englishmen (4: XI), coupled with plays on words referring to how the "barbarians" desecrate the statue of St. Barbara for its gold (5: XXXIX), point to English savagery, cruelty, and iconoclasm. The vivid description of the death of Drake's Protestant preacher friend falsely prophesying Drake's victory offers a conglomeration of monstrous and evil traits in someone whom the English consider a good man: "with a horrid and fierce face / the dogmatizer lost his life; / he departed to see his inventor, Luther / lying more than ever in his departure. / And being a vile perjurer and sorcerer … / anathema, lascivious and rebellious, / they praised his passage as glorious"[24] (7: LXV). The implication here is that because the English are "monsters of Luther," barbarians, and hell-bound heretics, they fail to see the evil before them ("horrid and fierce face," "lascivious and rebellious") and laud the death of a man going to hell ("to see his inventor, Luther") as "glorious." In fact, the Black Panamanians in Santiago del Principe whom Covetousness in canto 1 calls "barbarians in works and reasoning" (XLIX) ironically reject Drake's alliance, calling it deceitful and, instead, swear fidelity to the "Catholic Lord" Philip II (6: XXXIX–XLII). In other words, even people categorized as barbarians are less barbaric and fraudulent than the English.

Moreover, the English queen, Elizabeth Tudor, is also cruel and belligerent. As mentioned, the final canto of the epic poem praises God for defeating the dragon, who is seated by the apocalyptic Whore of Babylon, presumably an indirect reference to Elizabeth Tudor because of her ruthless execution of martyrs addressed in Religion's opening plea. Additionally, alluding to the mythological story of Jason and the Argonauts referenced in the first canto, Elizabeth is associated with Medea, the sorceress who enchanted the dragon and cut up her own brother to escape with her lover Jason from her father, the King of Colchis. According to Greek myths, Medea's ties with magic are strong: she is the granddaughter of the sun god Helios; the niece of Circe, the enchantress; and the priestess of Hecate, goddess of magic (Martínez Berbel 480). Martínez Berbel points out that in early modern Spain the works of Jorge de Bustamante and Juan Pérez de Moya moralized the myth and focused on its negative aspects so that, in general, the sixteenth-century Medea is a deceitful and dangerous sorceress, rather than a woman who is willing to do anything out of love for Jason (481–2). One exception to this representation appears in Lope de Vega's play *El vellocino de oro*, where the playwright humanizes her by focusing on her dilemma between love and duty and making her magical powers instrumental and not just cruel (Martínez Berbel 484–6). Nonetheless, Lope's Medea in *El vellocino de oro* may be more complex than her early modern Spanish counterparts because she is a central character in the play. In fact, Medea appears in at least forty other works by the same author, often aligned with the evil sorceress of Bustamante and Pérez de Moya (Martínez Berbel 479–80), which also seems to be the case in *La Dragontea* because of the epitaph "Medea, the cruel" that appears with the dragon (1: XXIX) and because of the link to the Whore of Babylon and the persecuting tyrant.

Religion links Elizabeth to the witch twice, and Covetousness calls Drake "dragon of Pallas, illustrious Queen,"[25] likening Elizabeth to the beautiful and astute maiden queen of war, Minerva or Athena (Lope de Vega, *Dragontea* 158, 162, 194, 196). Although within the larger poem[26] Covetousness offers the reference as a compliment fitting for the "Virgin Queen," probably because of her beauty, erudition, and ingeniousness to win over the Armada, when juxtaposed with Medea and cruelty, associating the queen with war ironically turns into a negative epitaph: she is a bloody queen, cruel to the point of having no scruples or familial affection, especially when the context of the poem pleads to God to look at England's persecutions and avenge them. Although somewhat less flat, this portrayal of Elizabeth is not unlike Ribadeneyra's picture of her after the theologian recounts her execution of her cousin Mary Stuart and invokes the heavens to wonder upon finding "such an horrific example of such rare crudeness" so great that "in Tartary and Scythia and in whatever nation, no matter how coarse, fierce, and inhuman it may be, the very barbarians, when they hear this, will not believe it"[27] (Ribadeneyra 1185, 1186). In fact, as will be discussed in detail below, Lope echoes this precise passage of Ribadeneyra's text *in La corona trágica*. In other words, Lope's Elizabeth is sourced in Ribadeneyra's monstrous portrayal, although her associations with Medea and Athena add that she is bewitching and ingenious, a fitting counterpart for the devilish clever Drake.

In sum, the analysis of English characters and events in *La Dragontea* reveals Lope's efforts to defend Roman Catholicism by assigning English figures, such as Elizabeth Tudor and Francis Drake, the metaphorical counterparts of the Beast and the Whore of Babylon of apocalyptic literature, the enemies of the church. Although these enemies are at war with the church and persecute Christians, through classical associations consistent with the decorum in the epic genre, they are portrayed as clever or attractively seductive. Nevertheless, rather than mitigating the evil deeds of these characters, these complex traits make them more deceitful and dangerous and remain consistent with biblical representations of the Devil (the astute angel of light) or evil queens (Jezebel and Athaliah). Conversely, *La Dragontea* links don Diego and his men to religious heroes such as St. George and the young David to account for their courage, faith, and victory in miraculous battles against powerful evil figures, and the framework for the poem is a plea for God to judge England's actions against the church, a plea that God answers in the demise of Drake. Additionally, *La Dragontea*'s obvious allusions to the classical works of the *Aeneid* and the mythology of Jason and the Argonauts create a national epic to honor Spain and its heroes that also applies Spanish Black Legend stereotypes of greed, arrogance, and barbarism to Drake, his men, and their queen. This analysis suggests that Lope's perceptions of England largely coincide with Ribadeneyra's – that the English queen is tyrannical, monstrous, and cruel; that God has allowed heresy to purge his church; and that the English are monstrous because of their opposition to Roman Catholicism. This kind of polarized representation of good and evil likely is driven by the epic poem genre but also coincides with Ribadeneyra's essentialism of Catholics vs. Protestants. Interestingly, Lope wrote *La Dragontea* simultaneously with a comedy titled *El amor desatinado* that dealt precisely with the story of Elizabeth's parents as narrated by Ribadeneyra but with a different representation of them that provides a fuller picture of Lope's engagement with and deployment of Ribadeneyra's view to address popular Spanish interests and concerns.[28]

El amor desatinado (1597)

El amor desatinado is an early comedy by Lope de Vega that has not received much scholarly attention. The only critical edition of the text was published in 1968 by Justo García Morales, and more recently, Joan Oleza has discussed the work in the context of Lope's early plays and their generic characteristics with respect to *Arte nuevo*.[29] What makes the comedy particularly relevant to this chapter is that it is almost undoubtedly drawn from Ribadeneyra's *Historia*, and as such it is the earliest play to engage with Ribadeneyra's view and is useful for comparison with Calderón's *La cisma de Ingalaterra*, a later play also sourced in Ribadeneyra's text. Furthermore, the work shows how the English Reformation was perceived and deployed by Spaniards. Justo García Morales convincingly argues that the title of *El amor desatinado* suggests an important line in Ribadeneyra's text describing Henry VIII's passion for Anne Boleyn – "In this ended the *love* [*amor*] so vehement and *reckless* [*desatinado*] that the King had for Anne Boleyn"[30] – and thereby suggests that the source of the comedy is the *Historia*, a common practice of Lope in naming his plays (xx–xxi; emphasis original). Beyond the title, strong textual parallels in the plot, characterization, and dialogue support the connection.

The three-act comedy is set in London in the court of "Roberto, King of England," a monarch who develops a "reckless love" (*amor desatinado*) for Rosa, a noble lady, even though he is married to Isabel, the virtuous queen and daughter of the King of France, Enrique. Roberto is said to be "bewitched" by Rosa into a violent, blind love that is blamed for the subsequent terrible decisions the king makes, such as repudiating the queen and later ordering her execution based on false charges of adultery from Rosa. Eventually, the king returns to his senses, sees Rosa as the deceiver that she is, and repents of his affair. Isabel, still in love with him, intercedes on his behalf before her father, who is ready to kill Roberto to avenge her, and the spouses are reconciled. Instead of being executed, Rosa is allowed to marry her lover, Teodoro, and they are banished from England together. Though the ending and names are changed, *El amor desatinado* echoes the characterization and many details of Ribadeneyra's narrative of Henry VIII's divorce from Catherine of Aragon in favor of Anne Boleyn to the extent that the audience would have recognized a parody of Henry VIII and his love triangle (Oleza, "Las posibilidades extremas" 9). Oleza suggests that Lope's Anglophobic perspective was probably behind such a burlesque characterization of Roberto, which may have been how Spaniards in general saw Henry VIII ("El amor desatinado" 8–9). Moreover, that the play is set in England and was written around the same time as *La Dragontea* indicates that thematic and textual parallels are more than coincidental, especially given Lope's Jesuit ties and the popularity of Ribadeneyra's *Historia*.

As discussed in chapter 2, Ribadeneyra describes Anne Boleyn as a beautiful, scheming, and licentious woman. Her counterpart in Lope's play, Rosa, catches the king's attention because of her great beauty, and the king enlists Teodoro, his servant (*camarero*) and Rosa's beau, to convince Rosa to be his concubine. In the first four scenes of the play, she does all she can to cleverly resist the king's advances to sleep with her, outwardly showing concern for her honor. By the end of the first act, however, she has already plotted with Teodoro to be the king's mistress and simultaneously have a love affair with Teodoro. Teodoro tells the king that Rosa only rejects the monarch to test Roberto's love (Lope de Vega, *amor* 13), which echoes Ribadeneyra's explanation that Anne's rejection of the king's offer to make her his mistress is not because she is chaste, since she is not, but because she is ambitious to be queen, and "with her exterior lukewarmness he burned more in his love"[31] (928–9).

In the second act of *El amor desatinado*, the queen describes Rosa like Ribadeneyra depicts Anne – seductive, intelligent, and promiscuous: "the woman certainly is beautiful, / and though of humble lineage / has rich understanding / and is a notable sorceress /... / but she lacks in that / she does not keep for the King / the decorum she owes him / and with other men interacts"[32] (Lope de Vega, *amor* 35–6). In the denouement of the play, the king becomes irate when realizing Rosa's licentiousness, and she and her lover are condemned for it, much like Ribadeneyra says Anne was condemned for adultery (Lope de Vega, *amor* 78; Ribadeneyra, *Historia* 1002–3). One major difference between Rosa and Anne is that the former is "of humble origin" and only ever occupies the place of a mistress, although Roberto metaphorically puts Rosa in the role of his wife and Queen of England with conventional early modern poetic discourse when he says "Rosa is my wife, Rosa is my owner [*señora*], / she is my Empress / little she is of England / absolute owner [*señora*] of the earth she is; / Rosa is for whom I live: / I am not king of Rosa, I am her captive!"[33] (Lope de Vega, *amor* 62). While the king here eloquently proclaims himself to be inescapably captive to Rosa out of love, so much so that she rules not only over a king, but also over England and the entire world, the dramatic irony that Roberto is cuckolded by Rosa and her lover makes his exaggerated declaration of love ridiculous and likely to elicit great laughs from the audience. Moreover, it shows that the king is enslaved to his passions, evidencing the recurring trope of an imprudent and bad king to be despised.

This aspect of the characterization of Anne and Henry as ridiculous in the play is a departure from Ribadeneyra's narrative, prompted by the comedic genre.

Lope's characterization of Isabel bears a close resemblance to Ribadeneyra's Catherine of Aragon, who because of her patience and constancy in the face of Henry's wrongdoings turns into an "example of saintliness" and "a mirror of Christian princesses and queens" (Ribadeneyra 899–900). Isabel is characterized as equally virtuous and an example for women: "she is a saintly woman / a martyr of the soul, and even, I believe, / of the body or of the desire / with which already her death she adores"[34] (Lope de Vega, *amor* 40, 71, 77). Isabel is described as a martyr in three ways: in her soul because Henry causes her to grieve, in her body because she will die from her suffering, and in her heart because she desires to die. Her constant, unfailing love for her husband is verbalized when she tells her father, the King of France, not to punish the repentant Roberto: "Do not deal with him with rigor / that, though it's true I've lost, / from suffering, my senses, / I have not yet lost my love! / Let me be repaid what I have lost, / if he has awakened from sleep! / You gave him to me as owner [*dueño*], / do not chastise me!"[35] (Lope de Vega, *amor* 83). Because she had never stopped loving him, Isabel believes that to punish Roberto is to punish her and to lose him again once she has recovered him from his "sleep" or "dream" (*sueño*). Furthermore, although she realizes that to love and honor him does not make sense ("I've lost … my senses") – contrasting with Roberto's losing his senses for love of Rosa – she still acknowledges him as her "owner" or "lord" (*dueño*), speaking like Roberto about Rosa.

Ribadeneyra's Catherine, too, respects Henry as her superior and beloved husband ("lord"), even after Henry followed through with the divorce. Before her death she writes to him as "My lord and my King and most beloved husband"[36] and concludes: "I certify and promise you, lord, that there is no mortal thing my eyes desire more than you"[37] (Ribadeneyra 1000). Moreover, just like Ribadeneyra places Anne and Catherine side by side to "compare life with life" and sees the differences as night and day, the subjects of the French king are shocked in the unequal comparison between Rosa and Isabel: that "such a vile and poisonous Rose / with our splendid *fleur de lis* compete"[38] (Ribadeneyra 1001; Lope de Vega, *amor* 45). In fact, the French also align Isabel with Penelope, the faithful wife of Odysseus, and Rosa with Circe, the enchantress who kept the hero away from his wife (Lope de Vega, *amor* 45). Additionally, as they look for Roberto's mistress, they link her to another sorceress, saying, "Where is the Medea who upon the miserable King / sows poisonous serpents in his chest?"[39] (Lope de Vega, *amor* 45).

Although it is common to poetically refer to women lovers as "enchantresses" and "Medeas," that Lope's *La Dragontea* also uses this imagery for Elizabeth Tudor seems significant given the similar topic and publication dates between the poem and the play. Like Elizabeth, Rosa is a deceitful witch associated with serpents and poison, but unlike Lope's poems, the slur is not connected to apocalyptic language and because of the comic nature of the play cannot be taken too seriously.

What seems clear, however, is that Rosa is the type of the bad, licentious woman, a foil to Isabel, who is the good, chaste one, and thus, the comedy reinforces traditional roles and behavior for women as those described in female conduct manuals by Luis Vives and Fray Luis de León. In fact, Rosa is raped and beaten, shockingly bringing tragic components into the comedy,[40] although several cues in the play indicate that this is an ironic, but comic punishment of Rosa's promiscuity and plot with Teodoro. At the height of Rosa's enchantment of the king and her and Teodoro's enjoyment of the king's benefits, the king brings Isabel to attend Rosa as a slave, and the queen humbly fulfills this role. The King of France, her father, enraged at this humiliation and further learning that Roberto plans to kidnap and kill his daughter, sends his noblemen disguised as merchants to kill Rosa. However, as the merchants flirt with Rosa and she welcomes their sexual advances and invites them to come to her house that evening after the king is in bed, they decide to rape and beat her instead. After this violent event, Rosa appears on stage, disheveled and bloody, in a scene that seems to be a precursor of Laurencia's sobering moment in *Fuenteovejuna* and in which she demands justice from the village men after her rape. But, instead of being solemn and tragic, Rosa's spectacle and words and Roberto's response result in a lightening of the situation and comical chaos. Rosa says:

> They say that they have forced me,
> although I have not felt it,
> because these men were sorcerers;
> but they have not robbed me
> for having hurt me
> then, of my true senses:
> that the fierce executioners,
> with the cruel sheaths
> of their cowardly weapons,
> have made my body – do not expect
> to see it alive in your arms as you do – as a lily
> with affronting and harsh martyrdom.[41]
> (Lope de Vega, *amor* 67)

Rosa's claim that they had forced her but "[she] ha[d] not felt it" minimizes the violence, and her phallic sexual innuendos of "cruel sheaths" and "cowardly weapons" that "made [her] body … as a lily" – a symbol of virginity – Oleza reasonably argues would have provoked great laughter ("Las posibilidades extremas" 17). While making light of a rape scene is rightly scandalous to a twenty-first-century audience, this was probably not true for an early modern one, especially if they recognized the play as a parody of Henry VIII and Anne Boleyn, characters who, as seen, were not positively represented in Spain and, therefore, were disliked and easy to disparage. The assumption is that Rosa was licentious, shown in her welcoming of sexual advances by the French as they trick her, and thus received what she deserved,[42] although Roberto, in an ironic twist, surprisingly refuses to acknowledge her defilement, intentionally done to separate him from Rosa, arguing that, like Lucretia, she was forced and could not be blamed (Lope de Vega, *amor* 65). Nonetheless, within the play, the rape ironically punishes Rosa not only for her licentiousness but also for her deception of the king and, most importantly, for the abuse of the innocent Isabel.

Although with fewer monstrous associations than Rosa, Roberto also resembles his counterpart, Ribadeneyra's Henry VIII, in being impulsive, stubborn, irrational, and foolish. Roberto, like Henry, attempts to divorce the queen and brings papal bulls "with false information" to his kingdom (Lope de Vega, *amor* 65, 80–1; García Morales xx). As noted in chapter 2, one of Ribadeneyra's thematic highlights is that Henry is a negative example of a powerful king driven by a blinding lust: "We see a powerful king who wants everything he craves and executes everything he desires; a blind and unbridled penchant" (Ribadeneyra 895). Lope also focuses on Roberto's power over his subjects – especially over Rosa, her father, and her brother, who must yield to his passions – and how his "reckless love" makes him act as a madman and blinds him to Rosa's "thorns" that everyone else can readily see. As such, he would be the exemplum of actions a Spanish king should avoid so as not to be despised, akin to a comic embodiment of Ribadeneyra's exhortation in his preface to Prince Philip in the *Historia*. When Roberto begins to repent of his actions, an incredulous subject asks him: "Well, say Lord, so blind and mad are you / that you did not see the evils of Rosa, / that if by chance you did not see them, / did you not hear them in the voice of the masses / and in the lampoons [*pasquines*] in your own house?" (Lope de Vega, *amor* 77). The king is persistently blind and crazy because he could not or would not see Rosa's bad deeds or listen to what his subjects were saying about them in his own house. Ribadeneyra describes this same "blind passion" of the king in even more emphatic terms, including the detail that Henry knowingly entered into an incestual relationship and would not listen to anyone's warnings, even those of his own council and his future father-in-law: "For it was not enough to deter him from his evil intent and mad determination neither the ugly traits of Anne Boleyn, nor her bad life and fame, nor to be considered his own daughter, nor all the means that his council and even Thomas Boleyn, Anne's putative father, took to detract him from such a strange delirium were part of bringing him to reason"[43] (Ribadeneyra 929). Anne's physical deformities, her promiscuity and bad reputation, the knowledge that she was his daughter, and all the warnings of those close to Henry were unable to dissuade the king from his "evil intent" and "crazy determination." In other words, though Lope's version is less sensational than Ribadeneyra's – perhaps because less is at stake – for both authors the scandalous, reckless love of the king was public and widely discussed in England and in France, but the king would not see or hear warnings. The fact that she is "bewitching" removes some of the agency from Henry and reflects the common notion, described in chapter 2, that all women are deceitful and dangerous and that men, especially kings, need to keep temptations in check.

Also, in both accounts, this reckless love causes personal and national havoc. Personally, the king's mad love turns him into a beast and a tyrant whose cruelty exceeds that of historically famous despots, again hinting at the Spanish Black Legend language applied to the English. As the first two chapters show, Sander, Ribadeneyra, and Yepes explain that Henry became tyrannical and even physically monstrous because of his lust. Lope includes a character who tells Roberto, "for an English Rose, / more dishonest than beautiful / you are transformed into a beast," while another character and the queen call him "tyrant" and "inhuman" and say that "in cruelty to Nero he exceeds" (*amor* 35, 64, 75, 83). Nationally, Roberto's reckless love will result in the destruction of England. He is warned as a deluded novice: "O King! O deceived youth, / fable of all the land, / what a bad end the heavens promise / to your reckless love!" (Lope de Vega, *amor* 39). The warning further connects the play with Ribadeneyra's text in saying that the king's "reckless love" is the "fable of all the land," alluding to the shocking nature of the English schism in all Catholic Europe that Ribadeneyra describes as "marvellous and horrifying things" (905). In fact, both the history and the play emphasize the destruction of England by a woman. Ribadeneyra calls Anne Boleyn, "most wretched [*infelicísima*] and abominable for having been the origin and fountainhead of the Schism and destruction of her homeland" (1004). Similarly,

Lope's characters say that Rosa is like the Cava, who destroyed Spain, and Helen, who was the demise of Troy (*amor* 34, 52, 68).

El amor desatinado, then, has clear connections to Ribadeneyra's *Historia* in theme (e.g., the love triangle of Henry, Catherine, and Anne), language (e.g., "reckless love"), and characterization (e.g., promiscuity of Anne and saintliness of Isabel). Less clear, however, is why Lope did not preserve his characters' historical names and changed some of the more scandalous details. García Morales suggests that Lope masked the play "for political reasons" and "respect to royalty," since England was still affected by the events narrated and was Spain's enemy at the time (xix). While this may be true, Lope's changes are not enough to elude noticeable links to Ribadeneyra's text, though perhaps the point is that he still would be able to deny them. Additionally, it could seem odd that in this play Lope, after how he presented Elizabeth Tudor in *La Dragontea*, would be hesitant to join Catholics all over Europe who were discrediting Elizabeth Tudor's right to the throne by exposing her parents' lust and sin in Henry's invalid divorce of Catherine and adulterous marriage to Anne. Moreover, Lope's portrayal of Roberto is much less scandalous than Ribadeneyra's description of Henry VIII: the Jesuit reproduces the incendiary rumor that Anne was born of Henry's affair with her mother. Lope does not even hint at an incestuous relationship between Roberto and Rosa, and his characters only commit common sexual sins that everyone already knew Henry practiced. Thus, given that Lope was not saying anything new or particularly scandalous about Henry or Anne, his characters should not have required pseudonyms, though perhaps fear of censorship[44] or the need for a royal position made discreetness necessary. Furthermore, if in *La Dragontea* Lope calls Elizabeth "Medea" and asks God to judge her while she is still Queen of England and at enmity with Spain, it seems strange that he would hesitate to present her parents in much milder negative roles that agreed with all historical reports.

In fact, in this play, in addition to avoiding reference to an incestuous affair between Henry and Anne, Lope did not take the opportunity to present the couple as monstrously as Ribadeneyra and Sander had done. While Lope allows his characters to say that Roberto had been turned into a "beast" because of Rosa and that he was "inhuman" and a "tyrant," the charges are temporary and trivial, even exaggerated, because they appear in a comedy and because the king will repent. Furthermore, this was common language to speak of a monarch who neglected his duty because he was unable to overcome a personal lust – a theme common in early modern Christian prince treatises and plays[45] – and its exaggeration could recall the Black Legend language reversal seen in Ribadeneyra's and Lope's texts. Ribadeneyra's portrayal of Henry VIII includes the idea of an imprudent king with unrestrained appetites but goes beyond to show in Henry's grotesque body the punishment of God as a serious spectacle for having transgressed human and divine laws and as a warning to readers not to do the same. For Lope, Roberto is ridiculous[46] but not monstrous. He is a kind of exemplum, a model of a bad king, but unlike Ribadeneyra's Henry VIII, his problem is not primarily sin, but yielding to a reckless love that makes him insane and blind, especially for a monarch. Isabel, for her part, is the example *par excellence* of Luis de León's "perfecta casada": the pious and devout wife who loves her husband at all costs and respects him as an authority ("lord") over her. However, she is primarily the example of a faithful lover. However problematic this particular story may seem to a modern audience, the comedy ultimately focuses on individuals in a domestic love triangle and celebrates undying love, rewarding Isabel's constancy and perseverance with her husband's repentance, his recognition of her value, and the renewal of his love for her. In the end, Isabel's love conquers all, and there are even references to point to the theme that married love is better than affairs,[47] despite the ironies of this being written by Lope.

In addition to political reasons, García Morales suggests that Lope's version of Ribadeneyra's account is aesthetic, since Spanish audiences generally preferred comedies to tragedies (xx, xl). This seems to be one important reason for the changes, especially because the comedic structure explains other adaptations to Ribadeneyra's narrative, such as Roberto not divorcing his wife and later reconciling with her and Roberto's characterization being ludicrous rather than monstrous and damning. Even if they have political weight, the name changes could be a clever way to distance Lope's story aesthetically from Ribadeneyra's and underscore that this is a new work: Rosa alluding to the red rose of the House of Lancaster and enabling the construction of witty puns,[48] and Isabel recalling Catherine's well-loved mother, Isabella of Castile, to honor by this allusion the memory of the repudiated wife of Henry VIII.[49] After all, Lope's commitment to create gusto and please crowds would ultimately make his adaptation a more universally appealing play while obliquely referring to a recent, scandalous event that was still of great interest throughout Spain. It would also indirectly disparage Elizabeth through ridiculing her parents and perhaps offer a covert moral and political lesson about the limits of monarchy and prudent ruling for Spanish kings and subjects.[50] Thus, Lope's changes to Ribadeneyra's story – that is, his portrayal of Henry Tudor as farcical and Anne Boleyn as a silly woman, rather than both being monstrous – seem to be driven by the comedic genre and the secular content of the play, especially because his perspective on Elizabeth and her parents in other works such as his poems was more serious, rancorous, and antagonistic.

Rimas humanas (1603)

In addition to how Lope characterized Elizabeth in *La Dragontea* and Henry in *El amor desatinado*, epitaphs on Henry VIII, Elizabeth Tudor, and Mary Stuart appeared in print sometime after 1603 in the second part of the collection of *Rimas humanas* (Lope de Vega, *Rimas* 523). The first part of this collection included two sonnets related to England from a Counter-Reformation perspective that indirectly allude to Henry and Elizabeth Tudor. The first (Sonnet XLVI), "A la jornada de Inglaterra," one of many laudatory poems written on the occasion of the departure of the Armada in 1588, calls the fleet "a jungle of the sea" leaving Spain on account of the faith of "Ulysses" (Philip II) "against the falsehood of a siren" (Elizabeth Tudor).[51] Using similar epic metaphors to those in *La Dragontea*, the English queen in the image of a siren appears again as deceitful, seductive, and deadly. The second sonnet (LXXXV), "Al conde don Tomás Porzey, mártir en Inglaterra,"[52] praises a Catholic Elizabethan martyr, Thomas Purcey, for "[going] against the fierce [*fiera*] Babylon … in defense of Christ and his temple" and ends announcing the destruction of "Julian and Babylon."[53] Whether "Babylon" here stands for Elizabeth herself or for Elizabethan England is unclear,[54] since both associations were used in Counter-Reformation debates, although "Julian," an allusion to the Roman Emperor "Julian the Apostate," who persecuted fourth-century Christians, may more properly correspond with the English tyrant queen who executed Percy. Nevertheless, the imagery of this sonnet clearly aligns with the apocalyptic representations of Elizabeth in *La Dragontea*.

More direct references to Henry and Elizabeth Tudor appear around the time of Elizabeth's death in the second part of *Rimas humanas* in epithets, pithy micro-poems that encapsulated information of a notable person and showed the rhetorical wit of a poet, often imitating classical epithets.[55] Of the English king, Lope writes:

Más que desta losa fría
cubrió, Enrique, tu valor
de una mujer el amor
y de un error la porfía.

¿Cómo cupo en tu grandeza
querer, engañado inglés,
de una mujer a los pies
ser de la Iglesia cabeza?
(*Rimas* 522)

This cold stone covered,
Henry, more than your worth [*valor*]
of a woman, the love
and of an error, the obstinacy [*porfía*].
How was there room in your greatness [*grandeza*]
to want [*querer*], deceived Englishman,
of a woman at the feet
to be of the Church the head?

According to the poet, Henry's life is summarized by his illicit love and his paradoxical attempt to be head of the church by placing himself at the feet of the woman he loved. At first glance, the poet seems to include two laudatory features that would be normal in an epithet of a king with "your worth/valor" (*valor*) and "your greatness" (*grandeza*) placed at the end of their respective lines, but these become ambiguous when connected to the words of the following line. The phrase "How was there room in your greatness / to want ... / ... / to be" either compliments the king, asking how in his moral or majestic grandeur he could want this sinful desire, or, in a hyperbaton, condemns his desire for greatness ("in your wanting greatness ... to be"). Moreover, "your greatness" could refer to the king's delirium of being great and could also be a witty allusion to the king's excessive weight at the time of his death. Likewise, the words "your valor" – which, if followed by a comma or a pause, would be translated as "your valor/ courage," perhaps referencing his courage to write against Luther[56] – are followed with "of a woman, the love," making the sense "your valuing of a woman's love." Moreover, the poem highlights Henry's obstinacy in continuing in his error and his blindness ("deceived"). Thus, the Henry of this seemingly laudatory but ultimately vituperative epitaph is precisely the Henry of *El amor desatinado*: a foolish and deceived king, wholly surrendered to a woman, persisting in his error even when warned – though the poem also shows an ambition to be head of the church and perhaps includes a joke about his weight, neither of which are present in the play.

The epitaph titled "Of Elizabeth of England" praises Henry's daughter's "ingenio" (wit, ingeniousness, cleverness) – a feature of the queen widely recognized – while equating her to wicked queens of the Bible who also were political maneuverers:

> Aquí yace Jezabel,
> aquí la nueva Atalía,
> del oro antártico arpía,
> del mar incendio cruel.
> Aquí el ingenio más dino
> de loor que ha tenido el suelo,
> si para llegar al cielo
> no hubiera errado el camino.
> (Lope de Vega, *Rimas* 523)

> Here lies Jezebel,
> here the new Athaliah,
> of the Antarctic gold a harpy,
> of the sea a cruel arson [*incendio*].
> Here [lies] the ingeniousness most worthy
> of praise that has had the land,
> if to reach heaven
> she would not have erred the way.

Epitaphs often began with "here lies" and focused on puns and allusions with the name of the deceased (Ponce Cárdenas 2, 5–6, 8). Catholics all over Europe referred to Elizabeth as "Jezebel" because of the similarity between the names *Isabel* and *Jezabel* and because the biblical Jezebel, wife of King Ahab, was a ruthless queen who promoted idolatry and persecuted God's prophets in the same way that Elizabeth persecuted Catholics and spread heresies (1 Kings 16–22). Burguillo helpfully traces the uses of "Jezebel" for Elizabeth Tudor in English Catholic polemic literature, which, as seen in chapters 1 and 2, was recurrent ("Lope y la causa" 196–8). However, the slur was also regularly used for Mary Stuart in Elizabeth's court, as is documented in Wentworth's 1576 speech (Hartley, 1.438 cited in Collinson, "Elizabeth I" [*ODNB*]). In fact, in the Commons during the 1572 Parliament, Mary was called "the monstrous and huge dragon, and masse of the earth" and "the most notorious whore in all the world" (Hartley, 1.312, 438 cited in Collinson, "Elizabeth I" [*ODNB*]), and in seventeenth-century England, Oliver Cromwell would be called "the Antichrist, the Babilon, the great dragon."[57] Thus, these terms were very common in the period to vilify opponents on various sides.

Lope adds a common Catholic association of Elizabeth with Athaliah[58] (*Atalía*), the daughter of Jezebel, who murdered her kindred to be the sole claimant to the Israelite throne of Judah (2 Kings 11). Similarly, it was said that Elizabeth had killed Mary Stuart in cold blood because Mary had a legitimate claim to the English throne. Moreover, echoing the imagery of *La Dragontea*, Lope references Elizabeth's greed in allowing her ships to intercept Spanish ships from America and steal their wealth by calling her "harpy" – alluding to the mythological greedy monster that was a bird of prey with the face of a woman – and "cruel arson" of the sea, jarringly depicting her naval rapaciousness as fire scorching water. Even Lope seems to acknowledge that Elizabeth's shrewdness was praiseworthy when he speaks of her "ingenio" being "most worthy / of praise that has had the land," perhaps referring to her cleverness in obtaining what she wanted and her political manoeuvring. The overall picture of the English queen is of a greedy, deceitful, and cruel woman who desired to reach heaven – probably indicating her arrogance and desire for greatness rather than her religious beliefs and creating a formal poetic parallel with the opposition of the words land and heaven – by all the wrong means. Because for Lope Elizabeth clearly had no sincere piety, the phrase "to reach heaven" likely links Elizabeth with the hubris of the builders of the tower of Babel, who said: "Come, let us make us a citie and a towre, the top whereof may reach to heaven" (Gen. 11:4).

Elizabeth Tudor is the foil of Mary Stuart, of whom Lope writes:

Esmalta esta piedra helada
sangre de un alma preciosa,
cuanto bien nacida hermosa
cuanto hermosa desdichada.
Murió santa y inocente
a manos de otra mujer,
que en todo (fuera del ser),
fue de su ser diferente.
(*Rimas* 524)

Enamels this cold stone
the blood of a precious soul,
as much well born as beautiful
as much beautiful as wretched [*desdichada*].
She died a saint and innocent
at the hands of another woman
that in all (outside of her being),
was of her being different.

The poem in a typical *laudatio* including lineage, beauty, and piety portrays Mary Stuart as a beautiful soul who is as unhappy and unfortunate ("wretched") as she is beautiful. She is also an innocent, martyred through a violent death, signaled by the word "saint" and the blood "enameled" on the tombstone, at the hand of Elizabeth ("a woman"), who was in everything her opposite. By way of contrasting parallelism, Elizabeth is worthless, of ignoble birth, repulsive, impious, and blameworthy, much like Lope and Ribadeneyra represent her in other texts. Presumably written to celebrate Elizabeth Tudor's death, these epithets display Lope's wit as a poet as well as the way Ribadeneyra's view and antagonism towards the queen persisted in his imagination and was broadcast for others at a time when Spaniards were turning their focus on James Stuart and negotiating peace with England. Nevertheless, over twenty years after writing this epitaph, Lope would still show a consistent antipathy towards the English queen and sustain this image in the imagination of Spaniards by expanding this opposition between Mary Stuart and Elizabeth Tudor in his religious epic poem *La corona trágica*, a work that, echoing these tropes, recounts the tragic life and end of the saintly Queen of Scots at the hands of her ruthless cousin.

La corona trágica (1627)

Lope's interest in writing about English matters related to Elizabeth Tudor apparently resurfaced when in 1626 a Jesuit gave him a copy of the recently published life of Mary Stuart by the Scottish canon George Conn (Lope de Vega, *corona* 123). This gift was obtained after a visit to Madrid from men close to Maffeo Barberini, who by the next year would be Pope Urban VIII, a party including Francisco Barberini, nephew of Maffeo, and Conn himself (Lope de Vega, *corona* 11–16, 123). Lope explains in his prologue to *La corona trágica* that he had enjoyed Conn's Latin narrative so much that he decided to write his own version in verse, "in parts following it and in parts adorning it with what is permissible according to the precepts of poetry in true history in our times" (Lope de Vega, *corona* 123). He fits the narrative into a religious epic poem of five books in which Mary is the central, exemplary figure and which follows Tasso's theory that an epic poem was to imitate "a notable action, great, and perfect; to be narrated in grandiloquent verses, to move whoever reads it or listens to it being read, to produce wonder and to be a model of exemplary conduct" (Lope de Vega, *corona* 55). Seeking some benefit, Lope dedicates the work to Urban VIII, including the poet's own translation of the once young Maffeo Barberini's epitaph of Mary Stuart as well as flattering mentions of the Pope throughout *La corona trágica*. In return, the Pope named Lope "Knight of the Order of St. John of Malta," which allowed the playwright to use the title "*frey*" (Lope de Vega, *corona* 16–17).

Although Lope claims that his primary source is Conn's text, scholars have found in *La corona trágica* similarities to other contemporary European sources on Mary Stuart's life and death, including plays (Lope de Vega, *corona* 39–47). These numerous accounts, published three decades after Mary's execution in 1587, stand as witness of the long-lasting political and theological effects of Henry VIII's decision to divorce Catherine and marry Anne Boleyn and how Catholics continued to deploy this story in different genres and settings. On the Catholic side, Mary Stuart became fixed as the innocent saint cruelly murdered by her tyrant cousin, Elizabeth, who had evidenced lack of all scruples and familial affection in her apostasy and thirst for power. Lope, consistent in his defense of Spain and Catholicism and in opposing the Tudor queen, as seen, eagerly took up this narrative, and among his sources of information seems to have been the ecclesiastical history of Ribadeneyra,[59] with which he was very familiar and which he had already referenced when writing *La Dragontea* and *El amor desatinado*. Surprisingly, critical studies of *La corona trágica* do not mention Ribadeneyra's *Historia* explicitly as a possible source, although Carreño includes it in footnotes and Paulson may allude to it when he says: "What is particularly interesting is the fact that much of the information contained is actually based on history – at least according to historical accounts by Catholic historians" (62). Nevertheless, this redeployment of Ribadeneyra's *Historia* thirty-three years after its completion offered a renewal of Ribadeneyra's vision for younger generations who had not been alive during the Anglo-Spanish War, bolstered the Counter-Reformation martyr myth of Mary Stuart in Spain's imagination, and extended the Jesuit's influence in Spain.

Material from Ribadeneyra

As the title indicates, *La corona trágica* presents Mary Stuart's life and death as tragic, echoing her description in the epithet of being "wretched"[60] (*desdichada*), because although she was innocent and pious, she stood in her wicked cousin's way and therefore was unjustly incarcerated and later killed. Lope's representation of Mary and Elizabeth, as is characteristic of epic poems, is flat and polarized, with Mary standing parallel to the saints and Elizabeth to the Whore of Babylon.[61] This representation corresponds with that in the ecclesiastical histories by Ribadeneyra and Yepes and with the English/Spanish portrayal in *La Dragontea*. Elizabethan England, for instance, is said to be at the height of heresy, cruelty, and monstrosity, replicating language in *La Dragontea*: "Never was the Caledonian wilderness seen / full of more beasts, nor more dressed / of monsters, that in her ruthless and fierce empire / Calvin sowed and Luther gathered"[62] (Lope de Vega, *corona* 177). For his part, Henry Tudor, on one hand, is a "British Nero" and appears as a bloody tyrant, killing martyrs whose blood calls out to God to be avenged, but on the other hand his agency seems limited, as in *El amor desatinado*, and he is called a "foolish Solomon" and lamented on account of "blindness" with the words: "Oh, Henry, whose senses blinded / lust and ambition, what unworthy death / of a man to whom always gave unjust love / years of infamy and atoms of pleasure!"[63] (Lope de Vega, *corona* 138–9, 154, 415, 418). Published decades after the king's death, the poem ironically attests to the "years of infamy" Henry sowed and implicitly renews the moral lesson to be drawn from his life: lust and ambition offer temporary pleasure but have permanent, tragic consequences.

Furthermore, certain details in Lope's poem strongly echo Ribadeneyra's *Historia*. Lope seems to repeat Ribadeneyra's debated indictment, avoided by Yepes, that Henry was Anne's biological father when he refers to Elizabeth as "incestuous birth of the Harpy," suggesting that Anne is the harpy (*corona* 141). As Carreño notes, this phrase could allude to the rumor that Anne was impregnated by her brother (Lope de Vega, *corona* 141); however, Ribadeneyra's account notes that no children were born from that union (Ribadeneyra 1002). Given that Lope was familiar with Ribadeneyra's narrative that asserted that Henry married Anne even after being warned that she was his daughter and that in another line Lope says "Elizabeth, of Anne Boleyn / and Henry born an adulterous fruit," indicating that Elizabeth was the child of Henry and Anne, Ribadeneyra's allusion to incest between the parents is more likely being referenced (Lope de Vega, *corona* 177). Another possible connection of Lope and Ribadeneyra is that they both remark that Elizabeth Tudor is Mary Stuart's "aunt" (*tía*) when, in fact, they were cousins (Lope de Vega, *corona* 143; Ribadeneyra 1186). Furthermore, the narrative of how Henry discovered that Anne was an adulteress and his subsequent command to execute her are nearly identical. Ribadeneyra writes:

> And since Anne had many lovers [*amigos*], and she was loose and very daring, her wickedness could not remain hidden from the King. But he kept silent with strange dissimulation until one day, being in Greenwich, at certain feasts and in great rejoicing, he saw that Anne threw from the window where she was her handkerchief [*lienzo*] to one of her gallants who was in the plaza, so he could wipe the sweat from his face. Then the king arose with great fury, and without saying anything to anyone he left with a few servants to London, everyone remaining

> marveled and Anne distraught from this sudden departure of the King. (Ribadeneyra 1002)

Ribadeneyra here closely follows Sander's account and then narrates her capture and execution. The image of a loose woman looking from a window was associated with the ungodly biblical queen Jezebel, a name that he also uses throughout this[64] and other texts for Elizabeth and that Calderón will also give to Anne (188).[65] Lope clearly replicates this narrative when he says of Anne:

> That cruel beast [*fiera*], that inhuman,
> So free in her lasciviousness acted
> That she gave, from the window in Greenwich
> A white handkerchief [*lienzo*] to her gallant one day;
> The King saw her, and the small occasion
> Opened the eyes that love had
> Kept shut in its deceit, and from this fate
> Gave just cause to her violent death.
> (Lope de Vega, *corona* 417)

Both accounts note Anne's lasciviousness and frivolity, the location of Greenwich, Anne throwing a white handkerchief from a window to her "gallant" (*galán*), and this event being a catalyst for Henry's disenchantment from his blind love, leading to Anne's condemnation. Additionally, the words "beast" and "inhuman" echo the monstrous language in the ecclesiastical histories given to Anne and Elizabeth that also points to their cruelty and lack of natural affection.

Finally, Lope also seems to replicate Ribadeneyra's astonishment at Elizabeth's ruthless execution of Mary, discussed above, where in an apostrophe he invokes the heavens to witness "such a horrific example of such rare crudeness," so great that "in Tartary and Scythia and in whatever nation, no matter how coarse, fierce, and inhuman it may be, the very barbarians, when they hear this, will not believe it" (Ribadeneyra 1185, 1186). Right before this point, the Jesuit uses anaphora in a series of rhetorical questions, such as "what greater inhumanity? … What greater hatred? … What greater hypocrisy?"[66] to emphasize that Elizabeth's actions against her cousin are indisputably unbelievable. Lope, very similarly, puts in the mouth of Mary Stuart the following lines:

> But, what part of the uninhabitable world,
> What Aymara so remote or fierce Islander [*igleo*],

What Tartar, what inhospitable Scythian,
What cruel Circassian, what vile Derbyshirean [*diarbeo*][67]
Does not know of my miserable tragedy,
Of a beastly [*fiera*] woman a vain trophy?;
Because if any part the sun ignores,
There it is known; there it is felt and mourned.[68]
(*corona* 148)

The anaphora using the word "what" mimics Ribadeneyra's rhetorical questions, and Lope alludes to remote parts of the world ("uninhabitable world"), listing, like the Jesuit, hostile and remote people groups ("Aymara," "Islander," "Circassian," "Derbyshirean"), including Tartars, Scythians, and, surprisingly, people from Derbyshire, the region where Mary was imprisoned for fifteen years under Elizabeth. However, while Ribadeneyra's *Historia* focuses on how Elizabeth's cruelty is unheard of in the most barbarous nations and those at the ends of the earth will not believe it, Lope hyperbolically asserts that all these people – the entire world – have heard of Mary's fate and weep for her. Moreover, Lope had already labeled Anne "cruel beast [*fiera*]" and "inhuman" and now uses "beastly [*fiera*] woman" for Elizabeth, exploiting the polysemy of the adjective "vain" to say that the latter queen's murder of Mary is a worthless trophy of Elizabeth's vanity. Assuming that Lope had read Ribadeneyra's text around the time of its first publication and given its final diatribe in favor of Mary Stuart and against Elizabeth Tudor, it is reasonable to conjecture that he drew these details from the Jesuit's work, which he may have consulted in addition to Conn's volume to write *La corona trágica*.[69] Upon reading *La corona trágica* Lope's adverse feelings towards Elizabeth Tudor and her parents, even decades after her death, are clear, and his defense of Roman Catholicism and Spain using apocalyptic language and Black Legend reversal language to grip the imagination of Spaniards is consistent with his early writings. Moreover, the Christian epic poem was dedicated to the upcoming Pope to display Lope's orthodoxy and militant Counter-Reformation imaginative appeal in exchange for religious recognition for defense of the church for himself and Spain – a work of letters akin to the work of arms by the Catholic Monarchs. Thus, rather than just gratuitous, elaborate insulting of Elizabeth Tudor and the English, *La corona trágica* can be seen as a response within the Counter-Reformation corpus of works responding to broader Protestantism's attacks on the legitimacy of the Catholic Church and on Spain as its loyal ally.

La cisma de Ingalaterra (1627)

Unlike Lope, Calderón de la Barca's stance concerning Elizabeth Tudor and her progenitors, Henry VIII and Anne Boleyn, is somewhat harder to ascertain because the only extant work involving these characters is the tragedy *La cisma de Ingalaterra*,[70] and his portrayal is complex. Alexander Parker states: "Calderón's treatment of the schismatic king is extraordinarily compassionate, and totally at variance with the source from which he learned his history"[71] (251). For Ignacio Arellano and Juan Manuel Escudero, this representation of Henry answers to the aesthetic need for dramatic decorum in tragedies, where monarchs, regardless of their wickedness, must be represented on stage with dignity commensurate to their position (Arellano, "Decid" 164, 173–4; Escudero 43–4).[72] Furthermore, Arellano sees continuity with Ribadeneyra's *Historia*, pointing out that Calderón employs certain strategies, primarily contrasts between him and Queen Catherine, to signal to the audience that this Henry certainly is not a positive character ("Decid" 173). The arguments of Arellano and Escudero are bolstered by comparing *El amor desatinado* with *La cisma de Ingalaterra* because even though Lope agrees with Ribadeneyra's monstrous representation of Henry and Anne in the *Historia*, his mitigation of that image in his play and poems can be explained through aesthetic choices, usually for more complex characterization. Thus, Lope's comedy shows that it is essential to consider the constraints of genre when exploring ideological reasons for offering a less monstrous representation of Henry or Anne in Spain during this time. The changing landscape of Anglo-Spanish relations certainly is also an important factor to understand Calderón's depiction. Calderón, unlike Lope, had only heard or read about Spain's war with the English queen – a history that some Spaniards attempted to whitewash when the queen was no longer a threat. As seen in chapter 3, already in 1610 Carvajal records that many Catholics, including priests, praised Elizabeth I and said her persecutions were not as bad compared to those currently under James Stuart in order to vilify the king[73] – a revisionist history that Carvajal condemns (*Epistolario* 298). Furthermore, Calderón's knowledge about England would have been filtered through the information and various opinions that spread throughout his hometown of Madrid about the Spanish Match and the new Anglo-Spanish War (1625–30). In the end, regardless of Calderón's intentions, the effect of his play was that it presented distant, yet well-known foreign characters and events in a way that was less polarized and, therefore, allowed for three results. First, the work renewed Ribadeneyra's narrative and moral lessons for Spaniards living in an era when hostility towards

Elizabeth Tudor may have been more distant. Second, the play offered a more nuanced perspective of England that potentially could move more moderate Spaniards away from objections to Anglo-Spanish political alliances, though after the failure of the Spanish Match negotiations and with the renewed Anglo-Spanish War, this moderation may have been more difficult. Finally, the historical tragedy was more relatable and could be used as a mirror for Spaniards to see themselves and reflect upon internal political and religious concerns.

El amor desatinado and *La cisma de Ingalaterra*

No evidence exists to assert that Calderón had encountered Lope de Vega's comedy, *El amor desatinado*. The play was written in 1597, and records show that it had received approval to be performed, at least, in Zaragoza and Madrid in 1602, Granada in 1603, and Ecija in 1606 (García Morales 87). Born in 1600, Calderón could not have seen any of these performances, though it is possible that the play was staged at a later time or that the playwright came across one of its manuscripts. Nevertheless, even if the plays are not directly linked, *El amor desatinado* and *La cisma de Ingalaterra* have a common source, namely, Ribadeneyra's *Historia*.

La cisma de Ingalaterra

The specific occasion for Calderón's interest in writing *La cisma de Ingalaterra*, a tragedy about the English schism, is not clear, although Calderón's use of Ribadeneyra's *Historia* as his primary source is not doubted.[74] As noted, Ribadeneyra's history was ubiquitous and appears in aristocratic library catalogues, so it is not unusual that Calderón was familiar with the text. In fact, the work was known to be a favorite of both Philip III and Philip IV (Escudero 29; Weinreich "Introduction" 87), and Mackenzie proposes that Philip IV possibly commissioned Calderón to write the corresponding play (5).

The precise dating of *La cisma de Ingalaterra* is also debated, but most scholars believe it to be the same theatrical work that was performed at court before Philip IV and Isabel of Bourbon on March 31, 1627 (Escudero 1; Shergold 277; A.A. Parker 283). This date seems plausible, especially given the Spanish interest in England renewed by the recent events of the Spanish Match negotiations (1614–23), the Prince of Wales' visit to Madrid,[75] and the current Anglo-Spanish War of 1625–30 (Mackenzie 2–3; A.A. Parker 283–7). Furthermore, as mentioned earlier, European Roman Catholic authors around this time were also focused on another related part of English history, namely, the life and death of Mary Stuart, martyred by Elizabeth Tudor, and Lope de Vega joined their voices in Spain with his own *La corona trágica*. In this historical and literary milieu of Europeans championing the Roman Catholic cause and Spaniards praising Spain's efforts in this task, *La cisma de Ingalaterra* could have been written as a visual reminder[76] of the warnings Ribadeneyra had included in his *Historia* about the danger of following heresy and lusts and turning one's back on God, his vicar, and his church. Moreover, as Ribadeneyra's *Historia* had suggested and emphasized with the actions of Wolsey, it renewed the political lesson about the dangers of over-relying on royal favorites (*validos*) and about the prudent king not letting personal desires overpower him – topics that were important to Spaniards at the time, that interested Calderón, and that would be more palatable in the defamiliarized and remote setting of the English court.[77]

La cisma de Ingalaterra opens with Enrique (Henry VIII) dreaming about a beautiful woman who erases what he writes as he defends the seven sacraments of the Roman Catholic Church against Martin Luther. The king is terrified of this sign, especially when coupled with another presage wherein he mistakenly places Luther's letter on his head and Pope Leo's under his feet. Volseo (Cardinal Wolsey) tries to assuage Enrique's anxieties, but in the end the oracles will tragically come true, and, because of a woman, Luther will have precedence over the Pope in England. Volseo, too, receives a prophecy that he will be destroyed by a woman who he assumes is Catalina (Catherine of Aragon). Seeing that Enrique is in love with Ana (Anne Boleyn) and allied with the English lady to promote himself, Volseo suggests that the king repudiate Catalina with the excuse that it is a matter of conscience because the queen had been married to Enrique's brother. The king follows this advice, repudiates the virtuous queen before Parliament, and marries the ambitious Ana, setting her in Catalina's place. After overhearing Ana in an amorous conversation with the French ambassador Carlos, the irate Enrique commands her execution and seeks Catalina in repentance, only to find that it is too late because the Spaniard has died. The best Enrique can do is to vindicate his and Catalina's daughter María as the rightful heir to the English throne. The play ends with Ana's corpse under the triumphant María's feet as the latter swears in before Parliament and becomes the Princess of Wales.

As various scholars have pointed out, the historical material is derived from Ribadeneyra's *Historia*, although the chronology and the selection and arrangement of the information is significantly modified to fit the tragic structure.[78] Volseo, for instance, is credited with the original idea to repudiate Catalina, but in Ribadeneyra's text he shares this information with the king's confessor, who helps the Cardinal, while in the play, Volseo acts alone, and the action is focused solely on him. Even the prophecy that Volseo will be destroyed by a woman is extracted from the ecclesiastical history,[79] though to provide thematic unity to the play, Calderón adds Enrique's initial dream and presage of his fate and glaringly omits mention of Elizabeth Tudor.[80]

Similarities between *La cisma de Ingalaterra* and *El amor desatinado*

Lope's *El amor desatinado* and Calderón's *La cisma de Ingalaterra* have multiple similarities. Calderón references the same comment from Ribadeneyra's *Historia* that gives its title to *El amor desatinado* when Enrique tells Volseo: "you only procure to give life / to your king who already has lost it / at the hands of a reckless [*desatinado*] love"[81] (Calderón 143). In another possible allusion to Ribadeneyra's *Historia,* both plays feature Anne taking the title of queen and Catherine being stripped of it, echoing Henry's command that "from then on under severe penalty, no one should call Doña Catalina queen or his wife, but the widow of Prince Arthur" (Ribadeneyra 969). In *El amor desatinado* Rosa asks for Isabel to bring her water, to which Teodoro replies, "You mean the Queen?" The king, who is present, rebukes Teodoro for calling Isabel queen and affirms, "only Rosa is and shall be / queen in my soul and my kingdom" (Lope de Vega, *amor* 37). Furthermore, when towards the end of the play Roberto uses the word "queen" for Isabel, his subjects note that he is beginning to repent and say that the king is coming to his senses again ("that lost light is returning to him") (Lope de Vega, *amor* 76). Perhaps ironically evoking the same passage in Ribadeneyra's *Historia,* Calderón's Volseo claims to accidentally call Ana "Majesty," but he purposefully does so to flatter her and begin a conversation to plot with her against Catalina (Calderón 131). After Ana's fall, Enrique opens a monologue referencing Ana as "queen" and immediately adds, "To the Queen? I misspoke! / To that woman, to that beast [*fiera*]"[82] (Calderón 182). As a thematic reference to Ribadeneyra's history, the function of this trope surrounding the title of queen would strengthen the sense of tragedy in Henry's error of displacing a virtuous and rightful queen in favor of an adulterous and illegitimate one.

Furthermore, both *El amor desatinado* and *La cisma de Ingalaterra* assign grisly names to Anne's character. In the same breath that Enrique calls Ana "beast" in *La cisma de Ingalaterra* he adds "blind enchantment, false sphinx, basilisk, asp, irate tiger" (Calderón 182), attributing to her monstrous, magical, and evil traits, not unlike the names Lope gives Rosa in *El amor desatinado*. Similar to Rosa and the Elizabeth of *La Dragontea*, Ana is a grotesque witch associated with serpents and poison. In fact, Calderón's Carlos calls Ana "Circe," just like the French labeled Rosa, and Enrique tells María that he will avenge her from "Jezebel," using Elizabeth Tudor's most common slur among Catholics to refer to Ana (Calderón 181, 188). As mentioned, when applied to Anne and Elizabeth, the ubiquitous poetic tropes of lovers who are cruel Medeas and enchanting Circes can only be damning, obliquely replicating the monstrous statements in Ribadeneyra's account. Moreover, even though Calderón does not mention Elizabeth Tudor, referring to Ana as "Jezebel" would have unavoidably linked the two for the audience. Thus, María's final victory over Ana is also a victory over Anne Boleyn's daughter, Elizabeth.[83]

Clearly, Lope and Calderón coincide in portraying Anne according to Ribadeneyra's description of her as beautiful, promiscuous, and highly ambitious, though Lope dwells on her sexual dissipation and Calderón on her arrogance and shrewdness.[84] In *La cisma de Ingalaterra* her French lover, Carlos, calls attention to Ana's haughtiness: "Ana is a haughty woman. / Her vanity, her ambition, / her arrogance and presumption / make her, at times, evasive, / arrogant, mad, and vain; / and though in public you see her / Catholic, I think that she is / secretly Lutheran"[85] (Calderón 92). Ana's pride is amplified by the conglomeration of synonyms and cognates used: *vanity/vain, arrogance/arrogant, haughty, ambition, presumption*. Like Lope before him, Calderón reproduces Ribadeneyra's comment that Anne does not refuse to sleep with the king because she is virtuous but because she seeks to be the next queen. In *La cisma de Ingalaterra* Volseo tells Ana that Enrique is an "easy man / and is blinded much"[86] and that she should pretend to love the king and tell him that she cannot favor him because of her blood and honor but that she would love him as a wife (Calderón 135). By placing these words in Volseo's mouth, Calderón enhances the cardinal's role in the tragedy, exposes Ana's duplicity, and highlights her ambition when agreeing to the plan.

Lope and Calderón also coincide in following Ribadeneyra's account in their portrayal of Henry. Enrique in *La cisma de Ingalaterra* is much like his counterpart Roberto in *El amor desatinado*: he is blind and mad so that he cannot see Ana's infidelity until the end of the play, when he condemns her to death. Though Rosa is ultimately exiled instead of executed, the body of Ana appears on stage as a spectacle of destruction and final justice. Calderón's Enrique says, "I confess / that I am mad, without sense [*seso*]," showing that he is aware of how reckless it is to follow his passions and yet he chooses not to restrain himself (141). In fact, in the chiastic soliloquy where Enrique opens and closes stating that he is "mad and blind," he admits that he does not really believe that his marriage to Catalina is invalid. In his reasoning that it was legitimate to marry her, he repeats twice "it is true" and "it is a plain matter [*cosa llana*]," alerting the audience to the fact that, logically, there is no sound argument for divorcing Catalina, but emotionally, Enrique is willing to believe that falsehood in order to marry Ana (Calderón 144–5).

While this comment dramatically underscores that Enrique is driven by passion rather than reason, it is also a crucial theological and political clarification within a Counter-Reformation context, probably necessary for the play to pass censorship.[87] This clarification prevented legitimating Henry's divorce and Elizabeth's right to the English throne – one of the strongest points of contention against the Church of England in Catholic polemic literature[88] – and undermining the authority of the Pope, who granted the bull authorizing Henry's marriage to his brother's wife. Thus, even though Calderón portrays Henry as more internally conflicted about his divorce than Ribadeneyra does, this monologue ensures that everyone understand that even the blind and mad Enrique, who had much at stake in the question, was certain that his marriage to Catalina was lawful. That it was legal was true (*verdad*) and clear (*cosa llana*). In fact, the only monsters in the play are the masses (*vulgo*) who believe that Catalina was not a legitimate queen[89] (Calderón 191).

The portrayal of Catherine of Aragon shows overlap between Lope and Calderón in their adaptations of Ribadeneyra's material: she is the model of a Christian woman, virtuous and loyal to her husband, and as such, she reinforced behavior for women prescribed in contemporary female conduct manuals.[90] In *La cisma de Ingalaterra* Tomás Boleno tells his daughter that Catalina is "a transparent crystal" for Ana to learn from the queen (Calderón 105), echoing Ribadeneyra's comment that Catherine is "mirror of princesses and Christian queens" (*Historia* 899–900). Like Isabel in *El amor desatinado*, Catalina is saintly, and even Volseo, who plotted against her, recognizes her piety (Calderón 142, 145, 174). Catalina, too, is the "perfecta casada" who loves and respects her husband deeply until the end, and as he publicly renounces their marriage before the court, she refuses to detach herself, emphasizing her possession of him when she calls him "My Enrique, my King, my owner [*dueño*] / my lord, my sweet husband"[91] (Calderón 150). Moreover, just like Isabel stands before her father and requests that he not avenge her by killing Roberto, Calderón's Catalina movingly avows that she would stand between Enrique and Emperor Charles' vengeance:

Though to Spain I could
go, where the victorious
Charles gave me his refuge
I do not ask him or invoke him
so as not to ask him for vengeance
against you; for if, lively,
he requested to avenge me,
my chest, my own chest
would be your shield, and on it
would be dissolved the angry
blows of the temperate steel,
after the burning lead.[92]
(Calderón 152)

As Enrique dismisses her, Catalina argues that she could seek refuge and revenge in Spain, but instead, even if her nephew, "the victorious Charles," sought her requital, she would stand between the men and shield Enrique with her own chest, a metonymy for her heart and her love, emphasized in an anaphora alongside images of strength ("steel," "lead"). In contrast to Isabel's situation, Calderón's Catalina did not have to defend Enrique against the physical threat from a powerful foreign king, but her affirmation that she would do so if necessary is backed by her constancy and virtue exhibited throughout the play. Catalina's words, too, written many years after the historical events, can be read as a poetic explanation for the Emperor's lack of response in the face of Henry's affronts to Catherine, Mary, and the Pope.

Differences between *La cisma de Ingalaterra* and *El amor desatinado*

Both theatrical adaptations of Ribadeneyra's material, *La cisma de Ingalaterra* and *El amor desatinado*, respond distinctively to generic demands. One important difference between early modern Spanish comedies and tragedies relates to the audiences' horizon of expectations and to the proximity between spectators and characters in the play. Citing Pinciano's *Filosofía antigua poética*,[93] Arellano explains that, while in tragedies, fears and deaths cathartically pass on to the audience, which feels them deeply, in comedies, the same events remain only with the actors, and the audience perceives them as entertainment ("Metodología" 12). The comedic genre allows for characters to behave badly and to be caricatured or abused by other characters because the audience is distant, knowing that the goal of the play is to entertain. The tragedy must adjust to the tragic decorum; the characterization of the protagonists and their actions bears more weight and cannot be taken lightly. Because the protagonists are noble, the audience feels the irreparable loss and undergoes catharsis.

El amor desatinado and *La cisma de Ingalaterra* adapt Ribadeneyra's narrative into these generic distinctions in characterization. Calderón's tragic characters, Ana and Catalina, are noble and more complex than Lope's comedic characters, Rosa and Isabel. Rosa, for example, is only a mistress and is raped and beaten by a group of Frenchmen, but the violence is minimized and the scene seems comical. Rosa's phallic jokes after at this action, which would have made audiences laugh, exhibit the comedic detachment of the audience from the characters.[94] In fact, Roberto succeeds in making Rosa his concubine, but Enrique cannot impose upon Ana until after they are secretly married, and although Rosa cleverly accuses Isabel of adultery, seizing the opportunity to interpret a dream of the king, she is not part of a complex plot like Ana's with Volseo. The *hamartia* of Calderón's Ana is her hubris and ambition, not her sexual promiscuity,[95] and therefore, she is a weightier character than Rosa, sexually untouchable, who becomes queen and attains power. Her differences with Rosa reveal a nobler and more complex Anne figure in Calderón than in Lope.

The character of Catherine in the plays by Calderón and Lope is very similar, but Calderón's queen seems more intellectually sophisticated because she is known for reciting good verses and speaking several languages (Calderón 122, 124–5). As a tragic figure, Calderón's Henry is more honorable than Lope's because, unlike Roberto, Enrique never forces himself upon a woman and is not ridiculous. Additionally, no character claims that Enrique's actions have turned him into a beast or directly calls him a tyrant. Only on one occasion, when Enrique repudiates Catalina before the court, do several characters exclaim, successively, "What tyranny! / What affront! / What marvel! / What astonishment!" (Calderón 153), perhaps alluding to Ribadeneyra's comment of the events of the English schism being "marvellous and horrific [*espantosas*] things" but avoiding Ribadeneyra's monstrous portrayal of Henry. Like Lope in *El amor desatinado*, Calderón averts any mention of an incestuous relationship between Henry and Anne. In other words, the tragic decorum in *La cisma de Ingalaterra* restricts the representation of the king so that he does not appear to be as base as he could be characterized in a comedy. Interestingly, even though early modern Spanish comedies tend to grant the dramatist greater artistic freedom than in tragedies, Lope's comedy, like Calderón's tragedy, does not present Henry as the monster that Ribadeneyra portrays but takes the decorum license to make him farcical.

In addition to characterization distinctions, *El amor desatinado* and *La cisma de Ingalaterra* reveal structural adaptations of Ribadeneyra's narrative to fit a comedic or tragic framework. In order to comply with a comedic ending, *El amor desatinado* turns the historical divorce and remarriage between Henry and Catherine into a temporary adulterous affair to allow for a simpler reconciliation between Roberto and Isabel. In *La cisma de Ingalaterra,* however, Enrique's *hamartia* bears the full weight of the irreversible tragedy described in Ribadeneyra's narrative. Enrique's moment of anagnorisis is intensified when the king discovers that Catalina is dead and pleads that she help him repent, calling her "Beautiful angel / who in the throne of light you serve," he immediately acknowledges: "but it is too late, I cannot. / How badly I've done! How badly I've done!"[96] (Calderón 187). This ahistorical repentance and commentary reinforce the saintliness of Catalina by transporting her immediately to heaven after her death. At this pathetic moment, Enrique realizes that he will not be able to make a satisfactory restoration to Catalina and must console himself with an attempt at restitution for María, to whom he turns and says: "since your mother, / though I loved her so much I was not able / to restore in her Kingdom, / in it I want to restore you"[97] (Calderón 188). In an imaginative addition to Ribadeneyra's text, Calderón presents María swearing in as Princess of Wales under conditions that she appears to receive but in an aside denies,[98] which suggests that, even though her reign will allegedly be successful, Enrique's actions have broken England in such a way that it will never be restored.[99] *El amor desatinado,* however, with its characteristically comedic, happy denouement of the restoration of chaos, seems to fully erase Roberto's gross mistake and even places him in a better position than he was before, now that his eyes have been opened and he has recognized Isabel's worth and rightful place on the throne. Even the titles of each play align Ribadeneyra's narrative with standard tragic and comedic themes.[100] *El amor desatinado* centers on love triangles and individuals, while *La cisma de Ingalaterra* highlights the actions of a monarch that have political implications for an entire nation.

Conclusion

As this chapter shows, even though both Lope and Calderón begin with Ribadeneyra's narrative, their respective adaptations of that text are shaped by the generic structure each author has chosen, the author's personal background relative to England, and the changing historical moments that affect Spanish interests and concerns. Lope's representation of Henry VIII, and especially of Anne Boleyn and Elizabeth

Tudor generally, is quite negative, even when he allots ingeniousness or beauty to these figures. In *La Dragontea*, Lope aligns Elizabeth with the cruel witch Medea and with Athena, the virgin goddess of war, implying that the English queen is harsh and bloody, even if beautiful and clever. *La Dragontea* also shares themes with Ribadeneyra's *Tratado de la tribulación* in that even though Religion recognizes that God's judgment upon his people is just, she pleads with the triune judge to take action against the tyrant Elizabeth, whose land is full of Catholic martyrs, which God answers by raising up Covetousness personified to entice Drake to costly expeditions so that he may have a great fall. Written simultaneously with *La Dragontea*, *El amor desatinado* references Ribadeneyra's *Historia*, as seen in the numerous details that correspond in both texts, including the basic characterization of the protagonists alluding to Henry VIII, Anne Boleyn, and Catherine of Aragon. The Anne Boleyn figure (Rosa) is beautiful, scheming, and licentious and is linked to Circe and Medea. Lope's Henry VIII (Roberto) is enchanted by her and becomes stubbornly blind and mad in a reckless love that threatens to destroy him and his kingdom. Isabel, the Catherine character, is a constant, devoted wife who loves and forgives her husband despite his rejection of her, and her undying love is ultimately rewarded by her husband's repentance. The departures from Ribadeneyra's narrative, including the changed names of the characters, the comedic ending, and the less negative portrayal of Henry VIII (including the refusal to show him as a monster or make mention of the incest with Anne Boleyn), appear to derive from Lope's stylistic choices often to enrich the characterization with complexity and generic necessities rather than an intentional desire to present them as less negative.

This last argument is further supported by Lope's description of Henry VIII and Elizabeth Tudor in a different genre, namely, the poems in *Rimas humanas*, where Henry VIII reflects the same characteristics found in Roberto, but the epitaph on Elizabeth calls her "Jezebel," "Athalia," and "harpy," echoing the monstrous representation of Ribadeneyra of a cruel, bloody tyrant and putting her in a polarized binary in contrast to Mary Stuart. Lope expands this flat and Manichean representation of Elizabeth Tudor and Mary Stuart in *La corona trágica*, a religious epic poem based on numerous European accounts, including that of Ribadeneyra, of the death of Mary Stuart by the hand of her cousin. In *La corona trágica* Lope maintains the monstrous characterization of Elizabeth found in the ecclesiastical histories, even alluding to the scandalous accusation of incest between Henry and Anne. Furthermore, the poem presents a Mary emulating saints and an Elizabeth depicting the Whore of Babylon. All of these works by Lope show that the playwright's stance concerning Henry, Anne, and Elizabeth is clearly and persistently antagonistic, and yet in *El amor desatinado* he chooses to present the pair Roberto and Rosa in a less monstrous way than does his source but takes the comic freedom to make them ridiculous. This particular representation points to aesthetic changes, often related to the comedic genre.

Also sourced in Ribadeneyra's *Historia*, Calderón de la Barca's tragedy *La cisma de Ingalaterra* shows a less negative and more complex portrayal of Henry VIII than its base text. When compared with *El amor desatinado*, *La cisma de Ingalaterra* reveals structural and characterization differences, most of which can be explained by generic distinction, the changing socio-political stance towards England, and the chronological distance from the English queen. As a tragedy, *La cisma de Ingalaterra* centers on actions that determine political outcomes, while the comedy *El amor desatinado* highlights individuals in a love triangle. The main characters in Calderon's tragedy also seem more noble than those in Lope's, so that Anne Boleyn's greatest fault is ambition and hubris rather than lasciviousness, and Henry is much more conflicted over the struggle between his passions and his duty than is Roberto. Nonetheless, like in Lope's works, in *La cisma de Ingalaterra* Anne is called "Jezebel" and "Circe," perhaps to connect her to Queen Elizabeth, who is not mentioned in the play, but neither the comedy nor the tragedy directly presents Henry as a monster or accuses him of incest with Anne. As a result, it is possible to conclude that these complex representations of Henry in both plays by Lope and Calderón largely respond to generic strictures and stylistic choices by each dramatist, as well as to their personal stance concerning Elizabeth Tudor and the goals of each literary piece within their changing socio-historical contexts. In the end, the fluctuating interest in England displayed by the Spaniards is highly concerned with using foreign, well-known stories for entertainment and authorial displays of skill, likely with moral or political lessons for Spanish introspection, and with promoting and defending Spain and Roman Catholicism in the wake of Protestant criticism and military victories, especially coming from England.

Chapter Five

A Novel Way of Looking at the English Reformation: Ribadeneyra and Cervantes' *La española inglesa*

As the previous chapters have showed, Ribadeneyra's representation of Elizabeth Tudor as a cruel tyrant associated with witches and monsters and the murder of Catholics was pervasive in early modern Spain. This seems clear not only from the publication success of Ribadeneyra's *Historia* but also because authors like Lope de Vega and Calderón de la Barca took the Jesuit's narrative as a point of reference when writing about characters and events related to the English Reformation. Moreover, as discussed earlier, for Spaniards siding with Ribadeneyra, the English schism was scandalous and theologically threatening, and the persecution of English Catholics was an atrocious massacre that unexpectedly persisted through the reign of King James and that Spanish monarchs (Philip II and III) and their diplomats sought to end or, at least, alleviate through different means, such as military invasion, the Treaty of London, and the Spanish Match. Within this context, the publication of *La española inglesa* (*The Spanish English Girl*), a *novela* by Cervantes, is quite puzzling. Printed in 1613 in the collection of *Novelas ejemplares* (exemplary novels), *La española inglesa* centers on a young Spanish girl named Isabela, captured during the sack of Cádiz, who is eventually brought to Elizabeth Tudor's court. In a curious scene, the queen's Protestant chambermaid warns the monarch of Isabela's intransigent Catholicism, complaining that "Isabela was Catholic, and so devout that none of their persuasions, which had been many, had turned her one bit away from her faith" (Cervantes, *Novelas* 268). Surprisingly, the queen answers in favor of the girl and tells her servant that "for that reason she esteemed her more, because she had kept so well the law that her parents had taught her" and that "her beauty and her many graces and virtues pleased her much" (Cervantes, *Novelas* 268). The English queen, in the Spanish ecclesiastical histories presented as a cruel persecutor of Catholics, here admires Isabela despite the girl's Catholicism, even precisely because she will not change her mind about it. Thus, the novel features a rather positive view of Queen Elizabeth and quite a softened representation of Catholic persecutions in England. While many scholars have pointed out this unusual portrayal of the queen, their explanations of this phenomenon remain incomplete because they lack a central piece of the historical puzzle that shaped Spain's imagination concerning Elizabethan and Stuart England and its own Catholic identity and role in the Counter-Reformation: Ribadeneyra's *Historia*. Thus, for example, Américo Castro and Melveena McKendrick, respectively, argued that *La española inglesa* shows Cervantes' ignorance of Elizabeth's court and hastiness in the writing of the novel (Castro 287–8; McKendrick, *Cervantes* 275), which, as this chapter will show, is an unlikely conclusion given Cervantes' biography and the literary production – including the Spanish ecclesiastical histories – of his time. I argue that, like Lope and Calderón, Cervantes was keenly aware of Ribadeneyra's *Historia* and writes in dialogue with that text. Moreover, like Ribadeneyra, Cervantes' story seems to be more interested in using English characters and settings for Spanish self-reflection and concerns.

La española inglesa

La española inglesa's title character, Isabela, is a Spanish girl who, after the sack of Cádiz, is taken captive to England by the English captain Clotaldo, who gives her as a gift to his wife Catalina. Clotaldo and Catalina adopt the girl as a daughter, and she learns to speak English "as if she had been born in London" (Cervantes, *Novelas* 244). Providentially, Clotaldo and his noble family are "secret Catholics," and this allows her to preserve her own faith and her language. The English couple keeps Isabela hidden from Queen Elizabeth out of fear of being found out to be Catholic. As Isabela grows up, she and Ricaredo, son of Clotaldo and Catalina, fall in love, but their marriage requires the blessing of the queen, and therefore, the young Isabela is brought to court. The beauty and discretion of the Spaniard fascinate the queen, who adopts her as a daughter in her court until Ricaredo proves his worth by privateering for the queen and bringing back riches. The couple must then overcome a series of obstacles to finally attain their marriage, and the explicit twofold moral of the story is that virtue and beauty can win over enemies and that God turns the greatest adversities into gains. The most prevalent themes of the narrative are that of providence, perseverance, and patience in adversity – themes also crucial especially in the second part of Ribadeneyra's *Historia* and in Yepes' volume.

Although Elizabeth Tudor had been dead for ten years by the time the novel appeared publicly, Cervantes' representation of Queen Elizabeth in this work remains extraordinarily positive for a Spaniard to write, as noted by critics. Carroll B. Johnson speaks of a "violent contrast" between the Elizabeth of history and that of Cervantes ("Production" 388). Américo Castro suggests that perhaps Cervantes does not care about history, calling Elizabeth's representation, "the historical unreality of the queen that he forges"[1] (288). Marsha Collins equates the queen to the young Isabela's "fairy godmother" (64). However, it has not been common to place this novel in its broader literary context to discern to what extent it adheres to or departs from other contemporary texts that represent the queen and Catholics around the time of the English Reformation. Among the authors who have analyzed *La española inglesa* from a historical perspective, until recently[2] none had discussed its relationship to Ribadeneyra's *Historia*, which is curious, especially in Johnson ("Production") and Ricapito, who extensively examine the situation of English Catholics. Only Américo Castro's amplified edition of *El pensamiento de Cervantes* appends a footnote directing the reader to compare Cervantes' representation of Elizabeth Tudor with Yepes' *Historia* as an example of "any of the accounts of the time" that contradicts Cervantes (323). Olid Guerrero references the "rampant presence of negative propaganda … about the British Isles and … their bestialized and evil Queen" but does not mention specific sources, such as the ecclesiastical histories (48).

The representation of Elizabeth in these histories is radically different from that of Cervantes. As discussed in chapter 2, according to these texts, Elizabeth is sensual, promiscuous, arrogant, deceitful, proud, and utterly cruel, which explains her tyranny and her bloody persecution of English Catholics. When we situate *La española inglesa* within this ideological context, Cervantes' novel appears yet more peculiar, especially if we consider the possibility that the novel is in dialogue with these ecclesiastical histories, which reflected more or less the Spanish position with respect to the English Reformation. Thus, the aim of this chapter is to place *La española inglesa* within the context of Ribadeneyra's vision, supported by Yepes, to show why these works are extremely important to understanding the configuration of the English queen in this novel, the potential implications of this positive representation, and what Cervantes' portrayal may reveal about Spanish perceptions of Spain and of England after Elizabeth Tudor was dead.

The Critical History of *La española inglesa*

One reason that the historical and theological context of *La española inglesa* has been understudied may have to do with the generic and literary features of the novel and its complex relationship between history and poetry and between verisimilitude and idealism[3] that largely affect how critics have understood the novel, especially the generally positive portrayal of Elizabeth. Because it includes sea voyages, strange lands, unexpected meetings, marvellous healing, anagnorisis, and a love story with a happy ending, critics have cogently argued that the novel resembles the Byzantine novel or at least shares some of its tropes.[4] For this reason, the old binary taxonomy of the *novelas* as "realistic" and "idealistic" relegated *La española inglesa* to this latter category and led scholars to believe that it was simplistic and less interesting than the other *novelas*, and it was, therefore, understudied (Torres 116; Johnson, "Production" 377). Even those who found the novel interesting tended to focus on the ideal and perceive the historical elements of the novel as fictionalized and less important to the overall aesthetic of the text. Moreover, Alban Forcione noted that scholars responded this way because of the influence of Américo Castro, who implied that the composition of the exemplary novels was for Cervantes an act of self-betrayal, where he simply conformed to the official convictions of his society (*Humanist Vision* 12–17). However, Castro's posture was challenged by the work of Ruth El Saffar – who argued that the older Cervantes privileged "romance" over novelistic writings – and of Forcione – who maintained that Cervantes' use of the romance was unconventional and, therefore, innovative.[5]

Stimulated by El Saffar's findings and following earlier studies by Icaza and Hanrahan, Johnson produced a valuable historical and economic reading of *La española inglesa* that demonstrated its complex intersection of fiction and history ("Production" 377). In Johnson's view, "the plot of *La española inglesa* could not be more improbable or romantic," yet its value lay in that it was "profoundly concerned with real historical and social issues" ("Production" 377, 379). Focusing on the historical markers of the novel and its innovative mix of poetry and history opened questions as to what the historical events could suggest to audiences about Spanish history or society. For Johnson, the story showcased Cervantes' quarrel with the aristocracy by associating it with the outdated economic system of feudalism while promoting the bourgeoisie, which was linked to the emerging capitalism ("Production" 415–16; "Catolicismo"). Other authors, such as Ricapito, argued that the historical alterations – for example, that of Queen Elizabeth – provide the setting for the dominant "secret Catholics" thread, which has a "subtext of disenchantment (*desengaño*)" exposing social problems, that is, the "presence and treatment of Spain's own minorities – Jews, Moors, *conversos*" in the great Spain of Lepanto (68). More specifically, the English setting of fear and secrecy of religion is considered an ironic mirroring and critique of the Spanish Inquisition's persecution of Jewish and Islamic converts on the peninsula (Castro 287–8; Johnson, "Production" 386; da Costa Fontes 743–4).[6] Another cogent political interpretation from a historical perspective was that *La española inglesa* was an attempt to rewrite the past in a period of Anglo-Spanish rapprochement surrounding the Treaty of London of 1604 (Icaza 144–5; Hanrahan; Lapesa 252–7; Johnson, "Production" 388–98; Ricapito 39–68). In this view, *La española inglesa* functioned as a sort of poetic "revisionist" history of Ribadeneyra and Yepes, deemphasizing some of Elizabeth's sins against Spain to encourage Spaniards to focus on a future of peace with England rather than to dwell on past grievances under a queen who was no longer on the political scene.[7] This position places the writing of the novel around 1604, a point accepted by many scholars, and assumes an older Cervantes, who has been disenchanted from the glory of the Spain of Lepanto and does not retain the bitterness that Lope shows against Queen Elizabeth even up until 1627 in *La corona trágica*.[8] In other words, this position would be similar to Calderón's stance in *La cisma de Ingalaterra* analyzed above.

Part of what opens up readings of political and social critiques is Cervantes' use of perspectivism and intertextuality in *La española inglesa* that infuses the work with ambiguity and complexity that appeals to active readers. Perspectivism in Cervantes' work allows readers to interpret a narrative from different points of view and often relies heavily on irony. *Don Quixote*'s episodes, for instance, vary depending on whether readers take the vantage point of Cide Hamete, Don Quixote, or another character. This strategy allows Cervantes to relativize the validity of any given interpretation and to distance himself from endorsing any particular view (Riley 31). As Spitzer described it: "We may assume that … [Cervantes] watches the story he narrates from his own private vantage point: the way in which the characters conceive of the situations in which they are involved may be not at all the way in which Cervantes sees them – though this latter way is not always made clear to the reader" (50). Perspectivism, then, could open readings that enable Cervantes to make his characters mouthpieces of political and social endorsements or critiques and to let readers make their own choice about these subjects without knowing which view Cervantes ultimately favors. While not as obvious as in *Don Quixote*, in *La española inglesa*, literary genres and tropes introduce this layer of perspectivism and ambiguity.

Fuchs, McKendrick, and others have argued that, especially in the second half of the sixteenth century and the first part of the seventeenth century in Spain, challenges to the political or religious status quo often had to be veiled in order to pass censorship, escape the attention of the Inquisition, or merely remain within the favor of nobles and the monarchy.[9] Fuchs suggests that sometimes literary genre provided a "screen" behind which authors could hide while sending an oblique political critique to alert audiences. Discussing *La española inglesa* and a similar novel, Fuchs states:

> [They] are fully engaged with their historical context … although the force of that engagement is often disguised by the trappings of romance: relentless idealization of the protagonists, coincidences, separations and marvelous reappearances, and so forth … the expected and comforting moves of romance serve Cervantes to challenge such ideological behemoths as the role of religious difference in national identity, or the exclusionary nature of Spain's Catholicism. Romance may pose its own explicit challenge to these ideologies, as in the many instances of individual knights who cross religious and national lines without impunity. Or it may simply present a pointed, striking contrast to the historical context in which its idealizing fictions are being invoked. (*Romance* 93)

Here Fuchs suggests that by inserting historical events in the imaginary world of a familiar genre – e.g., the "relentless idealization" of a historic Elizabeth or of a *converso* Isabela, who stands for the ideal Spaniard and Catholic when new Christians were suspect in Spain – Cervantes can subtly challenge entrenched ideas ("ideological behemoths") about religious and national difference and exclusion.

Intertextuality would allow Cervantes to open additional readings of the text and surprise readers with unexpected associations or go further with veiled critiques. When linked to another text (an *intertext*) by clear quotation, allusion, parody, or some subtler pattern, the meaning, value, and function of the primary text is modified (Venuti 157). If the intertext has positive or negative value, this value is read against the first text and makes it ambiguous, thus providing a "cover" for any critique that Cervantes would want to make. Thus, as will be shown, Elizabeth acquires certain positive value from the biblical intertext of Pharaoh's generosity towards Joseph or from Alemán's Isabella the Catholic who favors Daraja. If Cervantes intended to challenge political, religious, or racial prejudices in *La española inglesa,* the message would be more palatable to his audience – or would allow him to slip through the criticism of those strongly opposed to his view – through the ambiguity of perspectivism and intertextuality. However, since little is known of Cervantes' ideological convictions and precisely because of intertextuality and perspectivism, these veiled messages can only be suggested.

Moreover, Cervantes' *novelas* are hard to categorize generically, but they also invite active reading. They are not new merely because authors had not written before in this particular genre in Spanish. As Forcione and others have argued, they are new because they incorporate old materials – tropes, plots, genres – used in new ways. Cervantes brings heterogeneous literary materials, as he describes it, to his "table of tricks" (*mesa de trucos*) and puts them together into something new so that the ideal reader will be entertained "without harm to soul or body"[10] (Cervantes, *Novelas* 52). The reader is supposed to pick up these interesting clues that complicate the narrative, see how they have been revitalized, and maybe even arrive at certain conclusions about the changes, particularly the historical ones. These features of Cervantes' novels encourage the reading of *La española inglesa* in light of Ribadeneyra's and Yepes' histories.

Cervantes and the Ecclesiastical Histories

Although no evidence exists that Cervantes read the histories by Ribadeneyra and Yepes, he must have known of them for reasons similar to those of Carvajal, Lope, and Calderón. As pointed out in chapter 2, these works were widely read among lay Spanish aristocracy, considering that copies of the histories appear in catalogues of the libraries of Francisco Hurtado de Mendoza, Luisa de Carvajal's uncle, and Diego Sarmiento de Acuña, the first count of Gondomar and ambassador to London. Since the books in these libraries were often shared with literate friends in the noble's sphere,[11] those who had access to these volumes were not exclusively aristocrats. In fact, Ribadeneyra's *Historia* also appears among books in transatlantic ships that the Inquisition inspected, suggesting that these were also read aloud during long trips to the Americas, in which case literate and illiterate individuals on board would have had the opportunity to hear them (Leonard 57). Moreover, as discussed in the previous chapter, both Lope and Calderón drew directly from Ribadeneyra's *Historia* to write about England, and Lope and Cervantes maintained a friendship at least until 1602, when Cervantes wrote a sonnet for the introduction to the second edition of *La Dragontea*,[12] meaning that he had at least read it, and he also may have discussed it with Lope. If, then, the ecclesiastical histories were being published in multiple languages and editions and appear in book catalogues of ships and aristocratic libraries as well as in literary circles around Cervantes in his adult years, it seems highly probable that Cervantes would have known about them, especially since the histories were published, in part, as contemporary news about England, which

Spaniards were curious to know. In fact, Cervantes lauded the departure of the Armada in 1588,[13] and around the death of Queen Elizabeth in 1603, Cervantes was in Valladolid – the location of the court and of St. Alban's English College – which at the time was the center of Anglo-Spanish negotiations and news, making it nearly impossible for him to have escaped being interested in and hearing about these events.[14]

More important than this circumstantial evidence, however, is that the text of *La española inglesa* points to several internal connections with at least Ribadeneyra's ecclesiastical history but possibly also Yepes'. Most obviously, the three texts describe Elizabethan England and the persecution of English Catholics, the subject matter of the Spanish ecclesiastical histories. Additionally, the thematic focus of all these texts is providence and perseverance during times of trials, and the theological lesson to be drawn from each of the stories is that God will reward patience and virtue. Finally, *La española inglesa* and these histories are centered on the idea of exemplum, and particularly Ribadeneyra's *Historia* and the novel have uncanny textual parallels that signal a stronger link between these works. Even in the unlikely event that Cervantes did not draw his information about England from these texts – as Lope and Calderón seem to have done – readers who were familiar with negative portrayals of the queen would have immediately compared Cervantes' representation with that of Ribadeneyra and Yepes.[15] However, before one can reach a conclusion, it is important to examine the evidence that suggests textual connections.

La española inglesa and the Ecclesiastical Histories

La española inglesa echoes the ecclesiastical histories' descriptions of the persecution of Catholics, although it seems to soften some of the cruelty detailed in the theological sources. For instance, Cervantes' novel alludes to the persecution of English Catholics through the great consternation of Clotaldo and his wife in being discovered as "secret Catholics," but the text is not clear about the consequences for those who are detected – whether they would have to pay large sums, or be imprisoned, or suffer death. Once the family is informed that the queen wants Clotaldo to bring Isabela before her, they become full of "distress, fright, and fear," and they dread being "condemned"[16] (Cervantes, *Novelas* 247). In fact, although its certainty is ambiguous and perhaps could be read figuratively or as an exaggeration, Clotaldo states that they could be executed if discovered: "Clotaldo sought ways to assuage his great fear, and could not find them except in the great trust which he had in God and in the prudence of Isabela, whom he earnestly entreated that through every possible means she would avoid condemning them as Catholics: that *though in spirit they were ready to receive martyrdom, their weak flesh still refused its bitter way*" (Cervantes, *Novelas* 247; emphasis added). Clotaldo's paraphrase of Jesus' words in Matthew 26:41 ("Watch ye, and pray that ye enter not into temptation. The spirit indeed is willing, but the flesh weak.") is used to justify his lack of readiness to face the consequences of confessing his faith and explains why he and his family are secretive. These direct and indirect references to the fear that Catholics experienced under Elizabeth are consistent with the accounts in the Spanish ecclesiastical histories. Ribadeneyra's volume includes a famous letter from Edmund Campion from 1580 that lists reasons why Catholics were anxious: "While writing this letter, the most cruel persecution is becoming fiercer; the house is sorrowful, because no one speaks except about death, or prison, or of the loss of goods"[17] (1118). Campion notes that, though Catholics persevere, as the cruel persecution intensifies, the conversation topics are reduced to death, imprisonment, exile, and loss of possessions, which causes sorrow. Likewise, Clotaldo's family becomes grief-stricken, and their conversation turns to avoiding exposure. However, the vagueness and ambiguity surrounding the punishment of Catholics in Cervantes' novel seems to deemphasize the sufferings Ribadeneyra describes that are pivotal in his arguments against Elizabeth to indicting her as a cruel tyrant. For instance, after offering Elizabeth's execution of Mary Stuart as the ultimate proof of the former's ruthlessness, Ribadeneyra states: "Because since heresy is an infernal monster, all the fruits that are born from it are monstrous and infernal. And if to know this truth were not enough the innumerable examples that we previously had of cruelty, violence, and tyranny that the heretics have used in our times, this one only is enough for all, and will be enough in all the coming centuries"[18] (1186). Ribadeneyra here, almost at the end of his history, points out that even though Mary's execution is an extreme example of callousness, his narrative and other sources have exposed "innumerable examples ... of cruelty, violence, and tyranny." While it is unclear whether he is referring to the examples cited in his own work ("innumerable examples that we previously had") and to Elizabeth ("that the heretics have used"), the queen and her persecutions are implicit in this statement, since this passage comes at the end of his work where the suffering, perseverance, and death of the Catholic martyrs by Elizabeth and her magistrates has been extensively described. For Ribadeneyra, then, each brutal act against Catholics constitutes proof of Elizabeth's cruelty and is therefore worth documenting in detail for all to know.

One possible explanation for the lack of detail in the novel is that Cervantes did not know the particulars of the situation of Catholics in England, but the information Johnson argues he had during his time in Valladolid ("Literary Production" 399) and data from the ecclesiastical histories makes that claim unlikely.[19] Another plausible reason is that those details were simply not relevant to the story Cervantes aimed to tell. After all, the novel is short, and arguments from silence – in this case, why Cervantes omitted information – are sometimes feeble. While such argument is partially valid, when these omissions are considered alongside the many positive associations made for Elizabeth and when offered in a context of specific Anglo-Spanish relations, the novel seems to be deliberately deemphasizing the cruelty of Elizabeth Tudor so vivid in Ribadeneyra's and Yepes' histories and in the majority of Spanish accounts.[20]

La española inglesa does not tell readers directly what Elizabeth Tudor is like, but through her interactions and her subjects' statements, she is characterized as a queen that is feared but also loved. In the first mention of Elizabeth in the story, the text presents her religious stance as an "opinion" opposed to Catholicism, perhaps as a way to imply that the English religion is uncertain while Catholicism is true,[21] but uses a more neutral word than the common term "heresy" or another negatively charged word: "It was the will of good fortune that everyone in Clotaldo's house were secret Catholics, although in public they showed that they followed *the opinion* of their Queen" (Cervantes, *Novelas* 244; emphasis added). The narrator then notes that Clotaldo brought Spaniards to the house "secretly" to speak Spanish to Isabela so that she would not forget her mother tongue while she learns English (Cervantes, *Novelas* 244). The importance of keeping these secrets of being Catholic and bringing Spaniards to the house[22] is not revealed until a servant (*ministro*) of the queen brings the message that the monarch wants the Spanish girl to be brought to court, and Clotaldo's household becomes exceedingly alarmed about being exposed. This reaction shows that the Elizabeth of the story is a queen who is feared by her subjects, perhaps more accurately reflecting the feelings of English Catholics during that time, as described by Ribadeneyra and Yepes.

Clearly, the English queen also does not overlook her subjects' lack of submission, as is the case when Clotaldo hides Isabela and neglects to secure the queen's permission to marry his son, and she warns him: "be warned, Clotaldo, that I know that without my license you had her engaged to your son" (Cervantes, *Novelas* 250). Yet, in Cervantes' novel, Clotaldo's dread ultimately seems unwarranted because no Catholic is ever discovered or punished, and the queen acts graciously and favorably towards Spaniards. An unnamed character at court describes Elizabeth as "hard-hearted" and perhaps even materialistic for wanting gifts: "Now is confirmed what is commonly said, that gifts and presents split rocks, because the ones Ricaredo has brought have softened the hard heart of our Queen" (Cervantes, *Novelas* 262). However, even this negative comment is offset by a positive focus on the queen's softening.

In fact, Cervantes' Elizabeth has many positive traits that would enable her subjects to love her. She is fair and approachable: she listens to her subjects and grants them an impartial hearing and a fair chance. For example, she offers Ricaredo a reasonable opportunity to prove his worth and win Isabela. She is also just and uncompromising in keeping her word: she gives Ricaredo what he earned because even her chambermaid knows that is it "impossible … [for the queen] to break her word," and Elizabeth does not pervert justice even to favor her interests (Cervantes, *Novelas* 265). Though her chambermaid tells the queen that she poisoned Isabela because "in killing Isabela … she was removing a Catholic from earth," the queen justly punishes her subject by dismissing her and making her pay ten thousand golden *escudos* to Isabela rather than excusing the English woman's crime (Cervantes, *Novelas* 269, 272). Olid Guerrero calls this action of punishing an English subject and compensating Isabela for her loss a potential "political mistake" from a Machiavellian perspective, showing that the queen chooses to keep her word at all costs and displays the ideal balance between a Machiavellian and a Christian queen (46–7). If this is the case, then in an ironic twist of Ribadeneyra's and Yepes' focus on Christian prince treatises, Cervantes could be suggesting that Elizabeth is the exemplum of the Christian monarch lauded in those manuals.[23]

Further, Elizabeth also appears to be perceptive and wise, especially with respect to familial and romantic relationships, a trait that balances the fear of the queen. She understands how valuable Isabela is to Ricaredo when, upon his return to claim his bride, the monarch tells him: "the treasures bought with longing and whose worth is in the soul of the buyer, those are worth the value of a soul, for there is no price on earth to measure it"[24] (Cervantes, *Novelas* 260).[25] The queen also seems wise in understanding what great a shock it is for Isabela's parents to be reunited with their daughter and provides for them to stay in her palace so that "they would leisurely see and speak to their daughter and rejoice with her" (Cervantes, *Novelas* 264). In effect, Elizabeth is presented as a motherly figure, taking Isabela under her wing because she "esteemed her as a daughter" and giving her a courtly education[26] (Cervantes, *Novelas* 250).

Cervantes' monarch should be feared and loved, too, because she proves to be well educated, in accordance with the historical Elizabeth Tudor (Samson, "Upending" 301). She tells Isabela to speak to her in Spanish, adding "that I understand it well and will be pleased by it," showing that the queen knows and enjoys languages other than English (Cervantes, *Novelas* 249). She also seems well acquainted with literature when she speaks poetically to Ricaredo about lovers and war: "Happy would be the warrior king who had in his army ten thousand lover soldiers who longed that the prize of their victories would be to enjoy their beloved" (Cervantes, *Novelas* 251).

The education of Cervantes' Elizabeth contributes to the character of a respected and loved monarch, as does her generosity. The text shows the queen giving diamonds, pearls, and expensive dresses to Isabela as well as hosting the girl's parents in the palace, which gestures at the queen's generosity. Some scholars believe that the monarch's focus on riches – for example, when she chastises Clotaldo for keeping Isabela from her or when she forces Ricaredo to bring treasures in exchange for Isabela – is an oblique suggestion that she is greedy, and therefore, not such a positive queen.[27] This view is plausible, given that, as chapter 4 discussed, early modern Spaniards considered the English greedy because of the plundering of Spanish ships, and Lope de Vega makes these prejudices explicit in *La Dragontea*. However, from a sociological perspective, as Marcel Mauss has shown, the exchange of valuable objects between monarchs and subjects also has a complex social significance rather than just an economical one and is related to solidarity and obligations between groups.[28] From a literary perspective, these exchanges are positive in the idealized chivalric literature and Byzantine novels, two genres from which *La española inglesa* seems to borrow. Thus, although it should be acknowledged that the representation of the English queen is complex and not altogether positive, the novel's focus on valuable exchanges cannot be wholly cast in a negative light.

Most importantly, unlike portrayals in Ribadeneyra and Yepes, Cervantes' queen recognizes virtue and beauty in her enemies – that is, she can see beyond the outward identifiers of Catholics and Spaniards – and is able to respect and even love them. This quality allows Elizabeth to admire, rather than resent, Isabela's loyalty to the religion her parents taught her and to send off the Spaniards, whom she had received, "with much love" (Cervantes, *Novelas* 270). Additionally, as previously discussed, the generic feature of the Byzantine novel of thoroughly idealizing its protagonists invites readers to likewise admire the queen. Indeed, this is the most jarring aspect of Cervantes' representation of Elizabeth, especially when juxtaposed with the queen of the ecclesiastical histories and of Lope, who at times acknowledges her beauty and cleverness but never moral virtue such as honesty or generosity.

Ribadeneyra tells the "Christian and pious reader" in his preface that as a Jesuit, he must defend Roman Catholicism and oppose heretics, referencing Henry VIII, Anne Boleyn, and their daughter Elizabeth, currently on the throne, of whom he says: "Following the footsteps of such parents and filling up their measure, with extraordinary cruelty and tyranny she persecutes our holy Catholic Roman and apostolic faith, and butchers those who profess and teach it, tormenting, dislocating, and tearing them apart with extremely atrocious punishments and deaths"[29] (900). This short description of the persecution of Catholics in England at the time encapsulates all the violence, injustice, and prejudice that Ribadeneyra ascribes to the queen and that is explained in detail in the rest of his volume. Elizabeth not only "follows in the footsteps of her parents" but also "fills up their measure"[30] so that the charges against her parents are imputed to her and are even greater: their ambition, lust, and hypocrisy; their rejection of the Pope and the true church; their robbing of temples; and their cruel tyranny and persecution of Catholics. Ribadeneyra specifies Elizabeth's actions upon Catholics with vivid verbs ("butchers," "torments," "dislocates," "tears apart") and adjectives ("*extremely atrocious* punishments and deaths"), leaving no room in the monarch for moderation or mercy towards Catholics. Yepes, for his part, takes into account the disadvantages that he believed Elizabeth had (in her birth, her sex, and her counselors) that influenced who she became, yet still places her in an irredeemable position: "She resolved to leave God for the world, and the eternal Kingdom and its blessedness, for a miserable, temporal kingdom. And thus, she gave herself over to unbridled pleasures and indulgences, and her government to the soulless men that her misfortune and her parents' sins had given her as Advisors"[31] (12). This Elizabeth has turned her back on God and traded him for the world, completely given herself over to unrestrained lust, and handed over her kingdom to ruthless men. Because Elizabeth will not let go of her temporal reign and lust, she must oppose the Pope and those who follow him in challenging her choice. She cannot be tolerant towards the opposition if she is to continue as queen, and she cannot have affection for those who rebuke her sins if she is unwilling to repent. This queen's lack of control over her passions, as stated in Christian prince treatises, is precisely what makes her a tyrant (Arellano, "Decid" 161; Quintero, "Body" 83). In other words, this and Ribadeneyra's representation of Elizabeth seem fundamentally inconsistent with the queen of *La española inglesa* who – even if she is slightly hard-hearted and perhaps even greedy – is in full control of her passions, generous towards Isabela, faithful to her word, and imparts justice without bias.

In addition to the shared subject matter describing Elizabethan England, another marked connection between the histories of Ribadeneyra and Yepes and *La española inglesa* is their focus on the exemplum. The *Oxford English Dictionary* defines "exemplum" as "an example; spec. a moralizing tale or parable; an illustrative story," and the dictionary of the Royal Spanish Academy adds that the story is presented "either to be imitated and followed, if it is good and honest, or to be avoided, if it is evil." According to Maravall, the bulk of medieval didactic literature was collections of exempla, and in the sixteenth and seventeenth centuries these collections were continually being reprinted throughout Europe, thus showing the centrality of the exemplum in literature of this time (205–6). Rhetoricians that influenced Spain, such as Erasmus, Juan Luis Vives, and Saavedra Fajardo, discussed the greater power of the exemplum over the precept to move audiences[32] through vivid accounts, especially when these were historical and closer to the audience (Pineda 33–7; Maravall 208, 215). Maravall offers Ribadeneyra's work as a "very clear case" (*caso clarísimo*) of argumentation by exempla, where concrete stories have the force of empirical proof to support the doctrine proposed (206, 210), so one could say that Ribadeneyra's book is a model for the use of the exemplum. However, even though Cervantes' common focus with Ribadeneyra on the exemplum does not necessarily connect his text to the Jesuit's, that *La española inglesa* highlights Catholic exempla from Elizabethan England does seem to show a link between these works.

Complexities of the *Novela ejemplar*

As discussed in chapter 2, a relentless emphasis on the exemplum was one of the most important original adaptations of Ribadeneyra and Yepes of their source narrative by Sander. In both cases, the exempla are particular historical narratives related to the English Reformation framed as graphic paradigms of God's judgment and providence to teach readers what course of action they should follow or avoid.[33] Likewise, *La española inglesa*, published in the collection of "exemplary novels," is centered on the exemplum, especially as applied to Catholic readers and concerning the English persecution, but Cervantes' use of the exemplum seems more complex and ambiguous than the medieval one, likely because exempla were becoming increasingly problematic during this time.[34]

Despite extensive study of the topic, scholars find no consensus in ascertaining what Cervantes meant by "exemplary" when used to refer to the twelve *novelas* that comprise the exemplary novels. His prologue to that collection reads: "if you look carefully, there is no novel from which a profitable example cannot be extracted; and if were not that I wish to avoid overextending this subject, perhaps I would show you the delicious and honest fruit that could be extracted either from all of them together or from each on their own"[35] (52). Cervantes does not specify of what each novel is a "profitable example," but he indicates that they exemplify something all together as well as each individually if readers are actively engaged with the text ("if you look carefully"). The most obvious understanding of "exemplary" in the period – as recognized by the censor Fr. Juan Bautista, who wrote that Cervantes' stories "teach with their examples to flee vices and pursue virtues" – is in the sense of the medieval exemplum as used by the ecclesiastical histories – that is, learning from people and events – in which case the novels would provide both positive and negative moral models to follow (Cervantes, *Novelas* 45; Boyd 11–12). Cervantes, however, had already problematized exemplarity in *Don Quixote* (Cruz 18–19; Forcione, "Afterword" 334) and seems to do it again in the novels, since some have no explicit lesson and the actions of certain characters raise moral questions rather than answer them.[36] It is possible that the exemplary novels as a collection precisely resist this typical use, and as Stephen Boyd maintains, the adjective is ironic, satirizing Cervantes' contemporaries' obsession with literature always having to teach virtue (28).[37]

Most scholars believe that the exemplary novels are exemplary at least aesthetically, that is, that Cervantes is providing several examples of ways in which to write good *novelas* in Spanish (Boyd 12, 40–1). This notion is bolstered by Cervantes' explanation in the aforementioned prologue about being the first Spanish novelist: "I consider myself, and it is so, to be the first who has written novels in the Castilian language, since the many novels that are printed in Castilian have all been translated from foreign tongues, and these are my own, neither copied nor stolen"[38] (*Novelas* 52). Cervantes here seems to claim to write something new in the Spanish language, so critics posit that he intended the adjective "exemplary," at least in one sense, to describe his *novelas* as models for the creation of a new genre. Forcione, more specifically, argues that "exemplary" is a kind of *novela* that is different from the standard salacious Italian *novella* that was considered harmful to readers (*Humanist* 7–8; Boyd 11). Ruth El Saffar understood all of Cervantes' *novelas* as being morally exemplary. She saw *La española inglesa* as a more or less traditional romance concerned with depicting the meaning and complexity of marriage and, particularly, with exploring the depths of the social and religious implications of the marriage between Ricaredo and Isabela (151). Despite the apparent loss of freedom, El Saffar argued that within the romance, the characters' return to society and religion implicates their free will and choice because they come to understand that their search for a "liberty of flight" is illusory and that true freedom can only come through acknowledgment of "a reality beyond the self" (163). Therefore, when Isabela chooses to marry Ricaredo over entering the convent, she does so freely and thus reveals herself as a complex character, a position also held by Forcione.

La española inglesa, at least, seems to be responding to the moral exemplum as used by Ribadeneyra and Yepes with a measure of ambiguity that keeps the aesthetic and entertainment value of novels in play.[39] The signal that the story is an exemplum is clear in the novel's conclusion, where the narrator sums up the moral lesson that evil can be redeemed and won over by virtue and beauty: "This novel could teach us the extent of the power of virtue and of beauty, since they are sufficient together and each individually, to win the love even of enemies; and how Heaven can bring forth out of our greatest adversities, our greatest gain"[40] (Cervantes, *Novelas* 283). This passage explicitly refers to the story's ability to teach, and yet the conditional tense of the verb "could" (*podría*) may be deemphasizing the didactic aspect of the work.[41] In other words, the novel *could* teach something useful to the reader, but this lesson does not seem to be essential. If Cervantes had intended to stress the exemplum, alternative constructions could be "this novel shows us" or "we see in this novel," which would be closer to the unambiguous constructions that Ribadeneyra and Yepes use in these cases.[42] The effect of the ambiguous terminology of Cervantes could be, on one hand, to satisfy critics who believe that novels must have a moral lesson to be valuable or, on the other, to subtly undermine that position. That *La española inglesa* has an explicit moral lesson – unlike most of the exemplary novels – shows that Cervantes is interested in moral exemplarity and may be responding to the exempla of Ribadeneyra's history.

In fact, these two works may also be linked textually, since an uncanny resemblance appears in the conclusions to Cervantes' novel and Ribadeneyra's *Historia*, emphasizing that God can turn evil things to our advantage. The second part of Ribadeneyra's volume concludes: "In all of this is seen the ineffable mercy and boundless goodness of the Lord, who from the greatest evils of the world brings out the greatest goods"[43] (1325). Similarly, the last paragraph in *La española inglesa* reads: "This novel could teach us the extent of the power of virtue and of beauty … and how Heaven can bring forth out of our greatest adversities, our greatest gain" (Cervantes, *Novelas* 283). Both texts display the language parallels "greatest evils/adversities" and "greatest goods/gain." Granted, the lesson that God turns bad things into advantageous situations for his people is as old as the story of the patriarch Joseph. For centuries, the Joseph account – which, incidentally, has strong parallels to this novel, as will be discussed below – provided comfort to Jews, Christians, and Muslims.[44] Thus, the similar language may simply be derived from a common source, namely, the Genesis narrative. The wording of the biblical text, however, is not neatly summarized by a narrator. Instead, Joseph tells his brothers: "But as for you, ye thought evil against me; *but* God meant it unto good, to bring to pass, as *it is* this day, to save much people alive" (Gen. 50:20, *Authorized King James Version*). Despite these differences, it is possible that the textual similarities in Ribadeneyra's history and Cervantes' novel could stem from another common source, such as early modern sermons or devotional writings. Another widely read text that may be a source of *La española inglesa* is Ribadeneyra's *Tratado de la tribulación*, which outlined the theological basis for the second part of the *Historia* and Yepes' text. As discussed, the Jesuit explains in this volume that, as can be clearly seen in the Bible and in the writing of the church fathers, God sometimes uses calamity and evil for the good of his church, the crucifixion being the prime example, but Joseph's story is also specifically referenced[45] (Rivadeneira 224–5). In fact, he explains that God allows heresy for this purpose, using words similar to those in the final lesson of *La española inglesa* of "greatest goods/evils": "In what may better shine the immense and sovereign goodness of the Lord than in bringing out such great goods as those we have mentioned, of such a great and horrific evil as is heresy? That our God may be so good that the greatest evils in the world may serve him for such great goods!"[46] (Rivadeneira 224). Even so, at minimum, Ribadeneyra's *Tratado* shows that the theological lesson from Joseph was very present in the minds of early modern Spaniards and may even point to a more direct connection between Ribadeneyra's *Historia* and Cervantes' text, especially given the English persecutions context. Nevertheless, the additional lesson in the novel that beauty and virtue can even win the love of enemies – alluding to the possibility of friendship between adversaries – is very different from that in the ecclesiastical history: that enemies are completely irredeemable, and one can only learn from their destruction.

Some of the differences between *La española inglesa* and the histories hinge on generic distinctions. *La española inglesa*, probably written around 1605 (Johnson, "Production" 389–95; de Armas 92–4),[47] seems to be most closely aligned with the theme of providence and perseverance in Yepes' work and in the second part of Ribadeneyra's *Historia*. However, despite the story of Isabela being one of suffering, the overall tone of the novel seems much more optimistic than the histories because of the former's Byzantine novel tropes and the latter's devotional emphasis. Thus, the novel appropriately ends in a happy marriage, and while Yepes' text offers consolation in eternal and unseen realities – suffering will be rewarded in the afterlife – *La española inglesa* promises earthly reversals of fortune and rewards – that is, riches and happiness in this life as well as in the afterlife. Further, the focus of the exempla in the novel is generally positive and conciliatory in the midst of religious difference, with lessons like "virtue can conquer even enemies" and "even though very bad things happen, these can turn out to be very advantageous." The ecclesiastical histories, conversely, are largely concerned with negative exempla to avoid – because orthodoxy and the Pope's authority must be defended – and with the ultimate defeat of one's adversaries and heresy, whether in this life or the next, because ecclesiastical histories rely on continuity between biblical literature and church history that points to eschatological victory and justice. In other words, if the heretics are not ultimately punished, then, theologically, God is unjust.

Another important generic difference between the use of the exemplum in Cervantes' novel and in the ecclesiastical histories is that the exempla of the latter are based on characters that are rather static: saints, Catholics, and virtuous people (Catherine, Mary Tudor, Mary Stuart, Philip II) against heretics and monsters (Henry VIII, Anne Boleyn, Elizabeth Tudor). The Catholics are virtuous; the heretics are vicious. The actions of each group are fixed so that Catholic exempla seem to be free from wrongdoing, and heretic exempla are incapable of doing anything good. As discussed in the first two chapters of this book, these binaries were necessary to support the primary goal of the ecclesiastical histories – to rally around English Catholics and to oppose Elizabeth – by exhorting Spaniards to choose the "right" side and oppose the "wrong" one. As seen, in order to uphold this representation of the English Reformation, the ecclesiastical histories glossed over historical complexities, especially in the first part of Ribadeneyra's *Historia*, where military intervention was being promoted and Catholics had to be persuaded to support a new crusade.

The exempla of Cervantes' novel, however, are based on more complex characters that act in unexpected ways, as is characteristic of that author, and virtue and vice are not essentialist, that is, necessarily attached to a religious identity such as being Catholic or heretic. As seen in the discussion of Calderón's tragedy, complexity of characterization was more likely once Elizabeth had been removed from the scene and was no longer an active threat. Additionally, as Boyd argues, Cervantes does not use his characters merely to illustrate good and bad qualities and behaviors, but rather to "explor[e] vice and virtue, or, more accurately, the dynamics of their subtle coexistence, *in* his characters rather than *through* them" (29). Thus, Cervantes employs generic characters in complex and contradictory ways (Boyd 29). For instance, the Catholic Clotaldo is not a model of virtue – he shows greed, unreliability, and cowardice – and his son Ricaredo must undergo a series of tests to prove his virtue, perhaps even purging himself of his father's sins, as Clamurro suggests (112). In fact, Clotaldo seems to embody the kind of Catholic condemned by Carvajal as "lukewarm" (Zimic 157; Casalduero 125; Carvajal, *Epistolario* 238). Conversely, Queen Elizabeth is presented as a just, hospitable, and prudent queen despite being for Spaniards a heretic *par excellence* against Catholicism in her kingdom. In this sense, the use of exemplum in Ribadeneyra and Yepes appears to be somewhat static and predictable, while the use in Cervantes is more consistent with the complexity of characters of the modern novel and supports the idea that his novel is an unconventional romance, as Forcione argued. The protagonists of *La española inglesa* are more dynamic and closer to the reader than the stereotypes that Ribadeneyra and Yepes employ, and as was argued for *La cisma de Ingalaterra*, as such, the characters would be a better mirror in which Spaniards could see themselves. In fact, Canavaggio argues that Cervantes "gives us an infinitely subtler picture of the Muslim world than the caricature-like distortions to which we are more often exposed in the polemical writings of his contemporaries" (81–2). This seems to be the case in Cervantes' charitable portrayal of *moriscos*, the Muslim converts to Christianity – most notably, the episodes of Ana Felix and Ricote's encounter with Sancho Panza in *Don Quixote*.[48] Cervantes' refusal to caricature, then, also seems transferable to his portrayal of the English and of Elizabeth in particular.

Arguably, one reason for including a benevolent Elizabeth in *La española inglesa* is to move the plot forward, as Ruth El Saffar proposed, especially to show the explicit lesson of the novel – that virtue and beauty can conquer (or better, *enamorar*) enemies – in action.[49] A flat and utterly cruel Elizabeth would be difficult to win over. However, the strategy that most complicates Cervantes' exempla in *La española inglesa* is the gemination, or doubling, of the ideal Isabela and the English queen that displays the baroque obsession with mirroring so pervasive in the period and in the works of Cervantes.[50] Both characters share a name

("Elizabeth" is "Isabel" in Spanish), both display Christian virtues, both are wise and truthful, and each admires the other despite being enemies. In some respects, they are opposite images of one another – Spanish/English, Catholic/Protestant, queen/slave – and these qualities complicate the correspondence because it is unclear at which point the parallels suggest similarities or differences or are simply ironic.[51] In fact, the mirroring of Isabela and Elizabeth does not stop with them: Isabela also reflects the Virgin Mary and carries the name of Isabella the Catholic. By extension, Queen Elizabeth echoes these figures as well.[52] Ribadeneyra's Elizabeth, having no laudable qualities, would be too different from the young Spanish protagonist for the mirroring to be useful. Interestingly, in the novel Isabela is the one who becomes monstrous, rather than Elizabeth,[53] and instead of the outward state reflecting her inner self and sinful actions, it stands as a test for others to see beyond her outer ugliness into her pure soul, adhering to another baroque obsession with deception of the senses and disenchantment (*desengaño*).[54]

Also, this mimicking game can be extended to allusions to monarchs of other genres and texts, like the biblical Pharaoh and Solomon or Isabella the Catholic in *Guzmán de Alfarache*. *La española inglesa* has marked parallels to the biblical story of Joseph: both stories feature young exiles who learn another language and become very prominent before a foreign monarch, while the exiles' parents mourn their loss and finally become reunited with their lost children.[55] Elizabeth's generosity in welcoming Isabela's parents echoes Pharaoh's response to Joseph's family when they arrive in Egypt. References to Cervantes' queen being "hard-hearted" also recall the biblical epitaph of Pharaoh recounted in the book of Exodus and reiterated by Saint Paul (Exod. 4:21–2, 8:19, 14:4; Rom. 11:17–18). Elizabeth's greatness – which Ricaredo says Isabela's parents traveled to see – and wisdom could also gesture towards the greatness of Solomon as witnessed by the Queen of Sheba (1 Kings 10:1–13; 2 Chron. 9:1–12; Matt. 12:42; Luke 11:31).

While these connections may seem tenuous to the modern reader, they were ubiquitous in European Catholic literature, especially in the ecclesiastical histories of Sander, Ribadeneyra, and Yepes, as explained in chapters 1 and 2. In these histories, Henry VIII is the English monarch most often connected to these biblical figures, although Elizabeth Tudor sometimes is implicit in the imagery. Henry is equated to the wise and pious Solomon who fell into idolatry because of seductive women, particularly Anne Boleyn (Highley 162; Ribadeneyra 975; Sander 118). His hardness against and persecution of Catholics is likened to Pharaoh's futile attempts to destroy the Jews, and Queen Elizabeth in her role of tyrant against Catholics participates in this allusion (Ribadeneyra 994, 1201, 1306). Thus, Elizabeth's status as a monarch and daughter of Henry, coupled with clear textual parallels with the story of Joseph and more subtle references to her as "hard-hearted," would have linked her to these biblical kings.

Once more, the connections between *La española inglesa* and the ecclesiastical histories seem too strong to be coincidental, and Cervantes again disrupts the reader's expectations by ironically creating positive associations between the English queen and the biblical figures. Instead of coupling Elizabeth with the tyrant Pharaoh of the Moses story, like Ribadeneyra and Sander do, Cervantes puts the queen in the role of the earlier, generous Pharaoh who promoted Joseph and saved the Jews from extinction during the great famine. Even though the negative reference to her hard heart would also connect her to the tyrant Pharaoh, the statement that her heart was softened already is a change from the biblical Egyptian king, who is known for never having relented from his hardness. Even in the comparison with Solomon, if indeed a subtle allusion is intended in the novel, Elizabeth appears as the great and wise Solomon,[56] not the king who has fallen into idolatry because of his vices. Cervantes' characterization seems to be in direct opposition with Ribadeneyra's portrayal of her as a monstrous tyrant and with Yepes' argument that Elizabeth had given herself over completely to her lusts.

Additionally, if the mirroring extends to allusions to monarchs of other texts, it is possible to see a subtle connection between the Elizabeth of *La española inglesa* and Isabella the Catholic in *Guzmán de Alfarache*. First, when Elizabeth exclaims upon hearing Isabela's name that "she lacks nothing except to be called Isabela 'the Spaniard,' so that I would not desire any other perfection in her," the mention of "Isabela the Spaniard" recalls the well-known Spanish Catholic monarch (*Novelas* 250). More importantly, Cervantes' admiration for *Guzmán de Alfarache* is well known, and some of his works reflect this admiration, including *La española inglesa*, which displays numerous similarities with the interpolated story of Ozmín and Daraja. Both stories share tropes of "captivity tales"[57] and begin with a historical conflict of Spanish history: one against England, the other against the Moors. Like Isabela, Daraja is taken by Christians who "sacked great riches, capturing some people, among whom were Daraja, Moorish maiden, only daughter of the mayor of that fortress" (Alemán 215). Daraja, too, is the only daughter of an important man of the region and is counted among other valuable treasures ("great riches"). Although Daraja is seven years older than Isabela, both have rare beauty, grace, and discretion, and both speak two languages flawlessly. The narrator continues in a way that seems lifted from *La española inglesa*:

> She spoke Castilian so well that it would be difficult for anyone not to consider her an old Christian, for in a group of local maidens she could pass for one of them. The King esteemed her highly, believing her to be of great worth, so he sent her to the Queen, his wife, who did not esteem her less. The Queen received her joyfully, not only because of her merit and her lineage as a descendant of kings, being the daughter of such an honorable gentleman; but also to see whether the girl could help her win over the city without further damage or fighting. Thus, the Queen endeavored to treat Daraja very well, giving her the gifts and advantages that the monarch gave other women close to her. And so, not as a captive, but as a relative, the Queen began to dote on her, hoping that a woman of such merit and great beauty of body would not house an ugly soul.[58] (Alemán 216)

The parallels between these texts are striking: the king thinks Daraja is of great worth and gives the girl to the queen, who also sees her worth and lavishes her with gifts and advantages as she does with the closest women to her, as if the girl were her relative rather than a slave. Further, both texts have a subtext of passing and dissimulation, analyzed by Barbara Fuchs and others.[59]

The text has other strong echoes, but what is important here is that, given these similarities, it is reasonable to suppose that readers of *La española inglesa* and *Guzmán de Alfarache* would also see a resemblance between those texts in the scenes of Isabela before Elizabeth Tudor and of Daraja before Isabella the Catholic and connect the Spanish and English queens when reading Cervantes' novel. These positive associations of Elizabeth with the intertext of the biblical kings and of Isabella the Catholic would seem to indicate that, ironically, Elizabeth is the exemplum of a good Christian monarch. If taken as more than just a simple idealist representation in a kind of fairy tale, this compliment to Elizabeth could certainly be shocking to the original audience, but because it is subtle and elusively suggested by intertextuality, the connection could be understood as a playful literary experiment in imitation that merely strengthens the gemination in the text. If, then, *La española inglesa* shows intertextual connections with multiple sources, like Matteo Bandello's *novella* of Ligurina, the biblical story of Joseph, and the interpolated tale of Ozmín and Daraja, what would be gained by introducing additional echoes of the narratives in Ribadeneyra's and Yepes' histories, and what can be deduced from this choice? While it is impossible, of course, to reconstruct Cervantes' stylistic choices and even to affirm with certainty which sources he employed or allusions he intended, it is possible to offer suggestions about his use of the ecclesiastical histories based on the historical context of the time and what is known of Cervantes' interests.

Spain in English Events

To begin, it is possible to suggest several literary or aesthetic reasons for choosing to engage with the ecclesiastical histories in *La española inglesa*. The subtexts proposed for the novel in this chapter were all well known in early modern Spain, and weaving these together into one new, multifaceted story would show Cervantes' wit, or *ingenio*, in imitating sources in a new way and would certainly surprise and delight readers. As noted, the Spanish ecclesiastical histories were immensely popular in Cervantes' lifetime and for decades after his death, largely because they were truly entertaining. To engage historical narratives that bordered on the fictional – with six-fingered women, miraculous punishments, and monstrous births – may have appealed to Cervantes' strong interest in the intersection between poetry and history, idealism and verisimilitude.[60] Moreover, the ecclesiastical histories were Trent-approved stories that epitomized teaching and delighting, another dictum that, as discussed, is explored in *La española inglesa*, especially in its conclusion.

Additionally, it is possible that Cervantes wished to create his own "story of passing" in imitation of the narrative of Joseph or of Ozmín and Daraja, in which case the setting of England would be essential to the plot, since only there were Catholics persecuted and the English sack of Cádiz would explain Isabela's arrival in England. Moreover, around the time of the writing of this novel, Spaniards had a renewed interest in the topic of England because of the death of Elizabeth Tudor in 1603 and the Treaty of London of 1604. At that time, as mentioned, Cervantes was in Valladolid, the center of the Anglo-Spanish negotiations and information about English Catholics, and around the same time, Lope de Vega would publish his epitaphs on Elizabeth and Henry Tudor and Mary Stuart, so it would not be unusual that Cervantes' writing would turn to England.

Nevertheless, aesthetic reasons do not seem to be the only justification for reimagining Ribadeneyra's description of Catholic persecutions with a more positive English queen, given the particular historical context in which it was written of changing social and literary perspectives towards England. As discussed above, it is possible that *La española inglesa* is a reimagining of the life of Catholics in England after the time of Elizabeth, as some scholars propose, though given Cervantes' pride from his participation at Lepanto and his endorsement of Catholic ideals in the *Persiles*, among other things, it seems difficult to put too much weight on his positive representation of Elizabeth or to understand this as support for Anglo-Spanish rapprochement. Yet, as chapter 3 discussed, the death of Elizabeth Tudor and James Stuart's enthronement brought a truce with England and allowed Spaniards to hope that the persecution of Catholics in that country would end. Perhaps Cervantes was among these, and he explores this idea in the novel, though, as Luisa de Carvajal recorded, the persecutions under James persisted without Spaniards knowing it, to the point that Carvajal says they became worse than under Elizabeth Tudor. At minimum, Cervantes' novel could be seen as an illustration of the setting that many Spaniards imagined was true of English Catholics under James I, a perspective that Luisa de Carvajal endeavored to correct by sending information about the true condition of Catholics at that time. What can be suggested perhaps with more confidence is that the scandal of the sins of Henry VIII and Anne Boleyn with the resulting birth of Elizabeth Tudor seems to be more distant and less urgent in the Spanish imagination than it was during the lifetime of the English queen, as also noted with Calderón's play. Nevertheless, though Spanish popular opinion about Elizabeth Tudor was largely shaped by Ribadeneyra's view, in practice it was likely never monolithic. For many Spaniards, including Carvajal, with the arrival of King James I, the legitimate son of the Catholic Mary Stuart – that is, not the embodiment of heresy or incest – the door for political negotiation and, perhaps, fraternal and maybe even theological restoration was once more opened.

Yet another possible reason for Cervantes to set *La española inglesa* in England and to interact with Ribadeneyra's view in the Spanish ecclesiastical histories is to defamiliarize Spanish problems for reflection and self-critique. Given that the histories were explicitly mirrors of princes and encouraged Spanish readers to look at England to imitate good examples and to avoid bad ones, Cervantes feasibly has a similar aim that could involve different early modern Spanish concerns.

One concern obliquely addressed could be the challenges and consequences of imposing religion by force, which had been done in Spain and was being done all over Europe with the Wars of Religion. Other works by Cervantes gesture at this concern – for instance, the scene of the Toledan merchants in chapter 4 of the first part of *Don Quixote*[61] – and therefore, this idea would be within Cervantes' thematic concerns. As discussed, the setting of fear among "secret Catholics" in the novel ironically mirrors the condition of Jews and Muslims on the peninsula, who were forced to convert lest they be condemned. Putting this problem on English territory, in addition to being subtle and passing censorship, could invite readers to explore the complexities of the issue more dispassionately because it would now be distant to their personal experience. This allusion would underscore differences of opinions among Spaniards concerning religion that challenged Black Legend stereotypes in England about Spain's unity in alleged religious fanaticism and brutality.[62]

An additional Spanish problem defamiliarized in the novel is Spain's obsession with transparency of religion and nationality (Fuchs, *Passing* 106). In fact, scholars have cogently argued that since Isabela's parents were merchants and their name is not given, she probably was a *converso* – a Jewish convert to Christianity (Johnson, *Don Quixote* 8, 12; Da Costa Fontes 743; Johnson, "Fecundidad" 523). If so, her profession of faith in Spain would have caused suspicion, and it is ironic that she should be the model Catholic, never losing her faith, and the model Spaniard. It would also be ironic for a *converso* not to be forced to adopt a foreign religion (Protestantism), especially considering that Daraja appears to convert to Christianity in Guzmán's tale. Thus, through irony and defamiliarization Isabela's exemplary life can challenge some Spaniards' hypocritical claims that the faith of new converts should always be suspect and that a true Spaniard is one who has no Jewish or Muslim blood – as mocked in *El retablo de las maravillas*. In fact, in characters like Clotaldo and the queen, as discussed, the novel privileges action over identity – Catholic/Protestant or Spanish/English – to determine who is virtuous and should be emulated. Thus, Clotaldo's actions show imperfections among Catholic ranks and invite Spaniards to acknowledge these deficiencies, and he, along with Isabela and the other characters, challenge Spanish audiences to judge others based on their actions rather than their identity. Possibly, this could also be Cervantes' response to Spanish Black Legend stereotypes and attacks on Catholics: not a wholistic endorsement of all Spaniards, like Lope's seeming response, but a show of characters who break the stereotype, especially positive ones.

Perhaps a clearer justification for Cervantes' engagement with the ecclesiastical histories and redeployment of a modified representation of Elizabeth is a theological reason, since not all exemplary novels have an explicit moral lesson, but this one does. Furthermore, the moral lesson that God turns the greatest adversities to gain explicitly connects the novel to the biblical lesson of the patriarch Joseph, a connection that is also supported by narrative parallels between both tales, as discussed. Thus, the moral of the novel would have connected for the audience Isabela's story with that of Joseph and would have renewed the ancient exempla of virtue and providence to fit a contemporary context where Catholics were suffering in England or taken captive by corsairs, as Cervantes himself had been. In this scenario, the story would be less about the specific political situation in England and more universally about how to respond to adversity, especially at a time of growing skepticism towards faith and perhaps even virtue, as the novel *Don Quixote* illustrates. This message that hope, virtue, and perseverance are rewarded by providence also corresponds with the message of the last novel by Cervantes and the one he most prized, the *Persiles*.

Conclusion

As argued in this chapter, the shared subject matter and emphasis on Catholic exempla in Ribadeneyra's *Historia*, Yepes' *Historia particular*, and *La española inglesa* would have spontaneously linked these works in the minds of readers – especially because of their common theme of Christian providence in the suffering of Catholics. Thus, it is possible to recover lost connections that original readers would have made by analyzing *La española inglesa* within this literary context. In fact, *La española inglesa* cannot be fully understood apart from the Spanish ecclesiastical histories. Cervantes' exploration of the exemplum is derived, in part, from the histories and seems shaped by Cervantes' great interest in the relationship between history and fiction that is evident in *La española inglesa*. Thus, in the ecclesiastical histories the exemplum is extracted from real or fictional models – historical, biblical, literary – that are often presented as flawless and in polarizing binaries. Cervantes, however, seems to explore how history, or an alternative fictional representation of it, can teach without being slavishly dependent on flat characterization, hagiography, and essentialism.

Moreover, Cervantes shows that exempla such as Elizabeth and Isabela can be complex and complimentary rather than antithetical – that they can mirror each other in some ways while being opposites in others. Cervantes also seems to indicate that mirroring can be amplified almost infinitely, echoing various figures in multiple texts and perhaps suggesting that virtuous characters and hope can be found anywhere, across religious, racial, and literary boundaries. In the end, *La española inglesa* seems to unite the moral exemplum that virtue will be rewarded and that beauty and love will overcome enmities with the aesthetic exemplum that good novels may teach but that their artistic beauty is their own reward. Just like teaching and delighting are equally important, exemplum and entertainment appear to share equal weight for Cervantes.

What conclusion can readers make of Cervantes' changes to Spain's more or less "official" historical stance towards Elizabeth in the Spanish ecclesiastical histories? As discussed, the novel can be justified as an aesthetic experiment in blending traditional and new stories and in subverting readers' expectations with surprise (*admiratio*) and irony. As Zimic has pointed out, this novel follows the basic story of one of the novellas by Matteo Bandello, but *The Spanish English Girl* also echoes the Moorish story of Ozmín and Daraja in the popular picaresque novel *Guzmán de Alfarache* and, more importantly, the narrative of the Jewish patriarch Joseph in the Bible. Creating a new story with these subtexts and setting it in the context of English events, a popular topic at the turn of the seventeenth century, certainly would have caused *admiratio*, especially if Queen Elizabeth was now ironically sitting in the place of Isabella the Catholic or of the generous Pharaoh who helped Joseph and his family during the great famine. Doubtless, the Elizabeth of Cervantes is also consistent with the writer's masterful novelizing of characters that were often flat in literature, as he does with *moriscos* like Ricote. Thus, Cervantes may be suggesting that Ribadeneyra's Elizabeth, who is incapable of repenting, may be a more complex character, similar to how Lope and Calderón included "positive" traits in their characterizations. However, Cervantes surprisingly went beyond these authors and allowed for moral positive traits in Elizabeth, a heretic and enemy of Spain, such as being truthful, just, and generous towards enemies. This characterization of the English queen not only removes distance between herself and Isabela and makes them better doubles of each other, but also removes distance between Spaniards and the queen. In the end, Cervantes seems to suggest that England is a mirror for Spain to look into in order to examine herself, as Ribadeneyra also proposes upon the defeat of the Armada and the persecution of Catholics, and therefore, Spain should not be too quick to cast the first stone.

Conclusion

One of the goals of this book has been to show how transnational and interdisciplinary studies can enrich our understanding of Anglo-Spanish relations and perceptions. The literary production of a country is fertile ground for exploring how its people perceived and responded to their opponents, as well as what kinds of discourse shaped their thinking. Creative choices of content, genre, and rhetoric, especially when the same characters and events are adapted across different kinds of literary texts, belie particular biases of authors, including how they position themselves with respect to their social majority's ideological stance and, in turn, how they shape it. It is also vital to ground literary works not merely within their own ideological contexts but also in response to opposing ones to approximate the frameworks in which original readers of these texts likely accessed them.

Ribadeneyra's *Historia* decisively left a strong imprint upon the Spanish imagination and used the discourse of heresy and martyrdom to deploy not only an interpretation of England's actions but also an understanding of Spain's image and role in defending Catholicism. Although it is not surprising that an early modern theological text full of scathing indictments of heretics would become uninteresting to literary critics and eventually drop out of the literary canon, it is now necessary to bring back Ribadeneyra's *Historia* to attain a fuller understanding of the worldview it helped produce and which is embedded in literary artefacts of the period. As shown in this study, once Ribadeneyra's view is brought back into the canonical picture, the textual parallels and echoes of his work are everywhere. To be sure, some of these apparent echoes could arise from different sources – sermons, devotional works, plays – but when all the pieces are examined together, they point to Ribadeneyra's work, supported by Yepes', especially when a biographical document reveals a direct link with the author, such as Lope's praise of Ribadeneyra's style. The next necessary step towards gauging the breadth of Ribadeneyra's reception and influence is to read sermons and private letters from around the time to see if these parallels and echoes emerge.

This study also reveals that Ribadeneyra's and Yepes' strategies of representation that included monstrous characters and idealized saints categorized according to their allegiance to the Pope were carefully selected and were part of a national vindication of Spanish identity and Christian zeal as well as a transnational effort to defend Roman Catholicism from Protestant attacks. As such, they had to present a unified Catholic front, undermine divisions, and gloss over the failures and weaknesses of Catholics in England and Spain. However, these inconsistencies are only exposed when reading the histories alongside the private letters of Luisa de Carvajal, who had first-hand experience of Catholic work and persecutions in England and who reveals multiple networks and survival strategies that English Catholics used to persevere under dire conditions and persecution. Furthermore, the comparison of negative characterizations in this book suggests that in the early modern period flat characters were increasingly unsatisfactory, which may help explain why Lope and Calderón sometimes include "positive" traits in their characterization of "heretics" for depth and why Cervantes utterly transforms Ribadeneyra's monstrous queen into a more realistic, novel character. A similar concern seems apparent in ecclesiastical histories, especially of Foxe, but also of Catholics, who pattern their histories after Eusebius and shy away from medieval hagiographies that included supernatural saints that were difficult to relate to and model (Freeman, *Great Searching* 130–2).

Throughout this study, different Anglo-Spanish fraternal and antagonistic links emerge, revealing, as would be expected, that Spain's relationship to England has not always been defined by antagonism and that Spaniards like Carvajal remembered fraternal links with England and appealed to them to move their compatriots to support the English mission. Nevertheless, antagonistic relationships and prejudices also were present to the point that Spaniards at times refused to support the English, even if they were Catholics. Perhaps nowhere are both fraternal and antagonistic links more vividly evident than in the very relics of the English Catholic martyrs who were sent to Spain, which paradoxically contained a symbol of both the beloved English martyr and the hated English executioner.

Since most of Ribadeneyra's and Yepes' material was from England, this book has modeled and employed research that has been done on related topics in the field of early modern English history and literary and theological studies – for example, on the generic characteristics of ecclesiastical histories and the literary analysis of Foxe's *Acts and Monuments*[1] – because this kind of scholarship has been more developed with respect to England than to Spain. This book has also aimed to show the urgency of focusing on understudied texts and comparing them with similar works. Weinreich's 2018 translation and critical edition of Ribadeneyra's ecclesiastical history is a much-needed resource that will hopefully provoke further study of that volume. A similar undertaking is necessary for Diego de Yepes' *Historia particular* in conjunction with an analysis of its influence and reception, as well as the Catholic martyrdom accounts that only survive in his text. Freddy Domínguez's contributions of placing the works of Spanish and English Catholics within the political Anglo-Spanish context – most notably in *Radicals in Exile* (2020) – is very valuable, and his current project examining Carvajal and Counter-Reformation political thought is eagerly awaited. Finally, Olid Guerrero and Fernández's *The Image of Elizabeth I in Early Modern Spain* (2019), contains helpful essays suggesting multiple ways to study Anglo-Spanish perceptions.

As Susannah Monta and Alison Shell have pointed out, there has been a recent push to redefine the linguistic, geographical, and literary boundaries of English Catholicism;[2] and as Domínguez and Weinreich propose, there is now a keener interest in understanding the English Reformation and early modern ecclesiastical histories from a broader European vantage point.[3] One contributing factor to the rising interest among English scholars on these topics has been the valuable English translations of Spanish material, such as Glyn Redworth's *The Letters of Luisa de Carvajal y Mendoza* (Pickering & Chatto, 2012); Weinreich's *Pedro de Ribadeneyra's Ecclesiastical History of the Schism of the Kingdom of England: A Spanish Jesuit's History of the English Reformation* (Brill, 2017); and Victor Houliston's *The Correspondence and Unpublished Papers of Robert Persons, SJ (1546–1610)*, a multivolume project whose first volume was made available in January 2018 (PIMS).

My book aims to contribute to this renewed interest in early modern scholarship and to offer a more sophisticated view of early modern Anglo-Spanish conflicts and negotiations at a crucial moment in the history of Spain and England. This intricate construction is important for understanding the past but is also essential for understanding present international religious conflicts, which cannot be addressed using simplistic models. Moreover, the works of Cervantes consistently seem to provide a complex, alternative view of a Spain that is capacious enough to give credit to individuals of all nations, races, and religions by offering exceptions to established stereotypes. *La española inglesa* could be read as a literary paradigm that, bringing together early modern and contemporary ideas, provides an alternative view of the Other and could be used not only to examine personal and national prejudices and wrongdoing, but also to foster tolerance and generosity in the face of difference.

Notes

Introduction

1 As Wizeman remarks, the terms "Catholic" and "Protestant" are not unambiguous, but they are helpful terms to describe the confessional divisions in England and the Continent at the time (4–5).
2 For a description of some of these prayers and ceremonies, see Rey 874–6.
3 All translations are mine, unless otherwise noted.
4 One notable exception is that Ribadeneyra's *Historia* was included with other select works by the same author in the series *Biblioteca de autores españoles*, published in Spain in 1899.
5 Even though these texts have not been studied as a corpus, some valuable effort has been made to connect these works to one another. Anne J. Cruz states that Carvajal could have read Yepes' work, but she does not reference Ribadeneyra's (*Life* 54). Antonio Carreño mentions Ribadeneyra's *Historia* in footnotes in conjunction with Lope's *La corona trágica*, but only to reference the martyrdoms of Catherine's confessor, John Fisher, and of a heretic (Lope de Vega, *corona* 410–11, 413–14). Javier Burgüillo has recently published helpful articles on the influence of Ribadeneyra's *Historia* and its connection to Lope, and Justo García Morales describes several ties between *El amor desatinado* and Ribadeneyra's text (xviii–xxii). Calderon's debt to Ribadeneyra's *Historia* in *La cisma de Ingalaterra* has also been analyzed, most extensively by A.A. Parker and Juan Manuel Escudero Batzán but also by Ignacio Arellano, María Cristina Quintero, and Braulio Fernández Biggs, who compares the tragedy with Shakespeare's *Henry VIII*. Olid Guerrero and Fernández published in 2019 a collection of essays on Elizabeth I, which, despite limitations in scope (in that it deals with only one monarch) and in form (in that it is not a monograph), is a significant contribution. With respect to Cervantes' *La española inglesa*, Américo Castro lists Yepes' history in

a footnote as an example of Spanish views of Elizabeth Tudor (323), but to my knowledge no other scholar developed this or Ribadeneyra's connection in print before my 2015 conference paper or Samson's 2019 essay in Olid Guerrero and Fernández's book.

6 See *Charitable Hatred.*

7 Most of these sources came from Elizabethan English "radicals in exile," as Domínguez's book argues.

8 By 1630 the hopes of an Anglo-Spanish rapprochement stimulated by the Spanish Match negotiations (1614–23) to arrange a marriage between James I's son Charles and Philip III's daughter María Ana were dead.

9 Here I draw from Susannah Monta's methodological approach in her study of Protestant/Catholic literary interdependence in *Martyrdom and Literature.*

1. The War Brewing in Europe and Its Weapons: Ecclesiastical Histories and Martyrologies

1 My use of "sacred histories" follows Simon Ditchfield's description in "What Was Sacred History?"

2 Freddy Domínguez argues that English Catholic exiles most effectively intervened in the Reformation battles through texts, citing Sir Thomas Englefield's exhortation to his co-religionists Cardinal Allen and Robert Persons, "we must fight with pens and papers" (*Radicals* 10).

3 For details about these editions, see Allison and Rogers.

4 As Anthony Grafton pointed out: "the great religious debates of the sixteenth and seventeenth centuries turned in substantial part on historical questions: questions about the origins and development of Christianity" ("Church History" 4).

5 The Vatican archive was established in 1612 to gather documents supporting Catholic theology and historical continuity (Ditchfield, "What Was Sacred History?" 88–9). On the Protestant side, the main collectors of massive documentation for ecclesiastical histories were Flacius Illyricus, who with the Centuriators gathered lists of heretics and their ideas and liturgies; Matthew Parker, first archbishop of Canterbury under Elizabeth I, who built a massive library for documents he compiled; MP Robert Cotton, who as an antiquarian owned an extraordinary manuscript collection; and Thomas Bodley, who gathered manuscripts and contemporary tracts in a new library in Oxford (1602) (Grafton, "Church History" 16–17).

6 See Freeman and Evenden *Religion and the Book* for a complete discussion of how Foxe's *Acts and Monuments* not only overcame insurmountable

challenges of publication but also transformed England's publication industry thereafter.

7 Freeman sees the dropping of the label as a typographical change, while Woolf considers it a significant departure from Eusebius' model because of the vast amount of information in Foxe's work that made it difficult to sustain the model (Freeman, *Great Searching* 43–4; Woolf, "Rhetoric" 245–6).

8 King notes that Foxe wrote for both "true" and "false" readers, categorized according to doctrinal lines, and that Harpsfield's *Dialogi sex* would have included Protestants and Jesuit seminarians among its readership ("Guides" 144, 148).

9 Freeman's *Great Searching* details numerous instances of Harpsfield's criticism to which Foxe responded. For an example regarding the account of Sir John Oldcastle, see *Great Searching* 261–2.

10 See Richard Verstegan's letter to Robert Persons discussing this need, cited in Highley 151–2.

11 The first librarian of the Bodleian Library, Thomas James, collected documents because he believed that Catholic manuscripts of the church fathers had been doctored "according to the pleasure of their Lorde the Pope" (Grafton, "Matthew Parker" 30).

12 Also spelled "Parsons," though, as Houliston notes, usually by his opponents ("Rehabilitating" 421).

13 The sources of Sander's ecclesiastical history were not as carefully documented as those in his earlier works, such as *De visibili Monarchia Ecclesiae* (1571), a work where Sander defended his theological reasons for the invasion of England and from which Ribadeneyra and Yepes also drew for their histories (Veech 231). However, Veech notes that Sander's *Schismatis Anglicani* was written for circulation among exiles, so it is not as carefully documented as his books to be printed (234, 241). Highley suggests that the lack of precision in Sander's latter work was due to his premature death in 1581, Rishton finishing his work in 1585, and the lack of availability of primary sources to Sander and Rishton in their exile from England (158).

14 For a good summary of Sander's political involvement in England and Ireland, see Domínguez, *Radicals* 23–6. For a fuller account, see Veech 198–229, 259ff.

15 One extant Spanish version by Robert Persons printed by Pedro Madrigal is titled *Relacion de algvnos martyrios que de nueuo han hecho los hereges en Inglaterra y de otras cosas tocantes a nuestra santa y catolica religion* (1590).

16 Nonetheless, Woolf is quick to note that the gap between romance and histories has been overstated ("Rhetoric" 250).

17 Highley suggests that Sander's readability and literary strategies may be responding to Foxe's engaging literary style (157).
18 King notes that Foxe acknowledged that readers were "delited with heroicall stories," thus showing awareness that martyrologies were entertaining ("Guides" 135).
19 Highley notes that Sander's direct dialogues give the history an appearance of authenticity but also make readers question whether they are fabrications (158).
20 In Shakespeare's *Macbeth*, one strong condemnation of Lady Macbeth is that she wants to be "unsexed" so as to have no "natural" feminine weakness and feeling. In this sense, Catherine here illustrates the opposite of Lady Macbeth.
21 "The king having ruined a most admirable constitution by unsatiable gluttony, was now grown so unwieldy that he could hardly enter by the doors, and was wholly unable to mount up the stairs. They lifted him up, sitting in a chair, by machinery, to the upper rooms of the palace. It was said that he had no blood left in his body, that it was corrupted into humours."

2. How English Monsters Overtook Spain: Ribadeneyra's Adaptation of *The English Schism* and Yepes' Sequel

1 Spencer Weinreich convincingly argues that Ribadeneyra is also defending the reputation of the Jesuits ("Distinctiveness"), though I believe the Spaniard's goal is broader. For Ribadeneyra's broader contribution to Catholic literature, see Roldán-Figueroa.
2 The production of Spanish ecclesiastical histories about England is a good example of the kinds of unlikely and unexpected cultural contact and exchange that Anne Cruz notes occurred after the English Catholic exiles arrived in Spain ("Introduction" xx).
3 Walsham´s introduction to her book *Charitable Hatred* offers a good summary of these ideas: "In a context in which truth was held to be single and indivisible, the persecution of dissident minorities was logical, rational and legitimate … To take steps to correct religious deviance was a moral duty and a divinely ordained obligation, an act of compassion inspired by the conviction that heresy was, quite literally, soul-destroying. To allow men and women to persist in heterodox opinion was in effect to condemn them to eternal torment in hell. Cruelty was thus a form of kindness" (1–2).
4 Weinreich suggests that because of his first-hand experience in England, the danger of heresy for Ribadeneyra was "vivid, viscerally real" ("Introduction" 60).

5 Although similar theological explanations of the judgment of the gods have been used since antiquity, Weinreich frames this explanation as "trauma processing" which seems a helpful way to look at this from a modern perspective ("Introduction" 4, 27–30).

6 Kagan notes that in the 620s, Isidore of Seville finished a brief history of the Visigoths that traced their lineage to Japheth, son of Noah, and described their victories over Rome. This history set the standard for later histories of "Hispania" and had two specific features: 1) a nostalgic view of a unified, Christian Hispania that was also prosperous and 2) a Hispania that was strong in military achievements in the defense of Christianity and against infidels (Muslims) and in reclaiming land the infidels had usurped (Kagan 18–20). Kagan adds that following this historical tradition, Ferdinand and Isabella commissioned historians to write their chronicles in the service of imperial conquests (18).

7 For example, this is mentioned in Cervantes' *Don Quixote* and in the preface to the *Novelas ejemplares*.

8 See Riley, 94–102, 163–78. Teresa of Avila notes this objection in her *Vida*, chapter 2, and Juan Luis Vives dedicates his fifth chapter of *De Institutione Feminae Christianae* to warn maidens that reading books "of arms and love" is dangerous and "not Catholic." Anne Cruz discusses this subject and points out that Cervantes' nomenclature of "novelas ejemplares" for his stories aimed to signal to censors and readers that his novels were entertaining, but not harmful ("Trucos" 25–7). See also Forcione, *Humanist* 7–8.

9 This common term appears in the Captive's Tale episode in *Don Quixote*, vol. 1, chs. 38, 41–2, regarding the ideal story that everyone in early modern Spain likes to hear, which includes strange places, characters, and events.

10 Pole told the English that he had come "to reconcyle, not to condemne, … not to destroy but to build, … not to compel but to call agayne" (Weikel, "Mary I" [*ODNB*]). See Duffy and Wizeman for a discussion of the extensive restoration project by Mary with the help of Pole.

11 "Aquí no hacen otra cosa sino sacar en [comedias] mofas de España, las más infames que pueden, y predicar en los púlpitos que es tierra de bestias salvajes cruelísimas, y que beben sangre humana; idólatras, que adoran palos y piedras y, lo peor, que es la abominación del antecristo y ramera de Babilonia, que es el Papa, y un panecito que decimos que es nuestro Dios."

12 The first of Foxe's four questions to "Papists," as Catholics were called, was: "how the church of Rome can be answerable to this hill of Siō: seing in the sayd church of Rome is, and hath bene now so many yeares such killing and slaying, such cruelty and tyranny shewed, such burning

& spoyling of christen bloud, such malice & mischiefe wrought, as in reading these historyes may to all the world appeare" (Foxe 17).

13 See, for example, King, "Fiction and Fact" 21.

14 For details about this plot, see Goodare, "Mary [Mary Stewart]," *ODNB*.

15 See Walton 164–72 for a discussion of the political complexity of Elizabeth in giving refuge to Mary.

16 Of course, the reasons for the attack of 1588 were multiple and the expedition had been planned for many years. See Parker, *Empire* 21–33.

17 This is part of Robert Persons' argument in defense of the *infanta* Isabel Clara Eugenia in *A Conference about the Next Succession to the Crowne of England* (Wiesman 594–5).

18 See De la Fuente, XXI.

19 "El ser español me obliga a desear y procurar todo lo que es honra y provecho de mi nación, como lo es que se sepa y se publique en ella la vida de la esclarecida reina doña Catalina, nuestra española, hija de los gloriosos Reyes Católicos don Fernando y doña Isabel, que fue mujer legítima del rey Enrique VIII de Inglaterra, y repudiada y desechada de él con los mayores agravios que se pueden imaginar, los cuales ella sufrió con increíble constancia y paciencia, y dió tan admirable ejemplo de santidad, que con muy justo título se puede y debe llamar espejo de princesas y reinas cristianas."

20 See, especially, Ribadeneyra 1203.

21 This text is also known as *Philopater*. Rey mistakenly affirms that the second part of the *Historia* was entirely original work by Ribadeneyra with some material from the *Concertatio* (883–7; Ribadeneyra 1203). Weinreich explains how Ribadeneyra adapted the *Philopater* ("Introduction" 57–8).

22 For a good rhetorical analysis of Persons' work, see Houliston, "Lord Treasurer."

23 "Lo mismo [que los martyrologios e historias pasadas] ... se ha hecho, y va continuando en esta persecución de Inglaterra, y texiendo una historia Eclesiastica, para salir despues a luz, quando nuestro Señor sea servido, que se puedan manifestar muchas cosas, que agora se callan por justas causas" (Yepes, "Prefacion al Letor" 2). In all of Yepes' citations the contractions have been expanded, and the use of *u* and *v*, as well as the long *s*, has been modernized.

24 "Porque los sucesos particulares se leen con mas gusto, y se entienden mejor, quando se saben sus causas, y la travazon que tienen con otras mas universales" (Yepes, "Prefacion al Letor" 3).

25 For a more detailed bibliography of what has been written about Yepes and his *Historia particular*, see Forteza, "Particular Providence."

26 *Vida, virtudes y milagros de la bienauenturada virgen Teresa de Iesus, madre fundadora de la nueua reformacion de la Orden de los Descalços y Descalças de Nuestra Senora del Carmen*. En Caragoça: Por Angelo Tauanno, 1606. Although the authorship of Yepes for this work has been disputed, Carretero has published documents linking the work back to the Bishop (Barrón García 168–9; Forteza, "Particular Providence").

27 For specific changes, see Rey 867–71 and the footnotes throughout Weinreich's English translation of the *Historia*.

28 Rogers details the martyrdom accounts that only survive in Yepes' book.

29 Hillgarth notes that by the 1600s all Flemish and Waloons (French speakers from Belgium) knew Castilian (61–4).

30 The term "La empresa de Inglaterra" was coined by Don Guerau de Spes around 1571 in connection with the Rudolfi plot (Parker, *Imprudent King* 206).

31 Elliott notes that Philip II had begun plans for an invasion of England to subdue the Dutch in 1583, when the Marquis of Santa Cruz first proposed it (284).

32 For the history of the college, see Williams. Yepes' *Historia* includes the story of some English Catholic seminarians who came to Spain and were imprisoned because of "averse en España concebido tan justa indignacion contra el nombre Ingles, assi por lo que actualmente passava, como por las muchas y muy grandes insolencias, insultos, y robos, que los hereges de Inglaterra avian hecho y hazian en la mar, y las costas de España" (747).

33 "Pues destos Sacerdotes tan siervos de Dios han venido a España los días passados algunos, y piensan que sera forçoso el venir mas, por causa de las grandes persecuciones de Inglaterra ... Y como la nación Española es tan Christiana y Catolica, y tan defensora de la Fê, tienen confiança que hallaran en ella acogida y caridad; aunque el vulgo les tiene grande aversion, por el odio que estos años se ha concebido al nombre Ingles."

34 "Confiamos en Dios que mucho menos peligro avra en el negocio de la Fê, con recebir y amparar a estos perseguidos por la misma Fê; antes que sera de mucho merecimiento, gloria, y honra de España; assi para con Dios, como para con los hombres, al aver socorrido a una nación tan amiga, y tan afligida por Dios, y por la misma España; como lo es la parte Catolica Inglesa, y esto en tiempo de tanto aprieto y necesidad, quando no tienen otro refugio, ni pueden casi acudir a otra parte del mundo, por las guerras y heregias que ay en todas partes; y quando su total remedio, despues de Dios le esperan de España, y de Españoles."

35 Yepes' *Historia* recounts the Roman Catholic response in writing volumes in English to refute the "English Bibles" that were written to "deceive the people" (22). Ribadeneyra was clearly an advocate for publishing in the

vernacular, stating in his preface that he believed it important to recount Sander's story in Castilian because it would profit everyone (Ribadeneyra 895, 899). By the time Yepes published his volume, Ribadeneyra had already cleared the path, although the clear devotional content in Yepes' text allowed it to avoid political repercussions.

36 As seen in chapter 1, both Catholics and Protestants produced ecclesiastical histories that were read and disputed point by point by opponents.

37 Although theological concerns framed historical facts in a way that was appealing to co-religionists, writers of early modern ecclesiastical histories did not disregard the developing historical method that was increasingly more critical and careful in handling sources. See Grafton, "Church History" for a convincing argument on this point. Similarly, Kagan argues that "official" chroniclers cherry-picked evidence in their histories to place monarchs in a favorable light, but they rarely distorted the facts wilfully (5–7). Weinreich argues that though almost everything in Ribadeneyra's *Historia* had a source and his sources were carefully vetted, he did not hesitate to exaggerate, omit inconvenient details, or frame the story according to his theological purposes, as was common in histories of the time whose goal was verisimilitude rather than factual precision ("Introduction" 75–98).

38 Weinreich also notes this about Ribadeneyra's *Historia*, as he comments on the masterful rhetorical elements in the text ("Introduction" 103).

39 "Descubrense los embustes de los hereges para escurecer la Fè Catolica: y como començó otra vez a resplandecer la Fè. Cap.X" and "Capítulo XXV. La persecución que se levantó contra los católicos, por no querer reconocer a la Reina por cabeza de la Iglesia." Compare with the telegraphic style of Sander: "Chapter I. Hypocrisy of Elizabeth – Cecil – Oath of Supremacy – Headship of the Church – Delusion of the Catholics" (241).

40 King shows episodes of Foxe's martyrs being depicted as lambs and the Catholic persecutors as wolves ("Fiction and Fact" 29). Of course, this was a common biblical trope appearing in sermons and commentaries since New Testament times.

41 "Y sobre el quarto que estava colgado en una torre, en la plaça de Preston, viose por muchos días una como cara de hombre vivo" (Yepes 90).

42 "Semejante a este fue el fin de Francisco Valsingam principal secretario de la reina, grande perseguidor, y enemigo capital de los Jesuitas y seminarios, a quien en medio de su pujanza y prosperidad, hirio Dios con una plaga vergonzosa Y horrible: saliole la orina por la boca" (Yepes 72).

43 "Hizo el Martyr Dibdal al demonio sacar por la boca de una persona endemoniada, ovillos de pelos, y pedazos de hierro y otras cosas semejantes, que humanamente era impossible que huviessen entrado, ni despues podido salir de aquel cuerpo" (Yepes 97).

44 Interestingly, this statement about Sander's sources is a translation of a section in Sander's preface that Ribadeneyra seems to appropriate, which states: "that history, strange and surprising, I shall now tell in all sincerity as I have gathered it either from public records or from the testimony, oral and written, of men of the greatest consideration, or at least from my own knowledge and observation" (cxlvii).

45 Some were concerned about the prince, since the future Philip III already showed lack of interest in government affairs and greatly favored the soon-to-be powerful Duke of Lerma, and this had induced Philip II to make Lerma viceroy of Valencia in hope of separating the prince from the nobleman (Kamen 209; Benavides 7). Indeed, the age of the favorites began with Philip III, followed by Philip IV (Kamen 209–13).

46 This fear is especially seen in the numerous treatises on the ideal Christian prince that were written and dedicated to the future Philip III, including one by Ribadeneyra. Harry Sieber argues that the publication in 1599 of *El lazarillo de Tormes* in the same volume as the *Galateo español* (a manual including advice for acquiring a position in the court) was a deliberate ironic statement critiquing the prevalence of *validos* at court (149–60). Also, critics have argued that Lope de Vega's *Fuenteovejuna* (1619) (a play recounting a historical moment when Ferdinand and Isabella impart justice in a town abused by the corrupt *Comendador Mayor* Díaz de Guzmán) advocates that Philip III return to the ideal of personal involvement in ruling that was practiced under the Catholic Monarchs. See Blue for this last interpretation.

47 The histories of Ribadeneyra and Yepes both exhort the prince to emulate the Christian virtues of his father, Philip II. However, in other texts Ribadeneyra and others criticized Philip II precisely for compromising his stance as a Christian prince, particularly in his relations with Elizabeth I. See Domínguez, "History in Action" 17–22. Yepes, as confessor of Philip II, reinforces the glorious past of the monarch, but in his connecting the Roman Church at every turn with the New Testament, he focuses on an older glorious Christian past for Spain: that of the first-century church.

48 In fact, this nostalgic appeal was often brought up in early modern Spain at a time of weakness or internal crisis. For example, it was employed in 1609 with the signing of the decree for the expulsion of the *moriscos* on April 9, celebrated on the same day the Twelve Years' Truce with the Dutch was signed. This strategic move diverted attention from the lack of

success in Flanders and commemorated the date as the victorious end of Moorish dominance in Spain (Elliott 301).

49 "Las analogías que se pueden establecer entre los hechos del presente y los del pasado permiten comprender el alcance de una situación determinada y prever sus posibles efectos. De manera indirecta el ejemplo actualiza el pasado y ofrece la posibilidad de inferir verdades generales de casos particulares, fenómenos ambos de especial relevancia en el discurso histórico" (32).

50 "Porque si las vidas de los santos antiguos, y los valerosos combates de los sagrados Martyres, que en otros siglos han ilustrado la Iglesia, son de tanto provecho, como la experiencia enseña a los que los leen con atencion: mucho mas seran estos exemplos, que (corriendo sangre) no solo en nuestros días sino delante de nuestros ojos renuevan la fidelidad y constancia de los primeros Christianos."

51 "O mozos valerosos y constantes, corred con esfuerzo y alegría, pues habéis asentado debajo de tan gloriosa bandera: y en el juramento que habéis hecho de fidelidad, habéis juntamente prometido derramar vuestra sangre. Por cierto que cuando os miro, y os veo ir con largo paso al martirio, y casi vestidos de la nobilísima ropa de púrpura de vuestra sangre, querría seguiros, y digo, muera mi anima la muerte de los justos, y mis postrimerías sean como las destos gloriosos caballeros" (51).

52 "And he shal convert the hart of the fathers to the children, & the hart of the children to their fathers: lest perhaps I come, and strike the earth with anathema." This text and all subsequent English verses are taken from the 1610 Douay-Rheims version. Incidentally, this phrase is also used in the declaration of the Council of Trent to express the purpose of the council.

53 "Vese un rey poderoso, que quiere todo lo que se le antoja, y ejecuta todo lo que quiere; una afición ciega y desapoderada, armada de saña y poder, derramando la sangre de santísimos varones y profanando y robando los templos de Dios, y empobreciéndose con las riquezas de ellos; quitando la verdadera cabeza de la Iglesia, y haciéndose a sí cabeza monstruosa de ella, y pervirtiendo todas las leyes divinas y humanas."

54 Ribadeneyra explains this in his brief preface to the reader in *Tratado de la religión y virtudes que debe tener el Príncipe Cristiano.*

55 "Es tan grande bien el de todo el reino, cuando Dios le da de su mano un rey piadoso, celador de su Gloria, favorecedor de buenos, perseguidor de malos, justo, pacífico y moderado, que ninguna otra felicidad de las de acá puede tener mayor: porque como el Rey es la cabeza del reino y como la vida y ánima de él, al paso que anda el Rey, anda el reino, que depende del mismo Rey."

56 "Finalmente os quiero advertir (Christiano lector) que aunque en algunas partes desta obra *nos avemos entretenido en materias mas doctrinales,*

que de historia y narracion, no por eso nos avemos apartado de vuestro provecho, ni de nuestro proposito; que ha sido de *mostraros con exemplo desta persecucion*, quan temidos han de ser los juyzios de Dios, y quan reverenciados los secretos de su providencia, y amada su eterna bondad, con que acude siempre al amparo de los suyos, guardandolos, y defendiendolos de tal manera con su gracia y protección, que ninguna criatura les puede ofender."

57 See King, "Fiction and Fact" 16–18.

58 "No se puede fácilmente creer la ruina y calamidad de los monasterios y casas sagradas, que en tiempo de este Nabucodonosor [Enrique] hubo en Inglaterra" (Ribadeneyra 1021).

59 "Pues ¿qué diré de otra utilidad maravillosa, que podemos todos sacar de esta Historia? Ella es la compasión por una parte, y por otra la santa envidia que debemos tener a nuestros hermanos, los que en Inglaterra, por no querer adorar la estatua de Nabucodonosor, y reconocer a la reina por cabeza de la Iglesia, cada día son perseguidos" (Ribadeneyra 899).

60 "No hay consejo contra el Señor; y es cosa dura y sin fruto tirar coces contra el aguijón, como lo probó Saulo antes que se convirtiese; y antes que él el rey Faraón, el cual cuanto más procuraba de extinguir el pueblo de Israel, tanto Dios le favorecía y multiplicaba más, y al cabo de tantos prodigios, milagros y plagas, con destrucción suya y de su reino, le libró" (Ribadeneyra 1306).

61 "Para que, pues en el principio de su reinado había representado a Salomón en piedad y sabiduría, no acabase, como él, engañado y pervertido de las mujeres."

62 In fact, this assumption is explicit in Calderón's adaptation of this scene in *La cisma de Ingalaterra*, which features Anne dancing a *gallarda*, a lewd dance prohibited by the church (Quintero, *Gendering* 140).

63 "Let women be subiect to their husbandes, as to our Lord: because the man is the head of the woman, as Christ is the head of the CHURCH. Himself, the saviour of his body. But as the CHURCH is subject to Christ: so also the women to their husbands in al things" (*Douay-Rheims 1610*).

64 "I wil therfore that men pray in every place: lifting up pure handes, without anger and altercation. In like manner women also in comely attire: with demurenesse and sobrietie adorning them selves, not in plaited heare, or gold, or pretious stones, or gorgeous apparel, but that which becometh women professing pietie by good workes. Let a woman learne in silence with al subiection. But to teach I permit not unto a woman, nor to have dominion over the man: but to be in silence. For Adam was formed first; then Eve, and Adam was not seduced: but the woman being seduced, was in prevarication. Yet she shall be saved by generation

of children: if they continue in faith & love and sanctification with sobrietie" (*Douay-Rheims 1610*).

65 "Por tanto como la muger sea naturalmente animal enfermo, y su juício no esté de todas partes seguro, y pueda ser muy ligeramente engañado, segun mostró nuestra madre Eva, que por muy poco se dexó embobecer y persuadir del demonio: por todos estos respetos y por otros algunos que se callan, no es bien que ella enseñe. Item, porque habiéndose puesto en la cabeza alguna falsa opinion, no la traspase en los auditores con la autoridad que tiene de maestra, y trayga á los otros en su mismo error, en especial que en el mal de grado siguen los discípulos al maestro."

66 "Agora el maestro ha de tener la nuestra virgen, yo por mi querría que fuese alguna muger ántes que hombre, y ántes su madre ó tia ó hermana que no alguna extraña … pero quando algo hubiere de faltar de esto, no falte la buena fama y las buenas letras; y quando ni uno ni otro se halle, búsquese con mucho cuidado algun hombre anciano, de fama, vida y doctrina aprobada" (libro I, cap IV, 24–5).

67 "¿Pues quánto mayor cuidado debemos poner en la crianza y vida de la muger christiana, siendo tan importante al vivir humano, que todo el bien y mal que en el mundo se hace, se puede sin yerro decir ser por causa de las mugeres, segun en el proceso de ésta obra se podrá comprehender?"

68 Following E.M. Forster, flat characters are two-dimensional figures that act predictably and can be summed up in a sentence (67–73).

69 This may be the case in Ribadeneyra's and Carvajal's reflections on Elizabeth discussed below. See also Weinreich, who argues that Ribadeneyra is not wholly negative in his portrayal of Cecil, Wolsey, and Hatton ("Introduction" 100–1).

70 The histories are careful to highlight that any good attributed to Henry refers to the time before his apostasy and is used to show the tragedy of Henry's actions.

71 There are brief statements recounting the execution of Cranmer, which is attributed as the just punishment for his treason and approval of Henry's divorce (Sander 222), and of other officials who were sentenced for high treason, but there is no attempt to address the other executions that gave the queen the title of "Bloody Mary." Weinreich adds other selective omissions to strengthen paradigmatic figures, such as Mary Tudor's opposition to the Pope and Jesuits and Campion's disclosure under torture of a recusant printing press ("Introduction" 82–4).

72 See Domínguez, "History in Action" 17–22; *Radicals* 68–9.

73 "Este fué el fin de la santa reina doña Catalina, esclarecida, cierto, por haber sido reina e hija de reyes, y de tan grandes reyes como fueron los Reyes Católicos, de gloriosa memoria; pero mucho más ilustre y bienaventurada por las excelentes virtudes con que resplandeció en el

mundo, y ahora reina con Cristo. Pasemos adelante, y veamos el fin de Ana Bolena, que le sucedió en el reino, y cotejemos linaje con linaje, vida con vida y muerte con muerte."

74 See Quintero for a discussion of Catherine's portrayal as the perfect Spanish wife in Ribadeneyra's history (*Gendering*, 128–9).

75 "Mas la muger no ha de tener muchos cuidados; sola una cosa le han encargado, que es la castidad: aquella ha de guardar y defender" (Vives, "Prefacion ... a la Serenisima Doña Catalina"). "Todo hombre queriendo ser casto debe templarse en su vivir, y desechar de sí todo comer, que instiga nuestros cuerpos á la carnalidad. Lo que he dicho de los manjares que de sí propios son calientes, digo de todo exercicio que escalienta y altera los cuerpos, como son danzas, olores, perfumes, pláticas y vistas de hombres, porque todas estas cosas son dañosas, y fácilmente pueden perjudicar á la limpieza del ánimo ... Se debe guardar que lo que trae no sea muy exquisito ni primoroso, ni busque nuevos trages, sino que se contente con sola la limpieza ... En las mugeres muy delicadas, que con esta limpieza no se contentan, sino que buscan cada dia ropas nuevas y atavíos muy ricos y pomposos ... estas tales no sé si tienen muy limpio el pensamiento" (Cap VIII, 63–4).

76 "Como en el alma, se yva desconcertando, y con la variedad de sus desenfrenados apetitos perdiendo su hermosura; assi en el cuerpo fue afeandose hasta llegar a tan monstruoso estado (causado de la destemplança de su vida)" (Yepes 8). "Habiendo sido cuando mozo muy bien dispuesto, gentil-hombre y agraciado, vino por su insaciable carnalidad y torpeza a ser tan feo y tan disforme o pesado, que no podía subir una escalera, y apenas había puerta tan ancha por donde pudiese entrar" (Ribadeneyra 1038).

77 See also Niccoli 30–59.

78 Retha Warnicke cogently argues that claims of Anne's physical deformities are untenable (3, 58–9).

79 "El resto del cuerpo era muy proporcionado y hermoso: tenía mucha gracia en los labios y gran donaire y desenvoltura en danzar y tañer, y extremada curiosidad en el vestido con nuevas invenciones y trajes y galas."

80 "Y para que la fe y creencia de esta mujer fuese semejante a su vida y costumbres, seguía la secta luterana, aunque no dejaba de oír misa como si fuera católica; porque siéndolo el rey, juzgaba que para sus intentos y ambición le podía aprovechar" (Ribadeneyra 928).

81 As Warnicke notes, however, at Anne's trial no one appealed to her physical deformities as proof of her involvement in witchcraft, and therefore, it is unlikely that these deformities were literal (3, 58–9).

82 "Bien veo que cuento algunas cosas que, o por ser menudas, o de la calidad que son, las podría dejar; mas, mirando en ello, me ha parecido las debía escribir, así por escribirlas un hombre tan grave y modesto como lo fué el Dr. Sandero, y ser provechosas para el hilo y verdad de la historia, como principalmente porque declaran más la ciega pasión del Rey."

83 Warnicke argues that the framing of this miscarriage as a monstrous birth was the catalyst for Anne's execution (191–233).

84 "All men see that this unhappy generation, and that most abandoned sect, have their Athalia, Maacha, Jezebel, Herodias, Selene, Constantia, and Eudoxia. But Elizabeth has surpassed them all, she has taken upon herself the supremacy in the things of God, over even bishops and priests" (240).

85 "[Ribadeneyra] lo va diciendo con tal lujo de considerandos y atenuaciones y envolviéndolo todo en un velo tan discreto de dolor y melancolía sacerdotales, que su tesis se abre insensiblemente camino en el corazón del lector, impelida por el generoso aliento de su oratoria." Samson notes that Ribadeneyra did not exploit Elizabeth's sexual scandals with Dudley or others ("Upending" 291–3). Weinreich agrees that Ribadeneyra had to measure his language but disputes Rey's point, noting, among other things, Ribadeneyra's inclusion of more vices to describe Henry VIII and his more militant, violent language against England ("Introduction" 29–30, 33–4).

86 Given the challenges to publish his text, they may have been political.

87 See Samson, "Upending" 289; and Weinreich, "Introduction" 34–5.

88 "Por habernos dejado una hija que así la imita, é hinche y colma la medida de su madre."

89 While unclear, it is possible to read this indictment of Elizabeth as a piteous lament for her own destruction, which, as noted, was considered inevitable given her birth, but which nonetheless was a threat for the Roman Church and its members.

90 "Vemos a una mujer, hija y nieta de Enrique VIII, e hija y hermana de Ana Bolena … como un abominable monstruo é ídolo, asentada en el templo de Dios, tomando el oficio y nombre de gobernadora y cabeza de la Iglesia."

91 "¿Quién jamás ha visto ni oído que una tía a su sobrina, y una reina a otra reina, le mandase cortar la cabeza por manos del verdugo ordinario …? ¿En qué historia de indios y bárbaros se lee que se hayan hecho luminarias, fiestas y regocijos por la muerte de una reina inocente; y que la misma reina que le da la muerte, se vista galana, y pasee la ciudad a caballo con alegría, como quien triunfa de su enemiga? … En Inglaterra solo se ha hecho esto en todo el mundo, y por mano de herejes se ha

hecho, y por ellos solo se podía hacer; porque como la herejía es un monstruo infernal, todos los frutos que nacen de ella son monstruosos é infernales. Y si para conocer esta verdad no bastaban los innumerables ejemplos que antes teníamos de crueldad, violencia y tiranía que han usado los herejes en nuestros tiempos, este solo basta por todos, y bastará en todos los siglos venideros; pues es tal, que en Tartaria y en Scithia, y en cualquiera nación por áspera, fiera e inhumana que sea, los mismos bárbaros, cuando le oyeren, no le creerán."

92 These ideas are more explicit in Ribadeneyra's letter to the Armada soldiers (Ribadeneyra 1352–3).

3. Who Gets to Be a Saint? Writing the English Reformation in Luisa de Carvajal's Letters

1 Carvajal's early biographers were her confessor, Michael Walpole, and the Jesuit Luis Muñoz. Modern biographies include Rhodes; Rees; Redworth, *She-Apostle*; and Cruz, *Life*.

2 Redworth points out that, in addition to endorsing the traditional monastic vows of poverty, chastity, and obedience for her London Rule, Carvajal adopted the Jesuit vow of papal obedience ("New Way" 282).

3 Cruz suggests that in Carvajal's case, the categories of gender, class, and religious background "function in collusion and in conflict with one another" (*Life* 34).

4 Cruz is the only biographer to document how Carvajal used her aristocratic connections to travel to England under a pseudonym (*Life* 61–6).

5 The right hand of the Duke of Lerma, Calderón became very powerful, but infamously fell from grace with Philip III (Carvajal, *Epistolario* 71–90). Abad posits that it would have been difficult for Carvajal to keep up with the internal governmental affairs in Spain involving her cousin (Carvajal, *Epistolario* 85).

6 Not all Spaniards admired the Jesuits; in fact, Weinreich argues that Ribadeneyra's *Historia* is a defense of the Society in the midst of much criticism ("Distinctiveness"; "Introduction" 35).

7 "[De la orden] yo tengo hermandad dada por el Reverendísimo maestro Laínez, su general" (Bouza 257).

8 "Mire, hermano, que sea devoto de la Compañía de Jesús (y de todas las religiones entiendo también); que yo no puedo sufrir que no se estimen y amen como se debe. Pero acuerdo a vuestra merced la particular obligación que tenemos a la Compañía, como medio de la salvación de nuestro abuelo y padre y otros deudos cercanos nuestros. Y por ella, en

estos últimos tiempos, ha renovado Dios la frecuentación de sacramentos, y llegado innumerables almas a Sí."

9 "Por enderezarme a virtud y destruir lo que puede impedirla."

10 Cruz highlights passages like these as instances where the adult Carvajal recasts her childhood pain into a narrative that explains it and justifies her nursemaid's actions (*Life* 24–5, 31).

11 "Gustaba mucho de hacer grandes penitencias, ordinarias y aun muy extraordinarias."

12 Though uneasy about Don Francisco's harsh corporal discipline of the girl, Luis Muñoz, one of Carvajal's early biographers, attributes to her uncle's "gardening" Carvajal's unusual devotion that moved her to travel to England: "[Carvajal] creció al lado deste gran maestro, fue hortolano que cultivó este vergel, al cual con continuos riegos y influencias fertilizó el espíritu Divino por su dirección, y su enseñanza, llegó a los grados de santidad que iremos viendo" (11).

13 Hurtado de Mendoza's involvement in Carvajal's "discipline" is controversial. Redworth (*She-Apostle* 29) and Rhodes (3–4) consider it sexually inappropriate. Cruz, however, argues that Carvajal's writings seem to preclude sexual abuse, though Cruz amply demonstrates that the marquis' discipline was excessive and alarming, even for Carvajal's early biographers (*Life* 27–31; "Chains" 100–2).

14 "Siendo de diecisiete años, y no sé si aún menos, en mi retirada oración empecé a tener grandes deseos de martirio: esto era, de morir por el dulcísimo Señor que murió por mí. Y por muy largo espacio, me hallaba algunas veces totalmente embebida en una profunda y viva consideración de que me estaban haciendo pedazos por la santa fe católica, en lo cual mi ánimo sentía la mayor satisfacción que se puede pensar; y grande deleite. Y de allí salía con gran propensión a una verdadera imitación de los trabajos y cruz de nuestro Señor."

15 Anne Cruz points to inconsistencies in Carvajal's autobiography that are clearly the result of mature reflections projected back on her life, at the request of men, patterned after hagiographies, and that present her and her loved ones in an acceptable light to her audience (*Life* 18–19, 30–1; "Willing Desire" 181–2). However, taking these caveats into account, Carvajal's narration is generally considered reliable (Redworth, "New Way" 288). For women and autobiographies, see Howe.

16 Redworth argues that the resemblances in the writings of Carvajal and Teresa "may be coincidental" ("New Way" 278). Cruz lists the similar sections in both women's biographical writings, including their memoirs of a pious mother, but notes that the crucial difference between their lives was social position (*Life* 11–12).

17 She says she possesses an English copy of the book, probably translated by Michael Walpole (Carvajal, *Epistolario* 331; Cruz, *Life* 3). For the English volume, see Spinnenweber.

18 For areas of disagreement between Carvajal and Teresa, see Redworth, "New Way" 280–5, and *She-Apostle* 148–59.

19 Abad notes that Don Francisco would translate from Latin into Spanish and that in this way the young girl came to master the academic language (Carvajal, *Epistolario* 45). See also Cruz, "Reading" 41–58.

20 "Mi más ordinaria compañía era la presencia de mi tío; y sentada junto a él pasaba gran parte del día: él en su silla, escribiendo a solas o con sus secretarios o escribientes; y yo en el suelo … Mi tío, cuando dejaba de escribir, o mientras sus escribientes sacaban en limpio lo ya escrito, se ponía luego a hablar en nuestro Señor conmigo … Muy ordinariamente leía la Sagrada Escritura y Sanctos Dotores de la Iglesia; lectura que él mucho amaba."

21 "Y no me meto en cosas temporales, que aborrezco mucho guerras y derramamiento de sangre; pero lo que es socorros de espíritu y que las misiones crezcan, y que estas almas se conviertan, y salven muchas de nuevo cada día, no me basta la paciencia con la letargia que en esto veo aún en los pechos muy católicos y celosos del bien de la Iglesia."

22 Some scholars question the reliability of Carvajal's statement that she desired to go specifically to England at such an early point in her life. The reasons given are that, first, Carvajal wrote her autobiography late in life and as an apology for her English trip, and second, she did not disclose this desire to anyone in her early letters. Anne Cruz argues that there is a marked discrepancy between the letters and the autobiography ("Willing Desire" 178; *Life* 54–60), while Glyn Redworth sees more continuity between the two sets of writings (*She-Apostle* 77–9).

23 While in England she requests someone to send her both the *Flos Sanctorum* of Basil and *Cayrasco* (Carvajal, *Epistolario* 135, 319).

24 For reasons why Walpole might have requested Carvajal to write her life, see Cruz, *Life* 9–10, and Bilinkoff.

25 For a fuller discussion of this medieval tradition, see Petroff, 3–59.

26 Redworth compares the rules for women that Carvajal and Teresa wrote for their communities and notes that while Carvajal's London Rule does not question the authority of male confessors, Teresa of Avila allowed a mother superior to select and replace at will general confessors for her community ("New Way" 281–2; *She-Apostle* 154).

27 See Cruz, "Willing."

28 "Tras esto me preguntó que por qué causa la reina Isabel no era tan verdadera y legítima sucesora del reino como el rey. Y dije que el rey descendía legítimamente de la hermana mayor del rey Enrique, cuyo

biznieto era, y que Isabel nació siendo viva doña Catalina, mujer del rey, padre de Isabel. Dijo que ¿quién me lo había dicho? Y dije que las crónicas impresas y historias de aquella edad. Dijo que aquello era no saberlas bien; porque doña Catalina no fue legítima mujer del rey, con que hizo a la reina María ilegítima reina. Y aunque había mucho que responderle, porque la reina Catalina tuvo dispensación del Papa, y para en caso de que fuera necesaria, que no lo fue, bastaba la plenitud con que la dispensación se dió, y el Enrique, antes de su muerte, declaró por bastarda a Isabel, su hija, e hizo que todo el reino junto, en forma de Parlamento, lo declarasen también, y se hizo ley de ello; pero él no apretó, ni yo quise meterme mucho en eso, ya que no podía hacerlo en las primeras y más graves materias."

29 The 1623 catalogue of Diego Sarmiento de Acuña's library (today at the Biblioteca Real de Palacio in Madrid) lists copies of the English ecclesiastical histories by Nicholas Sander, Pedro de Ribadeneyra, and Diego de Yepes. Although the catalogue was produced after Carvajal's death and her acquaintance with Don Diego as Spanish ambassador to London (1613–22) was brief, the inclusion of these books in his library attests to their popularity and accessibility, especially for Carvajal, who was an avid reader.

30 The collection also includes the ecclesiastical history of Eusebius, apparently in Spanish (Bouza 280).

31 The title in Spanish is *Historia de la vida y martyrio que padeció en Inglaterra, este año de 1595. P. Henrique Valpolo … el primer martyr de los seminarios de España. Con el martyrio de otros quatro sacerdotes* (Allison and Rogers 41).

32 Abad counts at least twenty-seven letters written between 1606 and 1612 among Carvajal's published correspondence (Carvajal, *Epistolario* 70–1).

33 For a full list of Creswell's works and translations, see Allison and Rogers 40–3.

34 Redworth argues that this includes Thomas Rogers' commentary (Carvajal, *Letters* 2: 169).

35 Rogers argues that Book V of Yepes' ecclesiastical history contains several unique accounts that survive nowhere else and that these are "specimens of the rich and detailed information which was available to Creswell through his correspondents."

36 For Robert Persons' role in the Catholic resistance, see Houliston, "Catholic."

37 "Las raposerías y ardides que ese mostruo de esa mujer suele tener, para solapadamente hacer guerra a Dios y a su Iglesia y a las almas de sus súbditos."

38 "Deberíase contentar esta mujer perversísima con la sangre que ha bebido de mártires y con la que bebe y podrá beber (si vive en su pertinacia) cada y cuando que cogiere en su reino algún sacerdote o religioso, o

otro de estos sus enemigos los católicos, sin pasar tan adelante y querer mañosamente y con dorada hipocresía inducir a tales, y tan cristianísimos y religiosísimos príncipes como los nuestros a que vengan en cosa tan ajena dellos cuanto propia y muy natural de su malicia y miseria della."

39 "Y la mujer estaba vestida de púrpura y de escarlata, y dorada con oro, y adornada de piedras preciosas y de perlas, teniendo un cáliz de oro en su mano lleno de abominaciones y de la suciedad de su fornicación; Y en su frente un nombre escrito: MISTERIO, BABILONIA LA GRANDE, LA MADRE DE LAS FORNICACIONES Y DE LAS ABOMINACIONES DE LA TIERRA. Y vi la mujer embriagada de la sangre de los santos, y de la sangre de los mártires de Jesús: y cuando la vi, quedé maravillado de grande admiración" (*Reina-Valera*).

40 According to Carvajal, heretics said that the Whore of Babylon was the Pope (*Epistolario* 374).

41 The annotations to the Apocalypse of the Douay-Rheims Bible state for verse six of chapter XVII: "It is plaine that this woman signifieth the whole corps of al the persecutors that haue and shal shede so much bloud of the iust: of the Prophets, Apostles, and other Martyrs from the beginning of the world to the end. The Protestants folishly expound it of Rome, for that there they put Heretikes to death, and allow of their punishment in other countries: but their bloud is not called the bloud of saincts, no more then the bloud of theeues, man-killers, and other malefactors: for the sheding of which by order of iustice, no Commonwealth shal answer."

42 This association is recurrent in Lope de Vega's poems, as the next chapter shows.

43 "¡Que poco que le habrá parecido, señora, a aquella mísera mujer el tiempo de su reinado y de su prosperidad, y qué de años le parecerá que dura su tormento! Infelicísima alma, por cierto, fue la suya, como lo será para siempre jamás. Y estupendo juicio, y muy particular, debió de ser el suyo ante el divino tribunal: y pienso que lo fue sobre todos los que de su sexo ha habido muchos años ha."

44 "Aquí no hacen otra cosa sino sacar en [comedias] mofas de España, las más infames que pueden, y predicar en los púlpitos que es tierra de bestias salvajes cruelísimas, y que beben sangre humana; idólatras, que adoran palos y piedras y, lo peor, que es la abominación del antecristo y ramera de Babilonia, que es el Papa, y un panecito que decimos que es nuestro Dios."

45 "Cosa dulcísima ha sido para mí ver el cuidado que ha mostrado Nuestro Señor tener de que esta miserable criatura suya, sea siempre proveída por mano de españoles, y entre ellos sonsacado uno acá y otro acullá. Parece que escogiendo los de más real ánimo y liberalidad, ha echado el resto,

a lo último, con la Majestad del rey nuestro señor y vuestra merced, de quienes totalmente carga ahora todo nuestro sustento y bien que se hace a otros" (Carvajal, *Epistolario* 328). "Guárdenos Dios a su majestad [doña Margarita] y Él sea bendito que nos la dió y tal rey. ¡Que de ello debe España a Dios aun en esto sólo!" (Carvajal, *Epistolario* 315).

46 "El señor de Montagudo, es notable en materia de celo de religión católica: no puede, cierto, haber hombre en el mundo que en eso lo haga ventaja, excetando, a nuestro gran Rey y señor Filipo tercero. ¡Gracias a Dios que nos le ha dado tal en estos míseros tiempos!" (Carvajal, *Epistolario* 293).

47 "¡Qué lástima es que no sea Rey de todo el mundo nuestro Rey de España! ¡Cuán respetada fuera la Santa Iglesia Católica y cuántas más almas se salvaran! Guárdele Dios larguísimos años, que locura sería no desear su vida más que la nuestra mil veces."

48 "[Don Diego] ha servido aquí mucho a Nuestro Señor y adelantado cuanto ha podido su santísima gloria y la honra de España, que no es tan difícil, en un gran extremo."

49 "Esta embajada es dificultosa, creo yo que tanto como otra cualquiera; en ella consiste no pequeña parte de la honra de España y de la Santa Iglesia Católica; que estas dos andan muy a una, gracias infinitas sean dadas a Dios."

50 Her letter to Creswell from April 23, 1608, introduces a detailed price comparison between the two countries, saying, "aquí son las cosas tan caras como en la corte de España; y muchas dellas, más" (*Epistolario* 244). She also expresses the altruistic and divine designs for her being in such a hostile place: "y cierto que ni me trujo a Inglaterra designio de lucidos sucesos, ni pensar de mí alguna cosa grande, ni querer que una sola persona se acordase de mí en este mundo; y en este estado permanezco, gracias a Nuestro Señor, deseando sólo el perfeto cumplimiento de su voluntad, aunque sea muriendo cada momento, como puedo decir que muero, todos los que me acuerdo que estoy en esta Isla" (*Epistolario* 183).

51 "La peste crece más estos días, que está ya vinculada doce años ha, según afirman; y, poca o mucha, nunca falta. ¡Qué lindas gracias tiene Inglaterra, que no le faltaba, cierto, sino ésta para echar el sello! Intolerable tierra es; no me defrauda en nada de la confianza que tenía de poder padecer un gran purgatorio en ella, porque para eso, sola la memoria de que se vive aquí, basta."

52 "Mucha merced y consuelo recibo con las de vuestra merced, y espero que vuestra merced habrá recibido consuelo, con las últimas mías, viendo la gran constancia de los santos mártires Garves y Fludder."

53 "Quiero, por vía del padre Baulduino, con un amigo que parte allá, dar la enhorabuena a vuestra merced de dos nuevos mártires" (Carvajal, *Epistolario* 240).

54 "El padre Al fue llevado con su criado fuera de Londres, y en un lugar do él solía vivir, fueron muertos los dos. En la horca declaró no haber jamás entendido cosa ninguna de la pólvora, y habló con tanto espíritu y ánimo, que se vieron llorar más de quinientas personas. Y Cecilio dijo después, que él diera trescientos ducados, por que no hubiera muerto; porque fue el provecho de las almas mucho con su muerte."

55 For example, right before her first incarceration, she recounts the dispute on this topic that she had with Londoners: "Uno de ellos empezó a llamar traidor al padre Charves a mis espaldas, hablando con Ana, mi compañera, que le llamaba mártir; y yo me volví a él y le pregunté por qué había muerto. Y díjome que por ser sacerdote papista. '¿Meramente?', dije yo. Y respondió que sí, sin mezcla de otro delito. Y dije: 'Siendo así, forzosamente es mártir y ha de ser tenido por tal; y no os habéis de indinar con esta doncella porque le llama así, y no quiere consentir en que le llaméis traidor'" (*Epistolario* 253).

56 Both Sander and Ribadeneyra discuss this in their ecclesiastical histories, but Ribadeneyra devotes an entire chapter to the explanation of how this was done, titled "Cómo la reina y sus ministros publican que los santos mártires no mueren por la religión, sino por otros delitos" (1143–6).

57 At the time that Creswell was appealing to Philip III for funds for the seminary in Madrid, he had to counteract the propaganda after the Gunpowder Plot that English Catholics were disloyal to their country (Allison 353; Loomie, *Toleration* 47–54).

58 "A mis carísimos y amados los ingleses católicos encomiendo por el amor de Nuestro Señor al real y benigno amparo de Su Alteza; a vuestra merced, como suelo, le suplico les haga cuanto bien pudiere en todas ocasiones."

59 "El licenciado Juan Manrique, a mi partida, me ofreció ayudarme en cualquier cosa del servicio de Nuestro Señor, si se lo escribía; y desde allá me ha escrito muy de veras, que diga si puede ayudarme acá en algo, porque vendría con toda verdad de buena gana a hacello; y en esta ocasión le tengo de tomar la palabra para ello. Y su celo de bien de las almas y de gusto de Nuestro Señor se mostraba allá bien grande; y si él quisiere ayudar con persona y dinero, será heroica cosa."

60 "Con el padre fray Juan, que se va a España, creo irá un mancebo gentilman llamado Brigman, hijo mayor de un cismático, que pienso tiene buena hacienda; y el mozo tiene fama de muy buen estudiante aquí en Londres, y eslo en el temple y con muy buena comodidad. Hále tocado Nuestro Señor, a lo que se puede juzgar, para dejarla y irse a un seminario: tiene agudeza de ingenio y muestra harta devoción. Va con esperanza que le ha de valer mi intercesión para ser recibido en

Valladolid: suplícolo así a vuestra merced de rodillas, que lo estimaré como se hiciera conmigo mesma."

61 "Si se supiese en España cuánto España debe a Dios y cuánta menos necesidad ahora tiene de semejantes ayudas de espíritu, no habría tanta aplicación a obras de allá, y tanta repugnancia de gusto en las de ayudar las almas de otras tierras."

62 "Entiende muy bien español, y háblado bien; y así le he podido apretar mucho, y servirse Nuestro Señor que me ayude la memoria de importantes y muy concluyentes razones que he leído y oído."

63 "Quiebra el corazón ver tantos millares de almas anegadas en un abismo de error, sin quien les diga palabra; porque los sacerdotes y religiosos por ninguna vía pueden hablar en público, y si de algunos herejes son conocidos, no pueden salir de día por las calles sin notable peligro de ser luego cogidos; y así parece que está librada la conversión de esta gente en las personas de tan poca importancia como yo y otras semejantes."

64 Cicero's directive that orators show submission and humility passed over into Christian literature, often as protestations of inadequacy followed by God's directive to write, but became especially important for women to justify their writing as not usurping men's prerogative, since God himself compelled them (Petroff 24–7).

65 "Si me viera vuestra merced delante el juez y en la cárcel, creo que se consolara muchísimo, Y lo que allí disputé y voceé en el corto inglés por la santa fe, acordándome de aquello del Santo Apóstol: que la palabra de Dios *no estaba atada en su prisión*."

66 Bale and Foxe equated Askew to Blandina, a female martyr in Eusebius, to justify her candid preaching at her trial. For a full discussion of these ideas, see Freeman, *Great Searching* 182–97.

67 "Sacerdote romano en hábito mujeril." Dolan argues that early modern English anti-Catholic literature presents Catholics as sexually disordered and ambiguous: priests and men are consistently shown as effeminate and women are presented as masculine, fulfilling priestly functions. Carvajal's insult, within this context, takes on weightier connotations.

68 Ward, who was twenty years younger than Carvajal, admired her elder and seems to have been influenced by her (Redworth, *She-Apostle* 155–6, 220, "New Way" 283–4). In addition to sharing correspondence, some argue that the women met personally, though this is disputed (Redworth, *She-Apostle* 155–6; Cruz, *Life* 89). For a summary of the life of Mary Ward, see Wallace, 133–200.

69 In many ways, Ward's conduct and beliefs mirrored Carvajal's. The younger woman, too, believed that the role of Catholic women in England was to complement the work of the Jesuits (Wallace 138–9, 165).

70 "Que la venerable doña Luisa en el modo que trató la causa de la Religion con los hereges, y el aprovechamiento de los Ingleses Catolicos, no excedio los limites que en esto tiene puesto la Iglesia a las mugeres. Cap.XV."

71 Freeman cites arguments by Stapleton, Harpsfield, and Persons that Protestant leaders like Latimer and Luther had no miracles to confirm their apostleship and details the struggle that Foxe faced to overcome the handicap in the *Acts and Monuments* (*Great Searching* 199–226).

72 "La obra de enterrar tales muertos y envolverlos en sábanas no se puede hacer en España, ni otras desta gran calidad. ¡Cuándo merecí yo, Señor, emplearme en ellas!"

73 In the case of Ribadeneyra's *Historia*, it also had to be approved by the Jesuits – an approval that, as the previous chapter showed, was not readily given.

74 Carvajal tells Creswell in some of her letters describing martyrdoms that she wrote the accounts to be shared with others or transcribed for broader circulation.

75 On one occasion, she conjectures that if the English start persecuting women, that will be to greater glory of God because they are determined to suffer (Carvajal, *Epistolario* 372).

76 "Las nuevas de por acá son todas lástimas y más lástimas y dolores sobre dolores; de manera que sucesos que allá espantan y de que no se enjugan las lágrimas en un año, aquí son pan cutidiano; y se miran los ojetos vivos con ojos serenos y enjutos por la mayor parte, porque no hay fuerzas ni aun para empezar a llorar tanto tropel y continuación de males de almas y cuerpos. Y es lo peor que el de las almas viene a llegar a algunos amigos, que, con la demasiada aflición flaquean y se rinden al pecado; aunque, gracias infinitas a Dios, muchos, y los más, están fuertes en la lealtad de la religión, y algunos se convierten de nuevo, aunque en estas apreturas, pocos."

77 "Confío muchísimo en que Dios le dará mejores sucesos al Rey nuestro señor, que dió a su padre; el cual, aunque fue bueno a los principios y años de su mocedad y en algunos otros tiempos, realmente no fue tan bueno y virtuosísimo como su hijo lo es y lo ha sido."

78 "Ofreciéronsele ocasiones fuertes en que quizá Dios se disgustó mucho, así en las domésticas como en otras muy grandes, tocantes a Estado. Y si fue así, que, por razón de Estado, como se dijo y entendió en el mundo, con favorecer a la reina Isabel y no contrastarla al tomar posesión de su reinado de Inglaterra (porque Francia no entrase con su derecho, que entonces tenía de la propietaria Reina de Escocia, María Stuarda, casada con el Delfín, heredera de este reino), se dio ocasión a tal perdición como la que se ve en este reino (aunque esto no se considerase en aquella

ocasión, que debiera considerarse); no debemos espantarnos que se perdiese una armada y armadas."

79 For a summary of Ribadeneyra's opinion on this subject, see Domínguez, "History in Action" 12–13.

80 "¿Piensa, que gustan los católicos de hablar en los tiempos de la reina Isabel? Raros veo, aun de los padres, que no gusten de alabarla y ponerla en las nubes. Y dicen que no había mucha persecución en su tiempo; como si no pudiesen desalabar al rey de ahora, que es lo que los lleva, sin alabar aquella miserable criatura, o no se pudiese tratar de esta persecución sin deshacer aquella. Yo les digo que creo no gusta Nuestro Señor de tales alabanzas y opiniones, de que se enojan bravamente algunos conmigo" (Carvajal, *Epistolario* 298). Though Carvajal here disagrees with the praises of Elizabeth, based on descriptions of the persecutions under James in other letters, she seems to agree that the Catholics at present experienced at least similar, if not worse, conditions than under the former queen. For instance, she tells Hernando de Espinoza in 1611: "La persecución está más fuerte que la he visto jamás en estos seis años. Las insolencias contra nuestra santa fe son cada día mayores y contra los que la profesan; verdaderamente, qué mártires hemos tenido tan dichosos, dos en la tierra y dos en Londres," mentioning also that now women were also persecuted, regardless of their rank (*Epistolario* 316). Incidentally, these letters reveal that, at least after the queen's death, not all Catholics hated Elizabeth.

81 "No sé lo que quiso ser: grandeza de Dios y consuelo grande para los católicos. Pues, prometo a vuestra señoría, lo han sentido de manera esta honra que se ha hecho a este santo cuerpo, que, con haber sido cosa tan pública, no hay una alma sola que hable en ello, de los herejes; y pocos católicos creo que lo saben. Yo lo publico lo que puedo y hallo que lo ignoran; o por lo menos los protestantes lo callan y muestran no saberlo. Esta traza tiene en todo" (*Epistolario* 378).

82 She recounts a dispute with Londoners on this topic: "Y uno de ellos me llegó con que este Rey les mandaba guardar su religión y que, 'si no era harto sabio para no hacerles seguir errores'; y yo, por huir el inconveniente que hay aquí en hablar del Rey, sobre que levantan mil caramillos, cautelosamente quise divertirlos de allí con fuerza, y no disimular la verdad; y dije que no me saliesen con el Rey, que había sido criado desde que era niño de un año entre puritanos, sin su santa madre y sin su católico padre; y que yo le quería bien, y ellos tenían mejor y más verdadero rey que la reina Isabel había sido." Even though Carvajal admits that she is being diplomatic in her comments about the king, she also affirms her commitment to the truth ("no disimular la verdad"), so

her words in 1608 can be taken as her opinion concerning James I, at least in her early days in London.

83 "Mucho se han fiado de su maldad del rey, pues se han determinado a hacerle su señor; porque, si no le tuvieran por infidelísimo, a la religión católica y a los padres por quien Dios le dio el ser, no se pudieran tanto dél asegurar; que, dicen, casi ninguno de ellos hay, digo de los que le han introducido en el reino, que no se halle culpado en la muerte de su madre, o que no sea hijo de los que la procuraron. Podría ser que Nuestro Señor se sirviese de tocarle en el corazón con el tiempo, que en el presente milagro sería no seguir la voluntad y consejos de los que le han hecho su rey, cosa de él tan deseada y pretendida."

84 "Las cosas de los católicos están bien apretadas en cuanto a hacienda, que los van dejando muy pobres; y eso es causa de la caída de muchos nuevamente, que, aunque en su corazón y en palabras se muestran católicos y dicen está con más viveza que nunca el amor de la fe en su pecho, van a la iglesia y toman el juramento nuevo, que es bien bellaco" (Carvajal, *Epistolario* 190).

85 "Aunque ha habido sacerdotes que quitan en esto el escrúpulo, aprobándole por lícito, pero no ninguno de la Compañía ni muchos de los sacerdotes importantes; porque, aunque estiman al principal, no quieren seguir su opinión en semejante materia."

86 "Uno de los carceleros principales se me llegó al oído un día y me dijo: 'Si queréis ir con el diablo, seguid a la religión nuestra; y si con Dios, la vuestra.' Y conocí que era cismático, que es ser católico en su corazón" (*Epistolario* 267).

87 See citation in 184n80.

88 "Cuando el Padre Ricardo Walpolo estaba en Valladolid, fiaba su celda, do se quedaban papeles y cartas sobre su mesa, de algunos estudiantes en quien había poco secreto; y menos, venidos ya a Inglaterra. Así, suplico a vuestra merced queme luego, en leyéndolas, mis cartas; que en ese colegio nuevo do hay tantos, habrá harto peligro desto; y algunos que, estando allá, dan satisfación y parecen muy devotos y santos, venidos acá se truecan muchísimo" (*Epistolario* 319).

89 "Deseo que no sepan los estudiantes ingleses estas cosas en particular; porque sepa que, venidos acá, todo lo cuentan en las casas de los católicos, en que hay gran inconveniente; y dicen que escribo larguísimo cuanto pasa en Inglaterra; y no todos los católicos son de fiar, aunque sean en la fe constantes, que tienen algunos cien impertinencias; y sacerdotes también."

90 This book is a Catholic response to James I's proclamation of 1610, long attributed to Creswell but recently conjectured to probably be from Michael Walpole (Allison). Its Spanish title is *Vando y leyes del Rey Iacobo*

de Inglaterra contra la fe católica. Con su respuests, y aduuertencias al letor prar la averiguación e inteligencia deste caso, provechosas para el mismo Rey, y para todos … traduzidal de Latin en varias leuguas por el D B. Claremond (Allison and Rogers 42).

91 "El libro contra la proclamación y leyes últimas es muy lindo; pero es en español, que acá vale poco o no nada. Pienso será de gran provecho en inglés para animar y fortificar los católicos. No son, sepa vuestra merced, tan fervorosos como allí los pinta; y éste es un inconveniente, porque ellos mesmos desestiman el libro en viendo algo que no es verdad en él, aunque sea en su favor; y yo lo he visto, cierto, y oído decirles en caso semejante: ¿Para qué escriben esas mentiras en los libros?"

92 "Bien parece que no lo padecen ellos. No sé porqué quieren cargar sus conciencias con caso tan grave, siendo motivo de tibieza y frialdad a los que allá pueden ayudar en diversas maneras a esta gente tan en extremo afligida y apretada."

93 "Veo que este rey trata de amistades con príncipes católicos, y al presente más que nunca; y, por otro cabo, jamás han sido tan apretados los católicos después que es rey, y crece notablemente su aflición de ellos; y hartos se rinden flacamente, cansados de sufrir con buscas y inquisiciones a todas horas infatigablemente … Espántome cómo el Consejo y Gobierno supremo lo sufre y permite; porque proceder tan tirano y exorbitante como estos oficiales tienen, aun entre herejes, puede condenarse por malísimo."

94 "No sé cómo allá se entiende esto de escribir. Yo escribo a los siervos de Dios, porque he menester sus oraciones; y a los que nos hacen limosna y escriben, no se puede tampoco dejar de escribirlos, si la limosna se ha de admitir, como es fuerza; y aunque no se admitiera, yo les mostrara gratitud y amor. Y no sé qué espíritu pueda ser, estando yo tratando siempre entre tan perversos demonios de gente como hay aquí y con tanta esterilidad de espirituales ayudas, retirarme de escribir a España a los que escribo, que son muy contados y sobre muy convenientes fundamentos. Y las cosas de aquí ahogan tanto, que tengo por muy especial discreción desahogarme en alguna manera."

95 "En dos casos hallo siempre muy dulce a Inglaterra, olvidándome que es un mar de hieles, con la gloria presente. Uno es cuando recibo a estos felices cuerpos y gasto las noches enteras, cansada en aderezarlos con las especias aromáticas, de limpiarlos primero del lodo, coger la sangre que aún brota de algunas de las venas, besando muchas veces sus manos y sus pies, vendando los despedazados miembros con holanda nueva, velando delante dellos y puniéndolos en su sepulcro de plomo, para que puedan conservarse, si así lo quiere conceder nuestro soberano señor, esperando acepta este pequeño servicio, a vueltas de su gran sacrificio y

holocausto dellos, que fuego se hace do queman sus entrañas y corazón. El otro es cuando estoy batallando, con las más eficaces razones que puedo, contra la ceguedad y error desta gente, puniéndoles delante la clara luz de la fe y doctrina católica y desbaratando con ella en sus entendimientos su opinión contraria, y veo que me escuchan y entienden y calan lo que digo; y que, verdaderamente, en esto hago aquello a que llega toda mi fuerza por muchas horas juntas, en una lengua áspera y trabajosa. Tienen poquísimo sentimiento de cosas eternas, no sé si es natural más en ellos que en nuestra nación, y cuando se llega a vencer a su entendimiento, queda una mucho más incontrastable muralla de amor y pegamiento a sus casas y huertas, y alegre cara de amigos, que, por no perderlo ni dar chica ocasión a ello, perderán a Dios mil veces. Entonces digo yo: Si os queréis ir al infierno, eso es otra cosa: yo no tengo de pagar por vos. Para mí basta justificar la causa de Dios y que no podáis decir: 'No tuvimos suficiente noticia.' Buscad, inquirid, preguntad."

96 "Puedo asegurar a vuestra excelencia de que la vocación de venir a Inglaterra que desde que era muchacha tuve, conforme a la doctrina de la Santa Iglesia ha sido muy probable y clarísima vocación de Dios, y con los sucesos se ha confirmado de día en día … Y así, suplico a vuestra excelencia que jamas concurra con los que, por su medio, procuraren mi salida deste reino, dejándolos a ellos que, a sus solas, hagan por violencia u maña lo que Nuestro Señor les permitiere" (*Epistolario* 416).

97 "Los bríos y valor de don Diego me han desbaratado una gloriosa corona que me parece llegué a ver desde muy cerca; y me deja en gran confianza de que ellos se buscarán modo y tiempo que don Diego ignore, si no es que Nuestro Señor quiera diferirlo más que el que él hubiere de estar aquí."

4. Monsters and Saints in Poetry and the Stage: Lope and Calderón

1 "Dos cosas me han obligado a escrebir este libro, y las mismas a dirigirle a Vuestra Alteza: la primera que no cubriese el olvido tan importante victoria, y la segunda que descubriese el desengaño lo que ignoraba el vulgo, que tuvo a Francisco Draque en tal predicamento, siendo la verdad que no tomó grano de oro que no le costase mucha sangre. En la una verá Vuestra Alteza qué valor tienen los españoles, y en la otra cómo acaban los enemigos de la Iglesia y en entrambas lo que debe a quien le ofrece su vida."

2 Hornedo discusses at length Lope's relationship to the Jesuits and cites two texts where Lope praises Ribadeneyra's language (413).

3 Though Lope's works imply these connections, no documents had been found to verify this information (Sánchez Jiménez, "Lope y la Armada";

Burguillo, "Lope y la causa" 180–2). However, this year Geoffrey Parker discovered a list of Armada soldiers that includes Lope de Vega's name (García Galero, "Un documento"). I am grateful to Burguillo for bringing this recent article to my attention.

4 For a summary of this position cojoined with the additional goal of presenting Drake as the model of the early modern Atlantic subject, see Wright, "From Drake to Draque."

5 E.C. Riley points to the sixteenth century as the time when verifiable facts gradually became important, but before that, the lines between history and fiction were blurred: "Writers of fiction continued the old tradition of asserting that the story they told was true (*adtestatio rei visae*) to impress and move their readers – a device evidently springing from the ancient idea of epic as designed to commemorate the deeds of famous men: the singer claimed that the deeds were true and revealed to him by the Muses" (164).

6 As mentioned in chapter 2, Ribadeneyra's history includes Sander's dubitable claim that Henry VIII was the father of Anne Boleyn – probably one reason the Englishman was nicknamed "Dr. Slanders" (Samson, "Upending" 288). Lope uses the *Relación de la Real Audiencia de Panamá* as his primary source, but because he sided with Diego Suárez de Amaya against Alonso de Sotomayor in the dispute of the glory for the victory over Drake and went against the official version, his poem is described as "very contrary to the truth" (Sánchez Jiménez, "Introducción" 65–78; "'Muy contrario a la verdad'"; García Rodrigo 329–31). Nevertheless, both Ribadeneyra and Lope strived to offer accounts supported by specific historical data, even if their construction of the overarching narrative was guided by their ideological goals.

7 "Canto las armas y el [varón] famoso, / que al atrevido inglés detuvo el paso, / aquel nuevo argonauta prodigioso, / que espantó las estrellas del Ocaso."

8 "De hoy más al fiero bárbaro disipo: / ya no estimo el Dragón ni los azores, / que el águila del Júpiter eterno / no teme al Anglia, al Asia, ni al infierno."

9 Another recurring trope in the poem is that of names, for example, when the great Spaniard don "Diego" is said to bear the name of Spain's great "Santiago" (9: XII) or the statue of St. "Barbara" being despoiled by "barbarians" (5: XXXIX). The trope is especially clear, however, in the episode of the attack on "Nombre de Dios," where a play on words indicates that those who do not love God's name cannot enter the town (5: V).

10 "Algunas veces levanta Dios á los malos, y les da el cetro y señorío para castigo del pueblo … Otras veces permite que los bárbaros y los hombres crueles é impíos tiranicen y aflijan el pueblo, y con sus crueldades purguen la escoria de sus grandes maldades, y por esto llama por Isaías

vara de su furor al rey de los asirios, y por Eçequiel á Nabucodonosor siervo suyo, porque se sirvió dellos para castigar á las diez tribus de Israel y á la tribu de Judá."

11 "Si son castigos, que a la tierra envías / con el poder inmenso de tu vara, / ¿hasta cuándo diré con Jeremías: / "¡Oh lanza del Señor descansa y para!", / y aquestas afligidas hijas mías / verán serena tu divina cara?"

12 "O cuchillo de Jehová, ¿hasta cuándo no reposarás? Métete en tu vaina, reposa y calla."

13 The word "rod" appears 118 times in the entire Bible scattered over twenty books. Psalms has the most occurrences of the use of this term in reference to God's rod (2:9, 23:4, 45:6, 89:32) – the most popular being in Psalm 23, the psalm of the Good Shepherd – and the word is also mentioned in Proverbs with reference to a parent's rod of discipline (10:13, 22:15, 23:13–14, 26:3, 29:15).

14 For example, part 1, chapter 5 includes citations on God's good discipline towards his children from Exod. 20; Ps. 9, 21, 98, 118; Prov. 3; Ezek. 16; Hos. 4; Amos 3; Mal. 3; John 9; 2 Cor. 12; Rom. 5; Heb. 13; Rev. 3.

15 "Costó sus vidas esto, inmenso Padre, / pero fue menester, pues se confirma / con esta sangre la divina Madre."

16 Some of those mentioned are the martyrs Peter, James the Great (*Santiago*), Andrew, Luke, and Mark, as well as the persecutors Nero, Diocletian, and Marcus Aurelius (1: XVII–XIX).

17 See Burguillo, "Ribadeneyra y la inestabilidad" 173.

18 "Pero vuelve a mirar a Ingalaterra / – que tan presto te amó .../ – verás de qué manera me destierra, / puesto que por tu fe y nombre divino / tantos mártires tiene jesuitas, / cartujos, sacerdotes y levitas. / ... / mira la reina del Dragón, Medea, / que las costas de América pasea."

19 For example, Ps. 35:17–25; Zech. 1:12–17.

20 "Agora que, del águila vencido, / ya no erizas las conchas arrogante, / su planta pone en tu cerviz britana / la Religión santísima Cristiana." In canto 1: V, Lope connects the eagle with Philip III, and Sánchez Jiménez points out that the eagle was the symbol of the Habsburgs (n. 113).

21 Gen. 3:15. Foreshadowing the defeat of the dragon in canto 5, the Virgin Mary is told: "Mirad, Señora, que hay enemistades / para siempre entre Vos y la serpiente, / que ansí lo dijo Dios, cuyas verdades / son más firmes que el cielo eternamente. / Si vuestras plantas para mil edades / y mil sin fin han de pisar su frente, / pisad este Dragón, pues que se atreve / a vuestros pies, más cándidos que nieve" (XXIX).

22 For a detailed argument supporting this idea, see Sánchez Jiménez, *Leyenda negra*.

23 "Agora es bien que en ese pecho infundas / mi espíritu de guerra y de codicia. / ¡Al arma, al arma, al oro, al oro, Draque, si hay tanto junto que la tuya aplaque!" (1: LXXVIII)

24 "Con rostro horrible y fiero / el dogmatizador perdió la vida; / partiose a ver a su inventor, Lutero, / mintiendo más que nunca en la partida. / Y, siendo un vil perjuro y hechicero, / … anátema, lascivo y revoltoso, / su tránsito alabaron por glorioso."

25 Sánchez Jiménez explains that the Greek Minerva was commonly depicted with a dragon in literature and in Lope's works (Lope de Vega, *Dragontea* 194).

26 The Black Panamanian men refuse Drake's alliance, saying that they do not fear his threats "nor the power of [his] belligerent queen" (6: XXXIX).

27 "Un ejemplo tan atroz y de tan extraña crudeza" tan grande que "en Tartaria y en la Scitia y en cualquiera nación por áspera, fiera e inhumana que sea, los mismos bárbaros, cuando le oyeren, no le creerán."

28 Even though *La Dragontea* was published in 1598, the poem had already received publication approval in 1597, the year that the comedy was written (García Morales xix).

29 See Oleza, *From Ancient Classical* and "Las posibilidades extremas."

30 "En esto paró el *amor* tan vehemente y *desatinado* que el Rey tuvo a Ana Bolena."

31 "Venciendo, pues, la ambición a la sensualidad, con gran sagacidad se determinó de no dar oídos a las requestas y combates amorosos del Rey, si no se casaba con ella … y cuanto ella más fuerte se mostraba, tanto el Rey más se enflaquecía, y con la exterior tibieza de ella se encendía él más en su amor" (Ribadeneyra 929).

32 "La mujer cierto es hermosa, / y aunque es de humilde linaje / tiene rico entendimiento / y es hechicera notable / … / pero en lo que falta tiene / es en que al Rey no le guarde / el decoro que le debe / y con otros hombres trate."

33 "Rosa es mi esposa, Rosa es mi señora, / ella es mi Emperadora / Poco es de Ing[a]laterra / señora es absoluta de la tierra; / Rosa es por quien yo vivo: / ¡no soy yo rey de Rosa, soy cautivo!"

34 "Es una santa señora / mártir del alma, y aun creo / que del cuerpo, o del deseo / con que ya su muerte adora."

35 "¡No lo trates con rigor / que, aunque es verdad que he perdido / de padecer el sentido, / aún no he perdido el amor! / ¡Cobre yo lo que perdí, / si ha despertado del sueño! / ¡Tú me le diste por dueño, / no me castigues a mí!"

36 "Señor mío y rey mío y marido amantísimo."

37 "Yo os certifico y prometo, señor, que no hay cosa mortal que mis ojos más deseen, que a vos."

38 "Una Rosa tan vil y venenífera / con nuestra flor de lis compita espléndida."
39 "¿Dónde esta la Medea que al Rey mísero / siembra en el pecho venenosos áspides?"
40 Oleza notes that the difference between tragedy and comedy in the baroque *Comedia nueva* was in whether the mimetic object of a play was a noble or a laughable action. He adds, therefore, that comedies could include tragic components (violence and even deaths) like the gang-rape in *El amor desatinado*, as long as they were meant to produce laughter (*From Ancient Classical* 27–9).
41 "Dicen que me han forzado / aunque no le he sentido, / porque eran estos hombres hechiceros; / pero no me han quitado / para el haberme herido / entonces, mis sentidos verdaderos: / que los verdugos fieros, / con las vainas crueles / de sus armas cobardes, / el cuerpo, que no aguardes / ver vivo entre los brazos como sueles, / me han puesto como un lirio / con afrentoso y áspero martirio."
42 Oleza cites Fadrique's harsh comment that early modern comic violence happens to people who are thought to be unnecessary in the world: "y ansí las muertes trágicas son lastimosas, mas las de la comedia, si alguna hay, son de gusto y pasatiempo, porque en ellas mueren personas que sobran en el mundo, como es una vieja cizañadora, un viejo avaro, un rufián o una alcahueta" (*From Ancient Classical* 29).
43 "Pues no bastaron para apartarle de su mal propósito y loca determinación las fealdades de Ana Bolena, ni su mala vida y fama, ni el ser tenida por hija suya, ni todos los medios que los de su consejo, y el mismo Tomás Boleyn, padre putativo de Ana, tomaron para divertirle de tan extraño desvarío, fueron parte para ponerle en razón."
44 McKendrick notes that the strictures of censorship varied according to time and that plays had to be passed by a censor and fiscal starting in 1615, which was after this play (*Theatre* 185–6).
45 Although from a later date, one of the most popular examples of plays that have this theme is Calderón de la Barca's *La vida es sueño*, where the prince, who cannot control his appetites, is likened to a beast and placed in a prison.
46 See Oleza, "Las posibilidades."
47 In addition to the example of Isabel as the faithful wife getting her husband back, Teodoro, Rosa's lover, at one point ironically sermonizes on the superiority of married love (Lope de Vega, *amor* 22).
48 For example: "¿mas quién no echará de ver / las espinas de la Rosa?" (Lope de Vega, *amor* 53).
49 On this point Lope coincides with Ribadeneyra since, as mentioned in chapter 2, honoring the memory of Catherine of Aragon was one

of the Jesuit's explicit reasons for writing the *Historia* (Ribadeneyra 899–900).

50 Yepes' *Historia particular*, for instance, was published in 1599.

51 For a discussion of this and other poems concerning England that show Lope's recurring interest in that land, see Burguillo, "Lope y la causa" 184–5.

52 "Fuiste contra la fiera Babilonia, / Aunque cordero tierno, por milagro, / nuevo, divino, heroico Meleagro, / de la escocessa silva Calidonia / … / en defensa de Cristo y de su templo, / Julián y Babilonia derribada / confiessen que ha vencido el Galileo" (Lope de Vega, *Rimas, Tomo I* 269).

53 For biographical information on Thomas Percy and a more detailed analysis of the sonnet, see Burguillo, "Lope y la causa" 188–91.

54 Pedraza Jiménez agrees with this assessment (Lope de Vega, *Rimas, Tomo I* 268), while Burguillo considers this a reference to Elizabethan England ("Lope y la causa" 190).

55 A good discussion with various examples of this genre in sixteenth- and seventeenth-century Spain, including Lope's familiarity with it, is available in Ponce Cárdenas, "El epitafio hispánico en el Renacimiento."

56 This achievement, referenced in Book IV of *La corona trágica* (Lope de Vega, *corona* 415), is important to the plot of Calderon's *La cisma de Ingalaterra*, which, like Lope and even perhaps inspired by this epitaph, plays with the symbolism of unintended reversals and paradoxes involving literal and metaphorical heads and feet.

57 See Knoppers, "The Antichrist, the Babilon, the great dragon."

58 One early reference to Elizabeth being worse than Jezebel and Athaliah appears in Sander's *Schismatis Anglicano*: "All men see that this unhappy generation, and that most abandoned sect, have their Athalia, Maacha, Jezabel, Herodias, Selene, Constantia, and Eudoxia. But Elizabeth has surpassed them all, she has taken upon herself the supremacy in the things of God, over even bishops and priests" (240). As mentioned in chapter 2, Ribadeneyra's *Historia* omits this comment.

59 Sander's and Yepes' ecclesiastical histories may have been used as a source, given their overlapping material with the other histories, although no specific reference seems to point directly to these texts.

60 For example, "reina sin dicha, aunque si más tuviera / más desdichada que dichosa fuera" (Lope de Vega, *corona* 129).

61 For instance, Elizabeth is implied in the lines "an inebriated woman sitting / upon the Beast, soaked in purple," and a few lines later, "she resembles Babylon, infamous mother of the lascivious fury" (Lope de Vega, *corona* 198), which clearly references the Whore of Babylon in the book of Revelation and, as discussed, which Lope had associated with the queen in earlier poems.

62 "Nunca la selva Calidonia llena / de más fieras se vio, ni más vestida / de monstros, que en su imperio atroz y fiero / sembró Calvino y cultivó Lutero."
63 "¡Oh, Enrique, a quien cegaron los sentidos / lascivia y ambición, qué muerte indina / de un hombre a quien dio siempre amor injusto / años de infamia y átomos de gusto!"
64 For example, in Book II Mary Stuart complains that the English do not respect her but that they respect "idolatrous Jezebel" (Elizabeth), and, continuing the same metaphor, the last stanza calls Mary the "Jehu" who "Jezebel" perceived as a threat (Lope de Vega, *corona* 263, 272; 2 Kings 9:30–3).
65 "And Jehu came into Jezrahel. Moreover Jezebel hearing of his entrance, paynted her face with stibicke stone, and decked her head, and beheld through the window" (2 Kings 9:30).
66 "¿Qué mayor inhumanidad ... ¿Qué mayor desamor ... ¿Qué mayor hipocresía."
67 Carreño notes that people in this region hated Mary, Queen of Scots (Lope, *corona* 148).
68 "Mas, ¿qué parte del mundo inhabitable, / qué Aimuro tan remoto o fiero igleo, / qué tártaro, qué scita inhospitable, / qué circaso cruel, qué vil diarbeo, / no sabe mi tragedia miserable, / de una fiera mujer vano trofeo?; / porque si alguna parte el sol ignora, / allí se sabe, allí se siente y llora."
69 Carreño seems to agree with this assessment when several of his notes reference Ribadeneyra's *Historia*, especially in the footnotes of Book IV (Lope de Vega, *corona* 409–13).
70 In this period, it was common to refer to England as *Ingalaterra*. Covarrubias' *Tesoro*, for instance, has an entry with this spelling (Lope de Vega, *Dragontea* 124). In plays, the longer name was often used to comply with the metric of the meter, and both Góngora and Quevedo only used "Ingalaterra" (Lope de Vega, *corona* 126n40).
71 See also A.A. Parker 251–4, 280.
72 For support, these scholars reference Bances Candamo's comments on an early modern representation of Elizabeth Tudor, where he says: "Ninguna reina ha sido más torpe que Isabela de Inglaterra ... la comedia del Conde de Essex la pinta solo con el efecto, pero tan retirado en la majestad y tan oculto en la entereza ... Preepto [*sic*] es de la comedia inviolable que ninguno de los personajes tenga acción desairada ni poco correspondiente a lo que significa ... Pues ¿cómo se ha de poner una princesa indignamente? Y más cuando la Poesía enmienda a la Historia" (qt. in Arellano, "Decid" 174).
73 See citation in 184n80.
74 See A.A. Parker 252–3.

75 *La corona trágica* also references the visit of the Prince of Wales to Madrid (Lope de Vega, *corona* 448). Because of this context, Weinreich argues that the play can be read as a political commentary to think through the possibility of a workable, albeit imperfect Anglo-Spanish marriage alliance in the context of the Spanish Match ("Introduction" 89–98).
76 See García Morales xxii.
77 In fact, Mackenzie and Quintero, the latter citing Bances Candamo's idea that the playwright was to be an entertainer and precept of the king, point out that *La cisma de Ingalaterra* could have included a covert lesson to Philip IV about the dangers for his kingdom in the sexual affair begun that year with the Spanish actress, María Calderón (*Gendering* 48–51, 140–1, 144–5; Mackenzie 5).
78 See Escudero 39–40.
79 "Algunos dicen que también se movió a perseguir a la reina, porque un astrólogo le había pronosticado que una mujer sería causa de su ruina y perdición, y dando él crédito a sus palabras, y pensando que esta mujer sería la reina doña Catalina, quiso quitarle el poder y apartarla del rey" (Ribadeneyra 920).
80 See A.A. Parker 285. Quintero sees this exclusion as an example of how Calderón employs plays to offer a more palatable ideological perspective for his audience through selective historical memory (*Gendering* 124).
81 "Tú sólo procuras dar la vida / a tu Rey, que ya la tiene perdida / a manos de un amor desatinado."
82 "¿A la Reina? ¡Qué mal dije! / A esa mujer, a esa fiera."
83 In fact, Quintero cogently argues that even though Elizabeth Tudor is not in the play, the audience would have reinscribed Elizabeth in the lewdness of Ana dancing and in other characteristics they were said to share (*Gendering* 147).
84 Escudero aptly notes: "La caída de Ana se desarrolla en un cuarto bloque. Calderón atempera las razones de la ejecución de Ana, al reducirlas esencialmente a su ambición, capaz de relegar su sentimiento amoroso (bastante ambiguo por cierto) por Carlos, en favor del fingido que siente por el rey. No sigue a Rivadeneyra que centra las razones de su ejecución en el aburrimiento del rey (aficionado a Juana Semeyra), y a su lascivia sin límite" (38). See also A.A. Parker 254–6.
85 "Es Ana mujer altiva. / Su vanidad, su ambición, / su arrogancia y presunción / la hacen, a veces, esquiva, / arrogante, loca y vana; / y aunque en público la ves / católica, pienso que es / en secreto luterana."
86 "hombre fácil / y se ciega tanto."
87 McKendrick notes that for the Inquisition, heresy and subversion in Spanish plays were more important than moral issues (*Theatre* 185–6). This, coupled with Spanish anxieties about opening theological disputes

to the *vulgo*, as illustrated by Ribadeneyra's challenges to publish his *Historia* in the vernacular, make crucial the clarification in the play.

88 As pointed out in chapter 2, even a decade after Elizabeth had died, Luisa de Carvajal contended this point with English Protestants at the local shops in London (*Epistolario* 258, 272).

89 Enrique swears María in as princess to satisfy the "vulgo, monstruo que piensa / que la Reina Catalina / no fue legítima Reina."

90 For a good summary of how different critics interpret Catalina in *La cisma de Ingalaterra*, see Fernández Biggs, *Calderón y Shakespeare* 207–8.

91 Fernández Biggs justly points out that the character of Catalina was originally conceived from historical accounts and filtered through an English vision of her exemplary life, not primarily forcing upon her León's "perfecta casada" or a Spanish post-Tridentine construction ("La reina Catalina" 340). Nevertheless, she aptly illustrated León's model and was clearly set forth in Spanish literature and plays – and would have been received by audiences – as an exemplum of León's ideal female behavior.

92 "Aunque a España pudiera / irme, adonde el victorioso / Carlos me diera su amparo, / ni le pido ni le invoco, / por no pedirle venganza / contra ti; pues si animoso / solicitara vengarme, / mi pecho, mi pecho propio / fuera tu escudo, y en el / deshicieran los enojos / golpes del templado acero, / tras el ardiente plomo."

93 "La diferencia que hay de los temores trágicos a los cómicos es que aquestos se quedan en los mismos actores solos, y aquellos pasan de los representantes en los oyentes, y ansí las muertes trágicas son lastimosas, mas las de la comedia, si alguna hay, son de gusto y pasatiempo."

94 See Oleza, *From Ancient Classical* 28–9.

95 Parker notes that Calderón makes these characterization changes because, for the playwright, the sins of the mind are more serious than the sins of the passions (256).

96 "Pero es muy tarde, no puedo. / ¡Qué mal hice! ¡Qué mal hice!" This last phrase could also be translated, "what evil I've done!" and Calderón possibly had both meanings in view.

97 "Ya que a tu madre no / pude, aunque tanto la quise, / restituirla en su Reino, / quiero en él restituirte."

98 "Yo las recibo. *Aparte* (Sin ellas.)" v. 2983.

99 For a convincing argument on this point, see Escudero 22–3, 37.

100 I am indebted to Ignacio Arellano for drawing my attention to this point.

5. A Novel Way of Looking at the English Reformation: Ribadeneyra and Cervantes' *La española inglesa*

1 "La irrealidad histórica de la reina que [él] forja."

2 See Samson, "Upending" (2019) and Forteza, "Representaciones" (2015).
3 For a discussion of the intersection between history and poetry in the work of Cervantes, see Riley 163–99.
4 Zimic points out that most scholars hold this position, though he considers *La española inglesa* to be closer to the chivalric novels (*libros de caballería*) (143–4). Sometimes the Byzantine novel also included tales of captives and overlapped with the "stories of captivity." Isabel Lozano-Renieblas argues that this novel belongs in the older categories of *caso* or saga.
5 Both El Saffar and Forcione – as well as Barbara Fuchs (*Romance*) and others – have used the term "romance" to refer to early modern Spanish idealist fiction, especially to what others describe as the Byzantine novel. Anne Cruz remarks that this understanding of the English word "romance" did not exist in early modern Spain and therefore suggests careful historical contextualizing when using it to discuss Spanish *novelas* ("Trucos" 20–1).
6 Fuchs adds that this mirroring serves to critique the "Spanish obsession with religious transparency" and to complicate national vs. religious alliances (*Passing* 106).
7 Although, as I mentioned, these authors usually do not point to the ecclesiastical histories for the negative view of Elizabeth, in effect, that is the historical narrative about England that Cervantes would be whitewashing. Alvar Ezquerra and Montcher argue that Cervantes was aware of what Richard Kagan calls a "political turn of history" around 1580, where historians produced texts that revised the past in order to gloss over former conflicts and establish political alliances in the present (66; Kagan 206–7). If this is the case, Cervantes may be doing something similar with *La española inglesa*.
8 Ricapito states: "as time went on, the greatness of Spain, just as powerful as at Lepanto, evanesced under the incompetence and misjudgments of Philip II, his advisors and admirals. The reality of Spain, now militarily and navally crippled must have affected Cervantes, who had the experience of defending its colors against the Turks" (63).
9 See McKendrick, *Theatre* 199–200.
10 "sin daño del alma ni del cuerpo."
11 Diego Sarmiento de Acuña, for example, lent his books to other Spaniards in London.
12 See Zamora Vicente 152. See Madroñal for his argument on their friendship lasting until 1604 and the reasons for their distancing.
13 See Rey 875–6.
14 See Johnson for a convincing argument on Cervantes' knowledge of English events and, particularly, of the visit of Lord Admiral Charles Howard and his entourage to Valladolid in 1605 ("Production" 390–6).

15 Johnson notes concerning *La española inglesa* that "the names of [Cervantes'] characters evoked for the Spanish reader of 1613 a half century of conflictive relations with England" ("Production" 379).
16 "Una tarde turbó todo su regocijo un ministro de la reina, que dio un recaudo a Clotaldo, que su Majestad mandaba que otro día por la mañana llevasen a su presencia a su prisionera la española de Cádiz. Respondióle Clotaldo que de muy buena gana haría lo que su Majestad le mandaba. Fuese el ministro, y dejó llenos los pechos de turbación, de sobresalto y miedo" (Cervantes, *Novelas* 247).
17 "Estando escribiendo ésta, se embravece la persecución cruelísima; la casa está triste, porque no se habla sino de la muerte o de las prisiones, o del perdimiento de los bienes y de la huída de los de ella; y con todo esto van adelante animosamente."
18 "Como la herejía es un monstruo infernal, todos los frutos que nacen de ella son monstruosos é infernales. *Y si para conocer esta verdad no bastaban los innumerables ejemplos que antes teníamos de crueldad, violencia y tiranía que han usado los herejes en nuestros tiempos*, este solo basta por todos, y bastará en todos los siglos venideros."
19 As noted, Américo Castro and Melveena McKendrick, respectively, believed that *La española inglesa* showed Cervantes' ignorance of Elizabeth's court and hastiness in the writing of the novel (Castro 287–8; McKendrick, *Cervantes* 275). Johnson, however, disagrees with these positions ("Literary Production" 399).
20 See Olid Guerrero 50–2.
21 Covarrubias' entry of "opinion" (*opinión*) notes the philosophical distinction between "opinion" and "science" (*ciencia*): "science says certain and indubitable things and opinion is about uncertain things: this is the reason for contrary opinions concerning one thing."
22 For Catholics to associate with Spaniards during Elizabeth's reign was highly suspicious of treason, especially after the execution of Mary Stuart and the proclamation of 1591, as seen in chapter 2.
23 Domínguez's argument that Ribadeneyra's *Historia* seems to stray from the norm and provides "true exemplars of royal prowess" in "a queenly trifecta" of Catherine of Aragon, Mary Tudor, and Mary Stuart ("History in Action" 10–11) would make Cervantes' reversal more ironic.
24 "Las prendas que se compran a deseos y tienen su estimación en el alma del comprador, aquello valen que vale una alma, que no hay precio en la tierra con que aprecialla."
25 The language of commerce employed in this response ("bought," "buyer," "worth," "value") is prominent throughout *La española inglesa*. For a more detailed analysis of this theme, see Johnson, "Literary Production."

26 Torres rightfully notes that this position is primarily based on Isabela being a spoil of war and does not give Isabela agency (124). Nevertheless, the queen remains a motherly figure, if only a substitute.
27 See Samson, "Upending" 301.
28 See *The Gift*.
29 "Siguiendo las pisadas de tales padres é hinchando la medida de ellos, con extraordinaria crueldad y tiranía persigue nuestra santa fe católica, apostólica y Romana, y hace carnicería de los que la profesan y enseñan, atormentándolos, descoyuntándolos y despedazándolos con atrocísimos linajes de penas y muertes."
30 This expression "to fill up the measure" of an ancestor's sins recalls Jesus' indictment of the scribes and Pharisees in Matthew 23:29–31 for killing the prophets: "Wo to you Scribes and Pharisees, ye hypocrites: because you build the Prophets sepulchres, and garnish the moniments of iust men, and say: If we had been in our fathers dayes, we had not been their felowes in the bloud of the Prophets. Therefore you are a testimonie to your owne selves, that you are the sonnes of them that killed the Prophets. And fil you up the measure of your fathers" (*Douay-Rheims*).
31 "Resolviose de dexar à Dios por el mundo, y el Reyno eterno, y de su bienaventurança, por otro miserable y temporal: y assi se entregó sin freno à los deleytes y regalos, y el govierno à los hombres desalmados, que su desventura, y los pecados de sus padres le avian dado por Consejeros."
32 Citing Saavedra Fajardo, Maravall notes that the value of exempla was that "not only do they delight but they also sweep away (*arrastran tras sí*)" (208).
33 "Para tener delante, para huir los malos [ejemplos] e imitar and seguir los buenos" and "*mostraros con exemplo desta persecucion*, quan temidos han de ser los juyzios de Dios, y quan reverenciados los secretos de su providencia, y amada su eterna bondad[33] (Ribadeneyra 893, 1195; emphasis added).
34 Maravall argues that the medieval exemplum responded to a society that was "immovable and traditional," and that Baroque authors reappropriated it with "forced novelty" (*forzosas novedades*) in order to restore the broken, traditional order (210). Stierle compares the use of the exemplum in Montaigne, Bocaccio, and Petrarch with that of Cervantes and places the exemplary novels in a moment of "crisis of exemplarity."
35 "Si bien lo miras, no hay ninguna [novela] de quien no se pueda sacar algún ejemplo provechoso; y si no fuera por no alargar este sujeto, quizá te mostrara el sabroso y honesto fruto que se podría sacar así de todas juntas, como de cada una de por sí."

36 For specific examples of the questions raised within different exemplary novels, see Boyd 29–40.

37 Anne Cruz makes a convincing case for Cervantes' awareness of the early modern expectation that novels should have a moral lesson ("Trucos" 17–19).

38 "Me doy a entender, y es así, que yo soy el primero que he novelado en lengua castellana, que las muchas novelas que en ella andan impresas, todas son traducidas de lenguas extranjeras, y éstas son mías propias, no imitadas ni hurtadas."

39 Cruz argues that this ambiguity reflected in the title "exemplary novels" arises from censorship and competition in the publishing market but that it also allows the reader to have an interpretive choice ("Trucos" 23).

40 "Esta novela nos podría enseñar cuánto puede la virtud y cuánto la hermosura, pues son bastante juntas y cada una de por sí a enamorar aun hasta los mismos enemigos, y de cómo sabe el cielo sacar de las mayores adversidades nuestras, nuestros mayores provechos."

41 The conditional verb may also mean that the reader "could" learn only if he or she reads carefully, as the prologue suggests. However, because of Cervantes' interest in entertainment and aesthetics in literature, as well as his ambiguity with the exemplum, it seems plausible to suggest that the novel here is questioning the didactic onus of literature.

42 As noted in chapter 2, when Ribadeneyra highlights that Henry is a negative example, he says, "We see a powerful king who wants everything he craves and executes everything he desires" (Ribadeneyra 895).

43 "En lo cual todo se vé la inefable misericordia é inmensa bondad del Señor, que de los mayores males del mundo saca mayores bienes."

44 The patriarch Joseph was appropriated by Jewish and Arab traditions alike as the model of patience in exile. Michael McGaha's *Coat of Many Cultures: The Story of Joseph in Spanish Literature, 1200–1492* is a compilation of old Jewish and Arabic retellings of the story of Joseph in Spain. See also Vincent Barletta's *Covert Gestures: Crypto-Islamic Literature as Culture Practice in Early Modern Spain*, especially chapters 5–6; and Anwar G. Chejne's *Islam and the West the Moriscos, a Cultural and Social History*.

45 The references to Joseph's suffering and outcomes in the *Tratado* are brief but numerous: 86 [91], 89 [94], 92 [97], 105 [110], 180 [184].

46 "¿En qué puede resplandecer más la bondad inmensa y soberana del Señor, que en sacar bienes tan grandes como los que habemos dicho, de un mal tan grande y espantoso como es la herejía? ¡Que sea nuestro Dios tan bueno, que los mayores males del mundo le sirvan para tan grandes bienes!"

47 For a later date, see Lapesa 242–63.
48 See Castro 283–4. For an opposing view, see McKendrick, *Cervantes* 262–3.
49 For El Saffar, Cervantes' Elizabeth is understood "by the abstract conception of her role" as Isabela's benefactor (160). Johnson, however, disagrees, stating that an evil Elizabeth who creates obstacles for the protagonist "would have been much more effective" ("Production" 388).
50 For a detailed analysis of gemination in the story, see Johnson, "Production" 398–400; Collins 59–60; and Torres.
51 Johnson thinks of these correspondences as "reversible equations" ("Production" 398–9).
52 Elizabeth was already known as "the Virgin Queen," and her comparison to the Virgin Mary is already prominent, as seen in Edmund Spenser's *The Faery Queene*.
53 See Johnson, "Production" 399.
54 This is not to say that the literary trope of ugliness as a test is baroque, since it appears in old folk stories. However, it is to say that this trope aligns with the early modern Spanish preoccupation with the correspondence between internal realities and external appearances, a concern also very present in other parts of *La española inglesa*.
55 For a more detailed discussion of the parallels between the biblical story of Joseph and *La española inglesa*, see Forteza, "Juegos intertextuales."
56 Incidentally, Foxe refers to the queen as a female Solomon in his 1583 dedication to the queen in the *Acts and Monuments*, addressing her as "your Maiestie (most deare Soueraigne Queene ELIZABETH, our peaceable SALOME)."
57 These tales were very popular in early modern Spain. They generally involved kidnappings, sea journeys, and stolen treasures and brought together national, racial, and/or religious enemies. One example is "The Story of the Captive Man" in chapters 37–42 of the first part of *Don Quixote*.
58 "Tan diestramente hablaba castellano, que con dificultad se le conociera no ser cristiana vieja, pues entre las más ladinas pudiera pasar por una dellas. El Rey la estimó en mucho, pareciéndole de gran precio. Luego la envió a la Reina su mujer, que no la tuvo en menos y, recibiéndola alegremente, así por su merecimiento como por ser principal decendiente de reyes, hija de un caballero tan honrado, como por ver si pudiera ser parte que le entregara la ciudad sin más daños ni peleas, procuró hacerle todo buen tratamiento, regalándola de la manera, y con ventajas, que a otras de las más llegadas a su persona. Y así no como a cautiva, antes como a deuda, la iba acariciando, con deseo que mujer

semejante y donde tanta hermosura de cuerpo estaba no tuviera el alma fea."

59 See *Passing for Spain* and Fuchs, Brewer-García, and Ilika, "*The Abencerraje*."

60 See Wardropper's argument that Cervantes draws from history because history is morally complex (154–5).

61 See Johnson, *Quest* 12.

62 Hillgarth points out that people outside of Spain looking in saw "a monolith of unchanging Catholic orthodoxy ruled over by absolute monarch," and this obscured internal criticism of Spain like that of *arbitristas* (9–10).

Conclusion

1 Although it was brought to my attention late in the writing of this book, my methodology in studying Ribadeneyra's influence in literature has some parallels to Peter Lake's *How Shakespeare Put Politics on the Stage*.

2 Monta, "Early Modern English Catholicism"; Shell, *Catholicism*.

3 See also Van Liere et al., *Sacred History*.

Works Cited

Alemán, Mateo. *Guzmán de Alfarache I*. Ed. José María Micó. Madrid: Cátedra, 1987.

Allison, A.F. "Did Creswell Write the Answer to the Proclamation of 1610? A Note on A&R 265." *Recusant History* 17.3 (1984): 348–57.

Allison, A.F., and D.M. Rogers. *The Contemporary Printed Literature of the English Counter-Reformation between 1558 and 1640: An Annotated Catalogue*. Vol. 1. Aldershot, Hant, England: Scolar Press; Brookfield, VT, USA: Gower, 1989.

Alvar Ezquerra, Alfredo, and Fabien Montcher. "Miguel de Cervantes and the Political Turn of History (c. 1570–1615)." *Cervantes: Bulletin of the Cervantes Society of America* 34.2 (2014): 15–36.

Arellano, Ignacio. "Decid al rey cuánto yerra. Algunos modelos de mal rey en Calderón." *El teatro clásico español a través de sus monarcas*. Ed. Luciano García Lorenzo. Madrid: Editorial Fundamentos, 2006. 149–80.

– "Metodología y recepción: lecturas trágicas de comedias cómicas del Siglo de Oro." *Criticón* 50 (1990): 7–21.

Barletta, Vincent. *Covert Gestures: Crypto-Islamic Literature as Culture Practice in Early Modern Spain*. Minneapolis, MN: University of Minnesota Press, 2005.

Barrón García, Aurelio A. "Interrogantes en torno a un cuadro de la visión mística de Fray Diego de Yepes." *La Contrarreforma en la diócesis de Tarazona: Estudios en torno al Obispo Fray Diego de Yepes*. Coord. Rebeca Carretero Calvo. Tarazona: Centro de Estudio Turiasonenses, 2013. 165–84.

Bates, A.W. *Emblematic Monsters: Unnatural Conceptions and Deformed Births in Early Modern Europe*. Amsterdam; New York, NY: Rodopi, 2005.

Benavides, José Ignacio de. *Las relaciones España-Inglaterra en los reinados de Felipe III y Felipe IV*. Madrid: Ministerio de Asuntos Exteriores y de Cooperación, Área de Documentación y Publicaciones, 2011.

Bilinkoff, Jodi. *Related Lives: Confessors and Their Female Penitents, 1450–1750*. Ithaca, NY: Cornell University Press, 2005.

Blue, William R. "The Politics of Lope's *Fuenteovejuna*." *Hispanic Review* 59.3 (1991): 295–315.

Bouza, Fernando. "Docto y devoto: La biblioteca del Marqués de Almazán y Conde de Monteagudo (Madrid, 1591)." *Hispania – Austria II: die Epoche Philipps II. (1556–1558)*. Ed. Friedrich Edelmayer. Vienna: Verlag für Geschichte und Politik; Munich: R. Oldenbourg Verlag, 1999. 247–308.

Boyd, Stephen F. "Introduction." *A Companion to Cervantes's* Novelas ejemplares. Ed. Stephen F. Boyd. Woodbridge, Suffolk: Tamesis, 2005. 1–46.

Burguillo, Javier. "Lope de Vega y la causa de Inglaterra: Notas de contexto sobre los poemas de las rimas dedicados a la Pérfida Albión." *Lope de Vega y El Humanismo Cristiano*. Eds. Jesús Ponce Cárdenas and Patricio de Navascués Benlloch. Madrid: Iberoamericana; Frankfurt am Main: Vervuert, 2018. Biblioteca áurea hispánica, 124. 177–205.

– "Pedro de Ribadeneyra y la inestabilidad del discurso histórico-literario en torno a la empresa de Inglaterra." *Saberes Inestables: Estudios Sobre expurgación y censura en la España de los siglos XVI y XVII*. Ed. Dámaris Montes, Víctor Lillo, María José Vega Ramos. Madrid: Iberoamericana; Frankfurt am Main: Vervuert, 2018. Biblioteca áurea hispánica, 118. 173–200.

Burnett, Mark Thornton. *Constructing "Monsters" in Shakespearean Drama and Early Modern Culture*. Houndmills, Basingstoke, Hampshire; New York: Palgrave Macmillan, 2002.

Calderón de la Barca, Pedro. *La cisma de Inglaterra*. Ed. Francisco Ruiz Ramón. Madrid: Castalia, 1981.

Cameron, Euan. "Primitivism, Patristics, and Polemics in Protestant Visions of Early Christianity." *Sacred History: Uses of the Christian Past in the Renaissance World*. Eds. Katherine Elliot Van Liere, Simon Ditchfield, and Howard Louthan. Oxford: Oxford University Press, 2012. 27–51.

Cammarata, Joan. *Women in the Discourse of Early Modern Spain*. Gainesville: University Press of Florida, 2003.

Canavaggio, Jean. *Cervantes*. New York: W.W. Norton, 1990.

Carvajal y Mendoza, Luisa de. *Escritos autobiográficos*. Ed. Camilo María Abad. Barcelona: J. Flors, 1966.

– *Epistolario y Poesías*. Eds. Jesús González Marañón and Camilo María Abad. Madrid: Ediciones Atlas, 1965.

– *The Letters of Luisa de Carvajal y Mendoza*. Ed. Glyn Redworth. 2 vols. London: Pickering & Chatto, 2012.

Casalduero, Joaquín. *Sentido y forma de las "Novelas ejemplares."* 2nd ed. Madrid: Editorial Gredos, 1974.

Castro, Américo. *El pensamiento de Cervantes*. Ed. Julio Rodríguez-Puértolas. Barcelona: Noguer, 1972.

Cervantes Saavedra, Miguel de. *Novelas ejemplares I*. Ed. Harry Sieber. Madrid: Ediciones Cátedra, 1980.

Chejne, Anwar G. *Islam and the West: The Moriscos, a Cultural and Social History*. Albany: State University of New York Press, 1983.

Clamurro, William H. "Chapter Four: The Sins of the Father: *La Española Inglesa." Beneath the Fiction the Contrary Worlds of Cervantes's Novelas Ejemplares*. 7 vols. New York: Peter Lang, 1997. 99–121.

Collins, Marsha S. "Transgression and Transfiguration in Cervantes's *La española inglesa." Cervantes: Bulletin of the Cervantes Society of America*. 16.1 (1996): 54–73.

Collinson, Patrick. "Elizabeth I (1533–1603), queen of England and Ireland." *Oxford Dictionary of National Biography*. Ed. Lawrence Goldman. Oxford: Oxford University Press, 2004. Online ed. https://doi.org/10.1093/ref:odnb/8636. 21 Aug 2021.

Cruz, Anne J. "Cervantes's *Novelas Ejemplares*: Table of Trucos, Tricks of the Trade." *Cervantes: Bulletin of the Cervantes Society of America* 34.1 (2014): 15–39.

– "Chains of Desire: Luisa de Carvajal y Mendoza's Poetics of Penance." *Estudios sobre escritoras hispánicas en honor de Georgina Sabat-Rivers*. Ed. Lou Charnon-Deutsch. Madrid: Editorial Castalia, 1992. 97–112.

– "Introduction – Crossing the Channel." *Material and Symbolic Circulation between Spain and England, 1554–1604*. Ed. Anne J. Cruz. Aldershot, England; Burlington, VT: Ashgate, 2008. xvii–xxvii.

– "Luisa de Carvajal y Mendoza y su conexión jesuita." *Actas Irvine-92, Asociación Internacional de Hispanistas*. Ed. Juan Villegas. Irvine: University of California: Asociación Internacional de Hispanistas, 1994. 97–104.

– trans. and ed. *The Life and Writings of Luisa de Carvajal y Mendoza*. Toronto: Iter Inc.: Centre for Reformation and Renaissance Studies, 2014.

– "Reading Over Men's Shoulders: Noblewomen's Libraries and Reading Practices." *Women's Literacy in Early Modern Spain and the New World*. Eds. Anne J. Cruz and Rosilie Hernández. Farnham, England; Burlington, VT: Ashgate, 2011. 41–58.

– "Willing Desire: Luisa de Carvajal y Mendoza and Female Subjectivity." *Power and Gender in Renaissance Spain: Eight Women of the Mendoza Family, 1450–1650*. Ed. Helen Nader. Chicago: University of Illinois Press, 2004. 177–93.

da Costa Fontes, Manuel. "Love as an Equalizer in *La española inglesa." Romance Notes* 16 (1975): 742–8.

de Armas, Frederick A. "Heretical Stars: The Politics of Astrology in Cervantes' *La gitanilla* and *La española inglesa." Material and Symbolic Circulation between Spain and England, 1554–1604*. Ed. Anne J. Cruz. Aldershot, England; Burlington, VT: Ashgate, 2008. 89–100.

de la Fuente, Vicente. *Obras escogidas del Padre Pedro de Rivadeneira … con una noticia de su vida y juicio crítico de sus escritos*. 62 vols. Madrid: Impr. de Hernando y Compañia, 1899. Biblioteca de autores españoles.

Demers, Patricia. *Women's Writing in English: Early Modern England*. Toronto: University of Toronto Press, 2005.

Ditchfield, Simon. "What Was Sacred History? (Mostly Roman) Catholic Uses of the Christian Past after Trent." *Sacred History: Uses of the Christian Past in the Renaissance World*. Eds. Katherine Elliot Van Liere, Simon Ditchfield, and Howard Louthan. Oxford: Oxford University Press, 2012. 72–97.

Dolan, Frances E. *Whores of Babylon: Catholicism, Gender, and Seventeenth-Century Print Culture*. Notre Dame, Ind.: University of Notre Dame Press, 2005.

Domínguez, Freddy C. "History in Action: The Case of Pedro de Ribadeneyra's *Historia ecclesiastica del scisma de Inglaterra*." *Bulletin of Spanish Studies* (2015): 1–26.

– *Radicals in Exile: English Catholic Books during the Reign of Philip II*. University Park, Pennsylvania: Penn State University Press, 2020.

Duffy, Eamon. *Fires of Faith: Catholic England under Mary Tudor*. New Haven: Yale University Press, 2009.

El Saffar, Ruth S. *Novel to Romance: A Study of Cervantes's Novelas Ejemplares*. Baltimore: Johns Hopkins University Press, 1974.

Elliott, John H. *Imperial Spain, 1469–1716*. Harmondsworth: Pelican Books, 1970.

Escudero, Juan Manuel. "Introducción a *La cisma de Ingalaterra*." *La cisma de Ingalaterra*. Ed. Juan Manuel Escudero. Kassel: Edition Reichenberger, 2001. 1–49.

Fernández Biggs, Braulio. *Calderón y Shakespeare: Los personajes de* La cisma de Inglaterra *y* Henry VIII. Madrid: Iberoamericana; Frankfurt am Main: Vervuert; Pamplona: Universidad de Navarra, 2012.

– "La reina Catalina en *La cisma de Ingalaterra* de Calderón: ¿construcción política o representación histórica?" *Mujer y literatura femenina en la América virreinal*. Ed. Miguel Donoso Rodríguez. New York: IDEA (Instituto de Estudios Auriseculares), 2015. 327–41. http://dadun.unav.edu/handle/10171/41584.

Forcione, Alban K. "Afterword: Exemplarity, Modernity, and the Discriminating Games of Reading." *Cervantes's 'Exemplary Novels' and the Adventure of Writing*. Eds. Michael Nerlich and Nicholas Spadaccini. Minneapolis, MN: Prisma Institute, 1989. 331–51.

– *Cervantes and the Humanist Vision: A Study of Four Exemplary Novels*. Princeton, NJ: Princeton University Press, 1982.

Forster, E.M. *Aspects of the Novel*. New York: Harcourt Brace & World, 1954.

Forteza, Deborah R. "Juegos intertextuales con relatos religiosos en *La española inglesa* de Cervantes." Actas del XX Congreso de la Asociación Internacional de Hispanistas (AIH), Jerusalén 2019, forthcoming.

– "Representaciones del cisma de Inglaterra en el Siglo de Oro: Ribadeneira y Cervantes." *"Spiritus Vivificat." Actas del V Congreso Internacional Jóvenes Investigadores Siglo de Oro (JISO 2015)*. Eds. Maite Iraceburu Jiménez and Carlos Mata Induráin. Pamplona: Servicio de Publicaciones de la

Universidad de Navarra, Colección BIADIG (Biblioteca Áurea Digital), 36 / Publicaciones Digitales del GRISO, 2016. 33–41.

– "A 'Very Particular Providence: Anglo-Spanish Connections and Textual Production in Diego de Yepes' *Historia particular*." Ed. Freddy Cristobal Domínguez. *Spanish Elizabethans: Anglo-Iberian Entanglements during the Counter-Reformation*, Boston: Brill (Catholic Christendom Series), forthcoming.

Foxe, John. *The Unabridged Acts and Monuments Online* or *TAMO* (1583 edition). Sheffield: The Digital Humanities Institute, 2011. http//www.dhi.ac.uk/foxe. 1 March 2011.

Freeman, Thomas S. "'As True a Subiect being Prysoner': John Foxe's Notes on the Imprisonment of Princess Elizabeth, 1554–5. (Notes and Documents)." *The English Historical Review* 117.470 (2002): 104–16.

– *'Great Searching out of Bookes and Autors': John Foxe as an Ecclesiastical Historian*. PhD dissertation Rutgers, 1995.

– "Harpsfield, Nicholas (1519–1575)." *Oxford Dictionary of National Biography*. Ed. Lawrence Goldman. Oxford: Oxford University Press, 2004. Online ed. http://www.oxforddnb.com/view/article/12369. 3 Nov. 2015.

– "Hands Defiled with Blood: Henry VIII in Foxe's 'Book of Martyrs.'" *Henry VIII and History*. Eds. Thomas Betteridge and Thomas S. Freeman. Farnham, Surrey, England; Burlington, VT: Ashgate, 2012. 87–118.

Freeman, Thomas S., and Elizabeth Evenden. *Religion and the Book in Early Modern England: The Making of John Foxe's "Book of Martyrs."* Cambridge: Cambridge University Press, 2014.

Fuchs, Barbara. *Passing for Spain: Cervantes and the Fictions of Identity*. University of Illinois Press, 2003.

– *Romance*. New York: Routledge, 2004.

Fuchs, Barbara, Larissa Brewer-García, and Aaron Ilika. *"The Abencerraje" and "Ozmín and Daraja": Two Sixteenth-Century Novellas from Spain*. Philadelphia: University of Pennsylvania Press, 2014.

García Galero, Jesús. "Un documento prueba que Lope de Vega estuvo en la Armada Invencible." *ABC* 21 June 2021. https://www.abc.es/cultura/abci-lope-de-vega-armada-enf-202106200101_reportaje.html.

García Morales, Justo. "Prologo." *El amor desatinado*. Ed. Justo García Morales. Madrid: Biblioteca Nacional, 1968. v–xlviii.

García Rodrigo, María Luisa. "Algunas notas sobre la piratería en *La Dragontea* de Lope de Vega." *Studia aurea: actas del III Congreso de la AISO (1993)*. Eds. (coord.)Ignacio Arellano Ayuso, Carmen Pinillos Salvador, Marc Vitse, Frédéric Serralta. Toulouse: 1996. 329–338.

Goodare, Julian. "Mary [Mary Stewart] (1542–1587)." *Oxford Dictionary of National Biography*. Eds. H.C.G. Matthew and Brian Harrison. Oxford: Oxford University Press, 2004. Online ed. Ed. Lawrence Goldman.

May 2007. http://www.oxforddnb.com/view/article/18248. 3 Nov. 2015.

Grafton, Anthony. "Church History in Early Modern Europe: Tradition and Innovations." *Sacred History: Uses of the Christian Past in the Renaissance World*. Eds. Katherine Elliot Van Liere, Simon Ditchfield, and Howard Louthan. Oxford: Oxford University Press, 2012. 72–97.

– "Matthew Parker: The Book as Archive." *History of Humanities* 2.1 (2017): 15–50.

– *Worlds Made by Words: Scholarship and Community in the Modern West*. Cambridge, MA: Harvard University Press, 2009.

Guazzelli, Giuseppe Antonio. "Cesare Baronio and the Roman Catholic Vision of the Early Church." *Sacred History: Uses of the Christian Past in the Renaissance World*. Eds. Katherine Elliot Van Liere, Simon Ditchfield, and Howard Louthan. Oxford: Oxford University Press, 2012. 52–71.

Hanrahan, Thomas. "History in the *Española Inglesa*." *MLN* 83 (1968): 267–71.

Herrera y Tordesillas, Antonio de. *Historia de lo succedido en Escocia e Inglaterra en quarenta y quatro años que vivio Maria Estuarda Reyna de Escocia / Escrita por Antonio de Herrera, criado del Rey Nuestro Señor* … Lisboa: por Manuel de Lyra, 1590.

Highley, Christopher. "'A Pestilent and Seditious Book': Nicholas Sander's *Schismatis Anglicani* and Catholic Histories of the Reformation." *Huntington Library Quarterly* 68.1–2 (2005): 151–71.

Hillgarth, J.N. *The Mirror of Spain, 1500–1700: The Formation of a Myth*. Ann Arbor: University of Michigan Press, 2000.

Hornedo, Rafael María de. "Lope y Los Jesuitas." *Razón y Fe: Revista Hispanoamericana de Cultura* 166 (1963): 405–22.

Houliston, Victor. *Catholic Resistance in Elizabethan England Robert Persons's Jesuit Polemic, 1580–1610*. Aldershot, England; Burlington, VT: Ashgate; Roma: Institutum Historicum Societatis Iesu, 2007.

– "The Lord Treasurer and the Jesuit: Robert *Persons's* Satirical *Responsio* to the 1591 Proclamation." *The Sixteenth Century Journal* 32.2 (2001): 383–401. *JSTOR*, www.jstor.org/stable/2671738. https://doi.org/10.2307/2671738. 11 July 2020.

– "Rehabilitating Robert Persons: Then and Now." *Reformation Reputations: The Power of the Individual in English Reformation History*. Eds. David J. Crankshaw and George W.C. Gross. Cham: Palgrave Macmillan, 2020. 421–47. https://doi.org/10.1007/978-3-030-55434-7_10.

Howe, Elizabeth Teresa. *Autobiographical Writing by Early Modern Hispanic Women*. Burlington, VT: Ashgate, 2015.

Icaza, Francisco de. *Las "Novelas ejemplares" de Cervantes: Sus críticos, sus modelos literarios, sus modelos vivos*. Madrid: 1901.

Ives, E.W. *Anne Boleyn*. Oxford, Oxfordshire; New York, NY: Blackwell, 1986.

Johnson, Carroll B. "Catolicismo, familia y fecundidad: el caso de 'La española inglesa.'" Actas del IX Congreso de la Asociación Internacional de Hispanistas: 18-23 agosto 1986 Berlín. Coord. Sebastián Neumeister. Vol. 1. Frankfurt am Main: Vervuert, 1989.

– "'La española inglesa' and the Practice of Literary Production." *Viator* 19 (1988): 377–416.

– *Don Quixote: The Quest for Modern Fiction*. Boston: Twayne Publishers, 1990.

Kagan, Richard L. *Clio & the Crown: The Politics of History in Medieval and Early Modern Spain*. Baltimore: Johns Hopkins University Press, 2009.

Kamen, Henry. *Spain, 1469–1714: A Society of Conflict*. 4th ed. London; New York: Routledge, 2014.

King, John N. "Fiction and Fact in Foxe's *Book of Martyrs*." *John Foxe and the English Reformation*. Ed. D.M. Loades. Aldershot, Hants, England; Brookfield, VT: Scolar Press, 1997. 12–35.

– "Guides to Reading Foxe's *Book of Martyrs*." *Huntington Library Quarterly* 68.1–2 (2005): 133–50.

Knoppers, Laura Lunger. "'The Antichrist, the Babilon, the Great Dragon': Oliver Cromwell, Andrew Marvell, and the Apocalyptic Monstrous." *Monstrous Bodies/Political Monstrosities in Early Modern Europe*. Eds. Laura Lunger Knoppers and Joan B. Landes. Ithaca: Cornell University Press, 2004. 93–126.

Lake, Peter. *How Shakespeare Put Politics on the Stage: Power and Succession in the History Plays*. New Haven: Yale University Press, 2016.

Lapesa, Rafael. "En torno a *La española inglesa* y *El Persiles*." *De la edad media a nuestros días; Estudios de historia literaría*. Madrid: Editorial Gredos, 1967.

Loades, D.M. *The Tudors: History of a Dynasty*. London: Continuum International Publishing Group, 2012.

Loomie, Albert J. *The Spanish Elizabethans: The English Exiles at the Court of Philip II*. New York: Fordham University Press, 1963.

– *Toleration and Diplomacy: The Religious Issue in Anglo-Spanish Relations, 1603–1605*. Philadelphia: American Philosophical Society, 1963.

Lope de Vega. *El amor desatinado*. Ed. Justo García Morales. Madrid: Biblioteca Nacional, 1968.

– *La corona trágica: vida y muerte de la serenísima reina de Escocia María Estuarda*. Eds. Antonio Carreño-Rodríguez and Antonio Carreño. Madrid: Cátedra, 2014.

– *La Dragontea*. Ed. Antonio Sánchez Jiménez. Madrid: Cátedra, 2007.

Lope de Vega. *Rimas*. Ed. Felipe B. Pedraza Jiménez. I Vol. Castilla-La Mancha: Universidad de Castilla-La Mancha, 1994.

– *Rimas humanas y otros versos*. Ed. Antonio Carreño. Barcelona: Crítica, 1998.

Lozano-Renieblas, Isabel. "Tradición y experimentación en *La española inglesa*." *Visiones y revisiones cervantinas: actas selectas del VII Congreso*

Internacional de la Asociación de Cervantistas. Coord. Christoph Strosetzki. Alcalá de Henares: Centro de Estudios Cervantinos, 2011. 527–34.
MacCulloch, Diarmaid. *The Reformation*. 1st American ed. New York: Viking, 2004.
Mackenzie, Ann L. "Introduction." *The Schism in England (La cisma de Inglaterra)*. Ed. Ann L. Mackenzie. Warminster England: Aris Phillips, 1990. 1–44.
Madroñal, Abraham. "Entre Cervantes y Lope: Toledo, hacia 1604." *eHumanista: Journal of Iberian Studies* 1 (2012): 300–32.
Maravall, José Antonio. *Estudios de historia del pensamiento español, serie tercera: El siglo del barroco*. 2nd ed. Madrid: Cultura Hispánica, 1984.
Martínez Berbel, Juan Antonio. "'Puso el honor dragones de Medea.' Sobre ésta y otras Medeas en el teatro de Lope." *Criticón* 87–9 (2003): 479–92.
Mascuch, Michael, Rudolf Dekker, and Arianne Baggerman. "Egodocuments and History: A Short Account of the Longue Durée." *Historian* 78.1 (2016): 11–56.
Mancini Giancarlo, Guido. *La obra histórico-apologética de Fray Diego de Yepes*. Santafé de Bogotá: Inst. Caro y Cuervo, 1953.
Marshall, Peter. "The Other Black Legend: The Henrician Reformation and the Spanish People." *The English Historical Review* 116.465 (2001): 31–49.
Mauss, Marcel. *The Gift*. Eds. Jane I. Guyer and Bill Maurer. Expanded ed. Chicago: HAU Books, 2016.
McGaha, Michael D. *Coat of Many Cultures: The Story of Joseph in Spanish Literature, 1200–1492*. Philadelphia: Jewish Publication Society, 1997.
McKendrick, Melveena. *Cervantes*. Boston: Little, Brown, 1980.
– *Theatre in Spain, 1490–1700*. Cambridge; New York: Cambridge University Press, 1989.
Mendoza, Don Bernardino de. "Copia de carta descifrada de Don Bernardino de Mendoza á Su Majestad, fecha en Londres á 4 de diciembre de 1581." *Colección de documentos inéditos para la historia de España*. Eds. Marqués de la Fuensanta del Valle, Feliciano Ramírez de Arellano; Francisco de Zabálburu; and José León Sancho Rayón. 92 vols. Madrid: s.n., 1888. 200–1.
Monta, Susannah Brietz. *Martyrdom and Literature in Early Modern England*. Cambridge; New York: Cambridge University Press, 2005.
Muñoz, Luis. *Vida y virtudes de … Doña L. de Carvaial y Mendoça. su jornada a Inglaterra, y Sucessos en aquel reyno. (Poesias espirituales de Doña L. de Carvaial y Mendoça, etc.)*. Madrid: 1632.
Niccoli, Ottavia. *Prophecy and People in Renaissance Italy*. Princeton, N.J.: Princeton University Press, 1990.
Oates, Rosamund. "Elizabethan Histories of English Christian Origins." *Sacred History: Uses of the Christian Past in the Renaissance World*. Eds. Katherine Elliot Van Liere, Simon Ditchfield, and Howard Louthan. Oxford: Oxford University Press, 2012. 165–85.

Oleza, Joan. *From Ancient Classical to Modern Classical: Lope de Vega and the New Challenges of Spanish Theatre*. New York: IDEA (Instituto de Estudios Auriseculares), 2012.

– "Las posibilidades extremas de una traza grave 'El amor desatinado,' de Lope de Vega." *En buena compañía: estudios en honor de Luciano García Lorenzo*. Ed. Joaquín Álvarez Barrientos. Madrid: Consejo Superior de Investigaciones Científicas, 2009. 489–504.

Olid Guerrero, Eduardo. "The Machiavellian in-Betweeness of Cervantes's Elizabeth I." *Cervantes: Bulletin of the Cervantes Society of America* 33.1 (2013): 45–80.

Olid Guerrero, Eduardo, and Esther Fernández Rodríguez, eds. *The Image of Elizabeth I in Early Modern Spain*. Lincoln, NE: University of Nebraska Press, 2019.

Parker, Alexander A. *The Mind and Art of Calderón: Essays on the Comedias*. Ed. Deborah Kong. Cambridge; New York: Cambridge University Press, 1988.

Parker, Geoffrey. *Empire, War and Faith in Early Modern Europe*. London: Penguin Books, 2003.

– *Imprudent King: A New Life of Philip II*. Cambridge: Yale University Press, 2014.

Parsons, Robert. *Relacion de algvnos martyrios que de nueuo han hecho los hereges en Inglaterra y de otras cosas tocantes a nuestra santa y Catolica religion*. En Madrid: Por Pedro Madrigal, 1590.

Patterson, W.B. "The Recusant View of the English Past." *The Materials, Sources and Methods of Ecclesiastical History*. Ed. Derek Baker. Oxford: Ecclesiastical History Society, 1975. 249–62.

Paulson, Michael. "The Scope of Mary Stuart in Lope's *La corona trágica* and in Diamante's *La Reina María Estuarda*." *Language Quarterly* 30.3–4 (1992): 61–7.

de Pazzis Pi Corrales, Magdalena. "The View from Spain: Distant Images and English Political Reality in the Late Sixteenth Century." *Material and Symbolic Circulation between Spain and England, 1554–1604*. Ed. Anne J. Cruz. Aldershot, England; Burlington, VT: Ashgate, 2008. 13–27.

Petroff, Elizabeth. *Medieval Women's Visionary Literature*. New York: Oxford University Press, 1986.

Pineda, Victoria. "La tradición del exemplum en el discurso historiográfico y político de la España imperial." *Revista de Literatura* 67.133 (2005): 31–48.

Pollen, J.H. "Dr. Nicholas Sander." *The English Historical Review* 6.21 (1891): 36–47.

Ponce Cárdenas, Jesús. "El epitafio Hispánico en el Renacimiento: Textos y contextos." *e-Spania* 17 (2014). https://doi.org/10.4000/e-spania.23300. 27 June 2020.

Quintero, María Cristina. "'The Body of a Weak and Feeble Woman': Courting Elizabeth in Antonio Coello's *El conde de Sex*." *Material and Symbolic Circulation between Spain and England, 1554–1604*. Ed. Anne J. Cruz. Aldershot, England; Burlington, VT: Ashgate, 2008. 71–87.

Quintero, María Cristina. *Gendering the Crown in the Spanish Baroque Comedia*. Burlington, VT: Ashgate, 2012.

Rainolde, Richard, and Aphthonius. *The Foundacion of Rhetorike*. Ed. Francis Rarick Johnson. New York: Scholars' facsimilies & reprints, 1945.

Redworth, Glyn. "A New Way of Living? Luisa de Carvajal and the Limits of Mysticism." *A New Companion to Hispanic Mysticism*. Ed. Hilaire Kallendorf. Leiden, Netherlands; Boston: Brill, 2010.

– *The She-Apostle: The Extraordinary Life and Death of Luisa de Carvajal*. Oxford; New York: Oxford University Press, 2008.

Rees, Margaret A. *The Writings of Doña Luisa de Carvajal y Mendoza, Catholic Missionary to James I's London*. Lewiston, NY: E. Mellen Press, 2002.

Rey, Eusebio. "Introducción a la Historia eclesiástica del cisma de Inglaterra." *Historias de la contrarreforma*. Madrid: Editorial Católica, 1945. 855–88. Biblioteca de autores cristianos.

Rhodes, Elizabeth. *This Tight Embrace*. Milwaukee, WI: Marquette University Press, 2000.

Ribadeneyra, Pedro de. *Historias de la contrarreforma*. Ed. Eusebio Rey. Madrid: Editorial Católica, 1945.

Ricapito, Joseph V. *Cervantes's Novelas Ejemplares: Between History and Creativity*. West Lafayette, IN: Purdue University Press, 1996.

Rico, Francisco. "Contextos." *Lazarillo de Tormes*. Eds. Francisco Rico and Bienvenido Morros. 15th ed. Madrid: Cátedra, 2000. 45–77.

Riley, E.C. *Cervantes's Theory of the Novel*. Newark: Juan de la Cuesta, 1992.

Rivadeneira, Pedro de. *Tratado de la tribulación*. Barcelona: Daniel Cortezo y Ca, 1885.

Rogers, D.M. "Introduction." *Historia particular de la persecucion de Inglaterra*. Ed. D.M. Rogers. Farnborough: Gregg, 1971.

Roldán-Figueroa, Rady. "Pedro de Ribadeneyra's *Vida del P. Ignacio de Loyola* (1583) and Literary Culture in Early Modern Spain." *Exploring Jesuit Distinctiveness: Interdisciplinary Perspectives on Ways of Proceeding within the Society of Jesus*. Ed. Robert Aleksander Maryks. 6 vols. Leiden; Boston: Brill, 2016. 156–74.

Samson, Alexander. "A vueltas con los orígenes de la Leyenda Negra: La Inglaterra mariana." *España ante sus críticos: las claves de la Leyenda Negra*. Eds. Yolanda Pérez Rodríguez, Antonio Sánchez Jiménez, and Harm den Boer. Madrid: Iberoamericana; Frankfurt am Main: Vervuert, 2015. 91–116.

– "Cervantes Upending Ribadeneyra: Elizabeth I and the Reformation in Early Modern Spain." *The Image of Elizabeth I in Early Modern Spain*. Eds. Eduardo Olid Guerrero and Esther Fernández Rodríguez. Lincoln, NE: University of Nebraska Press, 2019. 287–311.

Sánchez Jiménez, Antonio. "Introducción." *La Dragontea*. Ed. Antonio Sánchez Jiménez. Madrid: Cátedra, 2007. 11–113.

– *Leyenda Negra: La batalla sobre la imagen de España en tiempos de Lope de Vega*. Madrid: Cátedra, 2016.

– "Lope de Vega y la Armada Invencible de 1588: biografía y poses del autor." *Anuario Lope de Vega* 14 (2008): 269–89.

– "'Muy contrario a la verdad': Los documentos del Archivo General de Indias sobre *La Dragontea* y la polémica entre Lope y Antonio de Herrera." *Bulletin of Spanish Studies* 85.5 (2008): 569–80.

– "Quevedo y Lope (poesía y teatro) en 1609: patriotismo y construcción nacional en *La España defendida* y *La Jerusalén conquistada*." *La Perinola* 17 (2013): 27–56.

Sander, Nicolas. *Rise and Growth of the Anglican Schism*. Trans. and notes David Lewis. London: Burns and Oates, 1877.

Shell, Alison. *Catholicism, Controversy, and the English Literary Imagination, 1558–1660*. Cambridge, UK; New York: Cambridge University Press, 1999.

Shergold, N.D. and J.E. Varey. "Some Early Calderón Dates." *Bulletin of Hispanic Studies* 38.4 (1961): 274–86.

Sieber, Harry. "Literary Continuity, Social Order, and the Invention of the Picaresque." *Cultural Authority in Golden Age Spain*. Eds. Marina S. Brownlee and Hans Ulrich Gumbrecht. London and Baltimore: Johns Hopkins Press, 1995.

Spinnenweber, Kathleen. "The 1611 English Translation of St. Teresa's Autobiography: A Possible Carmelite-Jesuit Collaboration." *SKASE Journal of Translation and Interpretation* 2.1 (2007). http://www.skase.sk/Volumes/JTI02/pdf_doc/1.pdf. 26 May 2017.

Spitzer, Leo. "Perspectivism in 'Don Quijote.'" In *Linguistics and Literary History: Essays in Stylistics*. Princeton: Princeton University Press, 1948. 41–85.

Stierle, Karlheinz. "Three Moments in the Crisis of Exemplarity: Boccaccio-Petrarch, Montaigne, and Cervantes." *Journal of the History of Ideas* 59.4 (1998): 581–95.

Torres, Isabel. "Now You See It, Now You … See It Again? The Dynamics of Doubling in *La española inglesa*." *A Companion to Cervantes's* Novelas ejemplares. Ed. Stephen F. Boyd. Woodbridge, Suffolk: Tamesis, 2005. 115–33.

Van Liere, Katherine Elliot, Simon Ditchfield, and Howard Louthan. *Sacred History: Uses of the Christian Past in the Renaissance World*. Oxford: Oxford University Press, 2012.

Veech, Thomas McNevin. *Dr Nicholas Sanders and the English Reformation, 1530–1581*. Louvain: Bureaux du Recueil, Bibliothèque de l'Université, 1935.

Venuti, Lawrence. "Translation, Intertextuality, Interpretation." *Romance Studies* 27.3 (2009): 157–73.

Vives, Juan Luis. *Instruccion de la muger Christiana*. Madrid: en la Imprenta de Don Benito Cano, 1793.

Wallace, David. *Strong Women: Life, Text, and Territory, 1347–1645*. Oxford; New York: Oxford University Press, 2011.

Walsham, Alexandra. *Charitable Hatred: Tolerance and Intolerance in England, 1500–1700*. Manchester: Manchester University Press, 2009.

Walton, Kristen Post. *Catholic Queen, Protestant Patriarchy: Mary, Queen of Scots, and the Politics of Gender and Religion*. Basingstoke, England; New York: Palgrave Macmillan, 2007.

Wardropper, Bruce W. "*Don Quixote*: Story or History?" *Cervantes'* Don Quixote: *A Casebook*. Ed. Roberto González Echevarría. Oxford [England]: Oxford University Press, 2005. 141–61.

Warnicke, Retha M. *The Rise and Fall of Anne Boleyn: Family Politics at the Court of Henry VIII*. New York: Cambridge University Press, 1989.

Weikel, Ann. "Mary I (1516–1558)." *Oxford Dictionary of National Biography*. Eds. H.C.G. Matthew and Brian Harrison. Oxford: Oxford University Press, 2004. Online ed. Ed. Lawrence Goldman. Jan. 2008. http://www.oxforddnb.com/view/article/18245. 3 Nov. 2015.

Weinreich, Spencer J. "The Distinctiveness of the Society of Jesus's Mission in Pedro de Ribadeneyra's *Historia ecclesiastica del schisma del reyno de Inglaterra* (1588)." *Exploring Jesuit Distinctiveness: Interdisciplinary Perspectives on Ways of Proceeding within the Society of Jesus*. Ed. Robert Aleksander Maryks. 1 vol. Leiden; Boston: Brill, 2016. 175–88.

– "Introduction." *Pedro de Ribadeneyra's Ecclesiastical History of the Schism of the Kingdom of England: A Spanish Jesuit's History of the English Reformation*. Trans. and Ed. Spencer J. Weinreich. 8 vols. Leiden: Brill, 2017. 1–98.

Wiesman, Bernard. "Father Robert Parsons, S.J." *Catholic Historical Review* 12.4 (1927): 583–629.

Williams, Michael E. *St. Alban's College, Valladolid: Four Centuries of English Catholic Presence in Spain*. London: C. Hurst; New York: St. Martin's Press, 1986.

Wizeman, William. *The Theology and Spirituality of Mary Tudor's Church*. Aldershot, England; Burlington, VT: Ashgate, 2006.

– "The Rhetoric of Martyrdom: Generic Contradiction and Narrative Strategy in John Foxe's *Acts and Monuments*." *The Rhetorics of Life-Writing in Early Modern Europe: Forms of Biography from Cassandra Fedele to Louis XIV*. Eds. Thomas Frederick Mayer and Daniel R. Woolf. Ann Arbor, MI: University of Michigan Press, 1995. 243–82.

Wright, Elizabeth R. "From Drake to Draque: A Spanish Hero with an English Accent." *Material and Symbolic Circulation between Spain and England, 1554–1604*. Ed. Anne J. Cruz. Aldershot, England; Burlington, VT: Ashgate, 2008. 29–38.

– *Pilgrimage to Patronage: Lope de Vega and the Court of Philip III, 1598–1621.* Lewisburg, PA: Bucknell University Press, 2001.

Yepes, Diego de, Obispo de Tarazona. *Historia particular de la persecucion de Inglaterra y de los martirios mas insignes que en ella a auido, desde el año del Señor 1570: en la qual se descubren los efectos lastimosos de la heregia y las mudanças que suele causar en las repúblicas.* En Madrid: por Luis Sanchez, 1599.

Zamora Vicente, Alonso. *Lope de Vega: Su vida y su obra.* 2 ed. Madrid: Editorial Gredos, 1969.

Zimic, Stanislav. *Las* Novelas ejemplares *de Cervantes.* Madrid: Siglo Veintiuno Editores, 1996.

Index

Toronto Iberic

1 Anthony J. Cascardi, *Cervantes, Literature, and the Discourse of Politics*
2 Jessica A. Boon, *The Mystical Science of the Soul: Medieval Cognition in Bernardino de Laredo's Recollection Method*
3 Susan Byrne, *Law and History in Cervantes'* Don Quixote
4 Mary E. Barnard and Frederick A. de Armas (eds.), *Objects of Culture in the Literature of Imperial Spain*
5 Nil Santiáñez, *Topographies of Fascism: Habitus, Space, and Writing in Twentieth-Century Spain*
6 Nelson Orringer, *Lorca in Tune with Falla: Literary and Musical Interludes*
7 Ana M. Gómez-Bravo, *Textual Agency: Writing Culture and Social Networks in Fifteenth-Century Spain*
8 Javier Irigoyen-García, *The Spanish Arcadia: Sheep Herding, Pastoral Discourse, and Ethnicity in Early Modern Spain*
9 Stephanie Sieburth, *Survival Songs: Conchita Piquer's* Coplas *and Franco's Regime of Terror*
10 Christine Arkinstall, *Spanish Female Writers and the Freethinking Press, 1879–1926*

11 Margaret Boyle, *Unruly Women: Performance, Penitence, and Punishment in Early Modern Spain*
12 Evelina Gužauskytė, *Christopher Columbus's Naming in the* diarios *of the Four Voyages (1492–1504): A Discourse of Negotiation*
13 Mary E. Barnard, *Garcilaso de la Vega and the Material Culture of Renaissance Europe*
14 William Viestenz, *By the Grace of God: Francoist Spain and the Sacred Roots of Political Imagination*
15 Michael Scham, *Lector Ludens: The Representation of Games and Play in Cervantes*
16 Stephen Rupp, *Heroic Forms: Cervantes and the Literature of War*
17 Enrique Fernandez, *Anxieties of Interiority and Dissection in Early Modern Spain*
18 Susan Byrne, *Ficino in Spain*
19 Patricia M. Keller, *Ghostly Landscapes: Film, Photography, and the Aesthetics of Haunting in Contemporary Spanish Culture*
20 Carolyn A. Nadeau, *Food Matters: Alonso Quijano's Diet and the Discourse of Food in Early Modern Spain*
21 Cristian Berco, *From Body to Community: Venereal Disease and Society in Baroque Spain*
22 Elizabeth R. Wright, *The Epic of Juan Latino: Dilemmas of Race and Religion in Renaissance Spain*
23 Ryan D. Giles, *Inscribed Power: Amulets and Magic in Early Spanish Literature*
24 Jorge Pérez, *Confessional Cinema: Religion, Film, and Modernity in Spain's Development Years, 1960–1975*
25 Joan Ramon Resina, *Josep Pla: Seeing the World in the Form of Articles*
26 Javier Irigoyen-García, *"Moors Dressed as Moors": Clothing, Social Distinction, and Ethnicity in Early Modern Iberia*
27 Jean Dangler, *Edging toward Iberia*
28 Ryan D. Giles and Steven Wagschal (eds.), *Beyond Sight: Engaging the Senses in Iberian Literatures and Cultures, 1200–1750*
29 Silvia Bermúdez, *Rocking the Boat: Migration and Race in Contemporary Spanish Music*
30 Hilaire Kallendorf, *Ambiguous Antidotes: Virtue as Vaccine for Vice in Early Modern Spain*
31 Leslie Harkema, *Spanish Modernism and the Poetics of Youth: From Miguel de Unamuno to* La Joven Literatura
32 Benjamin Fraser, *Cognitive Disability Aesthetics: Visual Culture, Disability Representations, and the (In)Visibility of Cognitive Difference*
33 Robert Patrick Newcomb, *Iberianism and Crisis: Spain and Portugal at the Turn of the Twentieth Century*

34 Sara J. Brenneis, *Spaniards in Mauthausen: Representations of a Nazi Concentration Camp, 1940–2015*
35 Silvia Bermúdez and Roberta Johnson (eds.), *A New History of Iberian Feminisms*
36 Steven Wagschal, *Minding Animals in the Old and New Worlds: A Cognitive Historical Analysis*
37 Heather Bamford, *Cultures of the Fragment: Uses of the Iberian Manuscript, 1100–1600*
38 Enrique García Santo-Tomás (ed.), *Science on Stage in Early Modern Spain*
39 Marina Brownlee (ed.), *Cervantes'* Persiles *and the Travails of Romance*
40 Sarah Thomas, *Inhabiting the In-Between: Childhood and Cinema in Spain's Long Transition*
41 David A. Wacks, *Medieval Iberian Crusade Fiction and the Mediterranean World*
42 Rosilie Hernández, *Immaculate Conceptions: The Power of the Religious Imagination in Early Modern Spain*
43 Mary Coffey and Margot Versteeg (eds.), *Imagined Truths: Realism in Modern Spanish Literature and Culture*
44 Diana Aramburu, *Resisting Invisibility: Detecting the Female Body in Spanish Crime Fiction*
45 Samuel Amago and Matthew J. Marr (eds.), *Consequential Art: Comics Culture in Contemporary Spain*
46 Richard P. Kinkade, *Dawn of a Dynasty: The Life and Times of Infante Manuel of Castile*
47 Jill Robbins, *Poetry and Crisis: Cultural Politics and Citizenship in the Wake of the Madrid Bombings*
48 Ana María Laguna and John Beusterien (eds.), *Goodbye Eros: Recasting Forms and Norms of Love in the Age of Cervantes*
49 Sara J. Brenneis and Gina Herrmann (eds.), *Spain, World War II, and the Holocaust: History and Representation*
50 Francisco Fernández de Alba, *Sex, Drugs, and Fashion in 1970s Madrid*
51 Daniel Aguirre-Oteiza, *This Ghostly Poetry: Reading Spanish Republican Exiles between Literary History and Poetic Memory*
52 Lara Anderson, *Control and Resistance: Food Discourse in Franco Spain*
53 Faith Harden, *Arms and Letters: Military Life Writing in Early Modern Spain*
54 Erin Alice Cowling, Tania de Miguel Magro, Mina García Jordán, and Glenda Y. Nieto-Cuebas (eds.), *Social Justice in Spanish Golden Age Theatre*
55 Paul Michael Johnson, *Affective Geographies: Cervantes, Emotion, and the Literary Mediterranean*

56 Justin Crumbaugh and Nil Santiáñez (eds.), *Spanish Fascist Writing: An Anthology*
57 Margaret E. Boyle and Sarah E. Owens (eds.), *Health and Healing in the Early Modern Iberian World: A Gendered Perspective*
58 Leticia Álvarez-Recio (ed.), *Iberian Chivalric Romance: Translations and Cultural Transmission in Early Modern England*
59 Henry Berlin, *Alone Together: Poetics of the Passions in Late Medieval Iberia*
60 Adrian Shubert, *The Sword of Luchana: Baldomero Espartero and the Making of Modern Spain, 1793–1879*
61 Jorge Pérez, *Fashioning Spanish Cinema: Costume, Identity, and Stardom*
62 Enriqueta Zafra, *Lazarillo de Tormes: A Graphic Novel*
63 Erin Alice Cowling, *Chocolate: How a New World Commodity Conquered Spanish Literature*
64 Mary E. Barnard, *A Poetry of Things: The Material Lyric in Habsburg Spain*
65 Frederick A. de Armas and James Mandrell (eds.), *The Gastronomical Arts in Spain: Food and Etiquette*
66 Catherine Infante, *The Arts of Encounter: Christians, Muslims, and the Power of Images in Early Modern Spain*
67 Robert Richmond Ellis, *Bibliophiles, Murderous Bookmen, and Mad Librarians: The Story of Books in Modern Spain*
68 Beatriz de Alba-Koch (ed.), *The Ibero-American Baroque*
69 Deborah R. Forteza, *The English Reformation in the Spanish Imagination: Rewriting Nero, Jezebel, and the Dragon*

www.ingramcontent.com/pod-product-compliance
Lightning Source LLC
LaVergne TN
LVHW041112090826
844660LV00061B/846/J

* 9 7 8 1 4 8 7 5 6 3 5 0 9 *